Miss Spokane

Elegant Ambassadors and Their City

Miss Spokane
Elegant Ambassadors and Their City

Tony Bamonte
Suzanne Schaeffer Bamonte

Tornado Creek Publications
Spokane, Washington 2000

Published in 2000
Printed in the United States of America
by
Walsworth Publishing Company
Marceline, Missouri 64658

Library of Congress Catalog Card Number: 00-092864
ISBN: 0-9652219-6-2

Front cover photo: Marguerite Motie, the first Miss Spokane, in 1912 at the age of 17.
(Photo courtesy Dorothy and John Marchi.)

Back cover: A 1915 advertisement designed by the Spokane Advertising Club using
Marguerite Motie's image to promote the opening of the Davenport Hotel.
(Courtesy Dorothy and Bob Capeloto.)

Tornado Creek Publications
P.O. Box 8625
Spokane, Washington 99203-8625
(509) 838-7114

Other Books by Tony & Suzanne Bamonte:

Spokane and the Inland Northwest: Historical Images

Manito Park: A Reflection of Spokane's Past

History of Newport, Washington

History of Pend Oreille County

Books by Tony Bamonte:

Sheriffs 1911-1989: A History of Murders in the Wilderness of Washington's Last County

History of Metaline Falls

The Authors:

Tony and Suzanne Bamonte have turned their pastime and passion for writing and publishing Northwest history into a vocation. This is their fifth publication together. They are always looking for access to private photo collections for future publications. If you are interested, they can be contacted at the address or telephone number listed on the facing page.

Tony was born in Wallace, Idaho, in 1942 and raised in Metaline Falls, Washington. He was elected and served as Pend Oreille County sheriff for three consecutive terms from 1978 until 1991. He has a Master's Degree in Organizational Leadership from Gonzaga University and a Bachelor's Degree in Sociology from Whitworth College. Tony began his law-enforcement career in 1966 as a Spokane city police officer. He has also been a logger, miner, construction worker and an army helicopter door gunner during his tour of duty in Vietnam. In addition to coauthoring and publishing history books with wife Suzanne, he is a licensed Washington State Realtor.

Suzanne was born in Ione, Washington, in 1948 and raised in Metaline Falls, Washington. She graduated from Central Washington University with a Bachelor's Degree in Accounting, subsequently becoming a Certified Public Accountant. Prior to their marriage in 1994, Suzanne lived in Seattle where she worked as the controller of an art glass studio from 1988-1993 and of a publishing company from 1982-1988. Previous to that, she worked in the field of public accounting.

Acknowledgments

The inspiration for this book came from a curiosity about the striking young woman in Native American dress whose picture appears in various early Spokane publications, on postcards, hanging on the walls of restaurants and in antique stores. Especially intriguing was the large stained-glass likeness of her, which hung in the entryway of the Cheney Cowles Museum for many years. Most local historians recognize Marguerite Motie as the city's first and most familiar Miss Spokane, but few knew much about her. We fell in that category and were eager to learn more.

As fortune would have it, in 1998 we were privileged to make the acquaintance of Marguerite Motie's niece, **Dorothy Marchi**. She loaned us a treasure trove of family photographs, with the permission to use them. She also put us in touch with Marguerite's daughter, **Dorothy Capeloto**. Both women were extremely gracious and willing to assist us in putting together a book about their mother and aunt. Their generosity in sharing photographs, memorabilia and even firsthand written family histories was touching. We felt honored to be entrusted with such treasures and deeply appreciate both women and their families for their contributions.

As we began our discovery process, the scope of the project expanded. We learned there had been more than one Miss Spokane contest and in the course of our inquiry, we had the good fortune of meeting and becoming friends with **Anne Anderson**, a former Miss Spokane and the only one to have become Miss Washington. She has been involved in the current Miss Spokane Scholarship Pageant since its inception in 1989, and became a significant player in our project, for which we are deeply indebted. In addition to sharing her own personal story, she became our project assistant, helping to engage the participation of other Miss Spokanes and proofread the entire manuscript. Because of Anne's dedication to this project, the authors will donate, upon their deaths, all rights to this book to Anne's employer, the Spokane Symphony.

Outside of content and equally important to any major writing project is the editorial assistance. We were fortunate to have one of the best. We extend our most sincere admiration and gratitude to **Laura Arksey**, retired librarian and archivist from the Eastern Washington State Historical Society. Laura served as both proofreader and editorial assistant throughout this entire project.

To all the Miss Spokanes who contributed to the project, we extend our heartfelt appreciation. A special acknowledgement goes to **Catherine (Betts) Williams**, Marguerite Motie's successor, who repeatedly went out of her way to assist us in our efforts.

We also wish to thank the **contributors of photographs**, who have been acknowledged in the credit lines throughout the book. Due to limited space, the abbreviation **EWSHS** designates photos from the collections of the Eastern Washington State Historical Society/Northwest Museum of Arts & Culture.

We also wish to acknowledge the following people (in alphabetical order) for various other contributions such as proofreading sections of the manuscript, checking for historical accuracy, providing research material or assistance: **Julie Bunch, Bob Capeloto, Nancy Compau, Culture Department of the Spokane Tribe of Indians, Karen DeSeve, Grant Dixon, Judy Dixon, Brenda Janke, John Marchi, Nancy Martin, Don Neraas, Al and Mae Schaeffer.**

Table of Contents

Introduction 9

Chapter 1

A Glimpse of Early Spokane..10

The environment in which the Miss Spokane concept was developed.

Chapter 2

The Concept, the Contest and the First Miss Spokane................32

The Motie Family History – Marguerite Motie, the First Miss Spokane, 1912-1939 – Marguerite Motie's Family Life

Chapter 3

Spokane's Official City Hostesses, 1939-1976..........................130

The original Miss Spokane contest designed to select an official city hostess and a representative selection of the Miss Spokanes from this contest: Catherine Betts, Margel Peters, Glenda Bergen, Marcia Gusman, Suzanne Thompson, Patricia Kelly, Shirley Eagle, Maureen Brown, Sally Amick, Natalie Monte, Leilani Wickline

Chapter 4

Spokane's Miss Washington and Miss America Contestants.......240

The Miss Spokane contests designed to select a Spokane representative to compete in the Miss Washington or the Miss America contests or both and a cross-section of Miss Spokanes from these contests: Glorian Smith, Eva King, Donnagene Herr, Anne Henderson, Amy Sturtz, Brenda Grizzle, Jennifer Fryhling, Victoria Nicacio, Sarahlynn Aanderud, Abigail Palmer, Fianna Dickson

Letter from Executive Director of the Miss Spokane Scholarship Progam 343

Index..344

Dedicated to:

Marguerite Motie
and her family

Introduction

In 1912 the Spokane Advertising Club sponsored a contest among local artists to choose a symbol to represent the young and rapidly-growing city of Spokane. The winning sketch depicted an Indian princess with a sheaf of wheat in one hand to show the agricultural wealth of the area and in the other hand a jug from which water was being poured to show the abundance of water from the Spokane River. Immediately following this competition, another contest was held to choose a face for this Indian princess. The chosen face was to be superimposed on the sketch to bring the princess to life. This living symbol would then represent Spokane.

Miss Spokane 1912

At the age of 17, Marguerite Motie was selected in 1912 from 138 entries to become the first Miss Spokane, the city's official hostess. She would become the most publicized woman in Spokane's history and one of its most beloved personalities. According to the rules of the contest, Marguerite was to reign until she married. In 1920 she married Walter Shiel, her high school sweetheart. Shortly after their marriage, the newlyweds moved to Seattle where they started their family. Although Marguerite's marriage officially marked the end of her tenure as Miss Spokane, she was periodically called back to Spokane to officiate at special events. During the Depression years, the role of Miss Spokane essentially fell into obscurity, but the contest was revived in 1939 and a second Miss Spokane was chosen.

Three separate Miss Spokane contests have contributed to Spokane's history. The original contest continued until 1977. In 1926 and 1927, the *Spokane Press* and the Clemmer Theater sponsored another Miss Spokane contest that qualified the winner to participate in the Miss America Pageant. By the late 1940s, a third contest emerged. This contest, sponsored by the Spokane Junior Chamber of Commerce, contained the necessary elements for the winning contestant to participate in the Miss Washington Pageant. By this time, contestants in the Miss America Pageant were representatives of the states, not cities. The last Miss America to represent a city was in 1947. For about three decades, this contest ran concurrently, albeit sporadically, with the original Miss Spokane contest. Although the sponsorship has changed over the years, it was the forerunner of the present Miss Spokane contest.

This book offers a unique perspective of Spokane's history taken from numerous interviews and photo albums, scrapbooks and memorabilia belonging to former Miss Spokanes. Beginning with a glimpse of early Spokane through the reign of Miss Spokane 2000, experience the pulse, customs, fashions and changing face of the city as the years unfolded and were greeted by Spokane's chosen representatives.

Chapter 1

A Glimpse of Early Spokane

The first significant City Hall building. Constructed in 1892 on the site where Spokane's first quality hotel, the California House, once stood. It was torn down in 1913, the year after the selection of Marguerite Motie as the first Miss Spokane. This building, which also contained the city jail, was located in the heart of Spokane's early "tenderloin district" (major area of prostitutes and saloons). Consequently, it was often an unpleasant experience to visit City Hall.

(Photo courtesy Jerome Peltier)

By the time the Motie family moved to Spokane in 1907, the city had grown from its start as a tiny two-man sawmill operation to a respectable city, growing in population and significance. A devastating fire in 1889 had destroyed most of the business district and the reconstructed downtown had taken on a sophisticated new appearance with its predominantly brick and stone buildings.

As the nation recovered from the economic panic of 1893, Spokane experienced a major economic boom. The mining and timber industries were exploding with activity. Vast mineral fortunes were being amassed from the Coeur d'Alene Mining District in northern Idaho. Timber barons from the eastern United States were harvesting the gigantic reserves of valuable timber, while at the same time, the region's agricultural potential was being recognized. As a result, means of exploiting these resources began developing. In anticipation of this untouched wealth, a northern transcontinental railroad had been completed from the East to West coasts in 1883. The military had quelled Indian resistance and uprisings, and people were streaming into the area in search of the "promised land."

From 1885 to 1912 the Inland Northwest experienced the largest economic boom in its entire history. By 1910 Spokane's official census had jumped to 104,400. The automobile had become popular and was competing with the trains and streetcars. Mining productions, including concentrator mills and smelters, were being built. The plethora of sawmills and planing mills were threatening the scenic beauty of the Inland Northwest but providing countless jobs. These solid industrial mainstays gave rise to an eclectic array of supporting industries. The majority of Spokane's mansions were also built during this period.

Some of Spokane's darkest and most violent times accompanied this sudden massive influx of people. Crime was overwhelming the community to such an extent that on November 3, 1898, Spokane's mayor, E.D. Olmsted, publicly called upon every able-bodied man in the city to take arms in defense of life and property and offered a $500 reward for the arrest and conviction of any criminal engaged in armed robberies.

Nine years later, on September 14, 1907, Spokane Chief of Police Ren Rice publicly ordered the entire Spokane Police Department to "shoot the burglar or highwayman first and collect the evidence afterward." Six Spokane policemen were killed in the line of duty during this era and more citizens were killed by Spokane police than any other time in Spokane's history. It was legal to shoot and kill a fleeing felon and the police could arrest almost anyone for very little cause – a right which was exercised often. Spokane was a wide-open town bustling with an air of lawlessness and reckless urgency.

Yet among the mass of human confusion during these rough and rowdy times was a core group of people who recognized what Spokane could and would someday be. They were city boosters with a vision and goal of promoting the city of Spokane to the world at large. An unsuspecting young Marguerite Motie would eventually figure prominently into this evolving vision, contributing an element of refinement and class that enhanced and furthered the promoters' objectives .

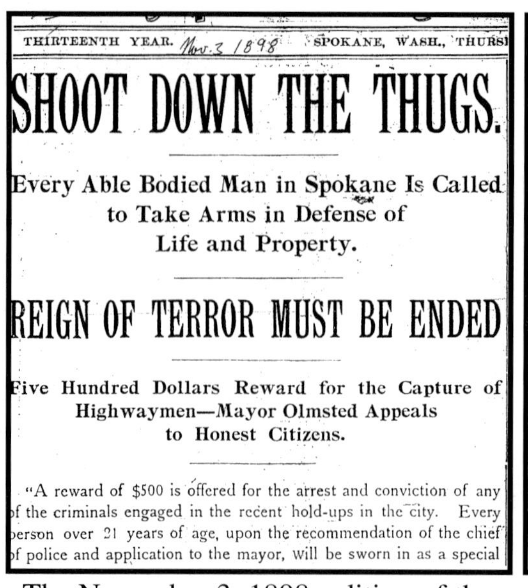

THIRTEENTH YEAR. Nov. 3, 1898 SPOKANE, WASH., THURS

SHOOT DOWN THE THUGS.

Every Able Bodied Man in Spokane Is Called to Take Arms in Defense of Life and Property.

REIGN OF TERROR MUST BE ENDED

Five Hundred Dollars Reward for the Capture of Highwaymen—Mayor Olmsted Appeals to Honest Citizens.

"A reward of $500 is offered for the arrest and conviction of any of the criminals engaged in the recent hold-ups in the city. Every person over 21 years of age, upon the recommendation of the chief of police and application to the mayor, will be sworn in as a special

The November 3, 1898, edition of the *Spokane Daily Chronicle*.

SPOKANE, WASH., SATURDAY EVENING, SEPTEMBER 14, 1907.

MUST GET THE THUGS DEAD OR ALIVE

"They Are Murderers at Heart," Declares Chief Rice.

"Shoot the burglar or highwayman first and collect the evidence afterward."

These are the instruction issued by Chief Rice to the night shift on the police force. Any man caught in the act of holding up a pedestrian or in

Chief Ren Rice.

the act of entering a house will have

RED WERE LOST

NO COAL FOR SALE

NEW YORK, Sept. 14.—The situation with regard to the proposals issued by the bureau of equipment of the navy department for supplying coal for the battleship fleet on its voyage to the Pacific, says the Journal of Commerce has assumed rather interesting shape here by the statements of several agents of the larger coal mining concerns, that they would not present bids.

Their reasons are that they have not the necessary quantity of coal on hand, aside from the quantity demanded by private contracts already entered into.

The companies claim that they have no reserve stocks on hand amounting to anything and that the labor, situation is such that they can not increase their mining capacity. The coal it was stated, can be obtained in England if it is necessary to go there, but prices will undoubtedly be what might be classed as "fancy."

INJUNCTION IS GRANTED

SEVERAL MA HAVE

ROBBED OF CASH

The local police received a wire from Missoula this morning stating that the Northern Pacific office at that place was entered last night by burglars who secured about $400, mostly in paper money. No description of the supposed burglars was received.

ON THE DEATH LIST.

The following deaths have been reported at the health office:

Phillips—At the Sacred Heart hospital, September 11, Howard Phillips, aged 40 years, of typhoid fever.

Campbell—At Hillyard September 12, Robert L. Campbell, aged 23, of injury of the spine.

RISK THE AM

The September 14, 1907, front page of the *Spokane Daily Chronicle*.

Looking across the Spokane River from Peaceful Valley at the Spokane County Courthouse in the early 1900s. Spokane's second "Shantytown," located on the north bank of the river, is in the foreground. *(Photo courtesy Jerome Peltier.)*

The Sprague House in 1883 located at the northwest corner of Railroad Avenue and Post Street. The hotel was built in 1882 and burned in August of 1884. (*Photo EWSHS, L89-267.*)

The Crescent Block immediately after the fire of August 4, 1889. Note the temporary business signs attached to the front of the building. (*Photo EWSHS, L88-362.*)

Harry G. Adams grocery at 700 W. Riverside in 1889. (*Photo EWSHS, L88-362.*)

Looking east on Riverside near Post Street in 1887. The tall building on the right is the Falls City Block and Opera House, Spokane's only theater for a short while.
(*Photo EWSHS, L86-768*)

Looking east on Riverside from Post Street with the five story Peyton Building in the right foreground, circa 1895. Note the dirt roads and trolley tracks. *(EWSHS, L84-112)*

F.O. Berg, owner of one of Spokane's first automobiles, circa 1898. *(EWSHS, L93-66.19)*

Northern Pacific Railway depot at First Avenue and Bernard Street, circa 1894.
(Photo EWSHS, L88-371)

Northern Pacific train wreck caused by collapsed trestle at Sixth and Cannon, circa 1890. *(Photo EWSHS, L87-321)*

Trying out the family car during an outing. *(Frank Guilbert photo, EWSHS, L97-63.195)*

Spokane Fruit Fair tents, 1896. Lincoln Street in foreground and the Auditorium Building, built in 1890, is the tall building beyond the tents. (*Photo courtesy Jerome Peltier.*)

Women's foot race at the Crescent employees' picnic in Spokane, circa 1913.
(*Frank Guilbert photo EWSHS, L97-63.110*)

Children attending Mildred Weston's birthday party, circa 1910. (*Photo EWSHS, L83-113.83*)

Natatorium Park baseball team in front of Nat Park trolley, circa 1900.
(Photo courtesy Jerome Peltier.)

Second Monroe Street Bridge, circa 1909. *(Photo courtesy Jerome Peltier.)*

The C & C Spokane Flour Mill, located on the north bank of the Spokane River at 621 West Mallon Street, in 1913. *(Frank Guilbert photo EWSHS, L97-63.85)*

The city of Spokane grew up around the Spokane Falls. Its first industry was a sawmill. Soon to follow, taking advantage of the abundant water power, was a flour mill built by Frederick Post in 1876. Flour mills quickly became a predominant industry. In 1885 F. Lewis Clark and Frank E. Curtis purchased the Post Mill and built a new, updated mill adjacent to it, called the C & C Flour Mill. In 1890 it was sold to another local company called Washington Water Power and Milling Company. Although the Washington Water Power Company was an electric utility, it was also in the milling business. The original C & C Flour Mill's capacity was 250 barrels a day. By 1893 the Washington Water Power increased that production to 700.

In 1895 the WWP sold the mill to the Portland Flouring Mill, which owned nine other mills around the country. By 1906 the C & C had merged with Spokane Flour Mills as the "C & C, the Spokane Flour Mills." The operation was moved to a building constructed in 1895 by Simon Oppenheimer on the north bank of the Spokane River opposite the site of the old C & C Mill. Due to financial difficulties, this large five-story red-brick building had stood empty for over a decade.

At the end of 1971, the Spokane Flour Mills went out of business. Today the building houses restaurants, shops and offices, and is among Spokane's favorite attractions.

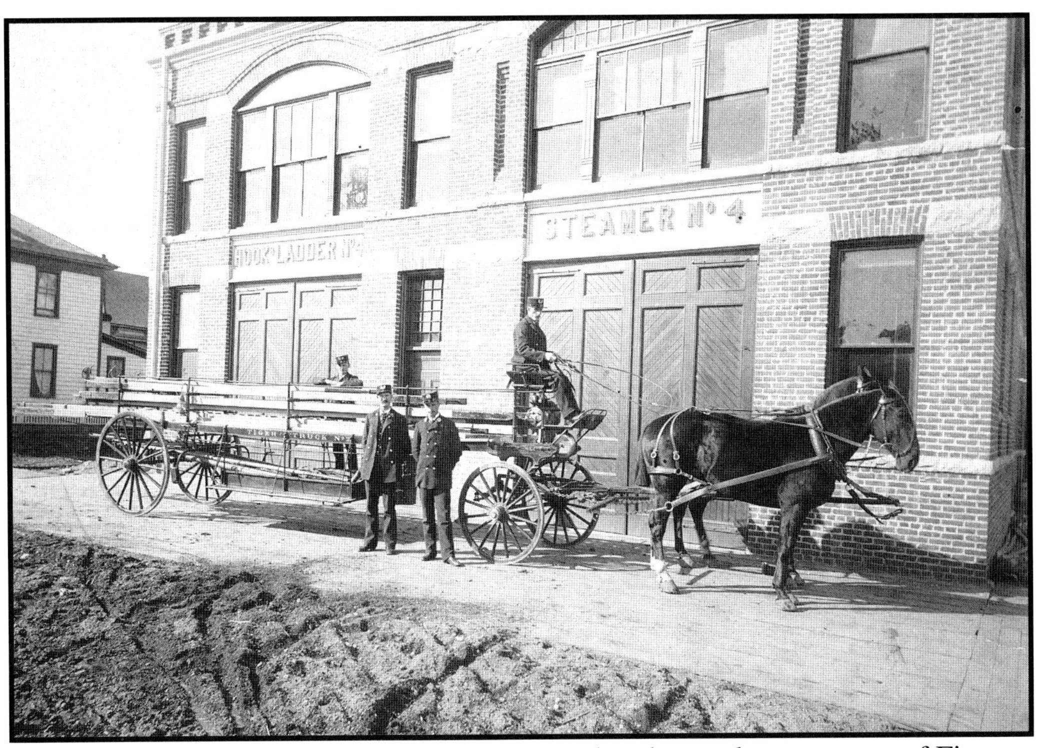

Fire Station #4 built about 1899 and located at the northwest corner of First Avenue and Adams Street. *(Photo courtesy Jerome Peltier.)*

Monroe Street near Maxwell in 1904. *(Photo courtesy Dean Ladd & Larry Elsom.)*

Interstate Fair in 1910. *(Libby Studio photo courtesy Jerome Peltier.)*

Carl Nelson, father-in-law of longtime radio and television personality Bob Briley, driving Spokane City water wagon, circa 1900. *(Photo courtesy Bob Briley)*

Northern Pacific locomotive near Spokane in 1903. *(Photo EWSHS, L84-368.6)*

Jim's Place, an oyster and lunch counter in 1907. *(Libby photo EWSHS, L87-1.19157.21)*

Levi and May Hutton home, 2206 E. 17th Avenue, built in 1914. *(EWSHS L94-19.131)*

Both Levi "Al" and May Arkwright Hutton were on their own in their early years and would come to know the bittersweet of life. In 1884 Levi worked for the Northern Pacific Railroad as a fireman on a locomotive running out of Missoula, Montana. Two-and-a-half years later, he took a job on D.C. Corbin's narrow gauge line (soon owned by the Northern Pacific) in the Coeur d'Alene Mining District. It was during that time he met, fell in love with and married May Arkwright, who ran a boarding house and cooked for the local miners and railroad employees.

The Huttons worked hard at their respective livelihoods, all the while investing in various mining claims, most of which proved worthless. In 1897, the year of the great Klondike Gold Rush in Alaska, they became partners in the Hercules mining claim. For the next four years, they sank every spare dollar into boring into a rocky mountainside. Against the advice of friends and mining experts, Levi was confident that the ore bodies of the district were continuous and, if they persisted, were bound to reach them. When the main vein was finally blasted into, the event did not carry a significant impact because this inexperienced group initially was unaware of what they had actually discovered. In fact, what the Hercules partners had reached was an ore body of high grade silver, one of the richest of the times. Before long, the significance of this discovery impacted the entire Inland Northwest. Hereafter, the Hercules mine became known as the "Mighty Hercules" and made this diligent group of partners wealthy.

The Huttons and other mining magnates brought their new-found mining wealth to Spokane and began building homes and business buildings. Following May Hutton's death, Levi built the Hutton Settlement in 1919 for orphaned children and established a trust to perpetuate it. The Hutton Settlement remains active to this day.

An electric streetcar in front of the Interurban Terminal at Main and Lincoln in 1907. *(Photo EWSHS, L87-245.3.9)*

St. Aloysius Church, 330 East Boone, was the Motie family's parish. It was located across the street and just east of the Motie's first Spokane residence.

(Postcard photo courtesy Don Neraas)

Construction of the Mission Street Bridge in 1908. *(Photo EWSHS, L93-18.153)*

F.O. Berg Company on Division north of Trent, circa 1905. *(Photo courtesy Jerome Peltier.)*

1910 International Motor Wagon with load of flour in 1911. Motor vehicles were beginning to become more practical and popular. *(Photo EWSHS, L83-113.20)*

The Farmers' Market at 400 West Second Avenue in 1908. *(Photo EWSHS, L90-208.2)*

The Monroe Street Bridge, 1912. *(Frank Guilbert photo EWSHS, L97-63.122)*

One of Spokane's most recognizable and historic landmarks, the present Monroe Street Bridge, completed in 1911, was the third bridge to span the Spokane River at that location. The first Monroe Street Bridge was constructed with wooden timbers and planks. Construction began in 1888 and it opened the following year. In 1890 the bridge burned and was replaced with a steel structure in 1891. By 1907 this bridge was becoming shaky and demolition began in 1910, during which the south approach spans collapsed. The present concrete bridge was built in its place and completed in 1911 at a cost of $500,000. At the time of its completion, the Spokane City fathers boasted the Monroe Street Bridge was the longest concrete bridge structure in the world.

From its inception, the Monroe Street Bridge has been a prominent Spokane landmark. It has and continues to be displayed on numerous official and promotional materials.

Interestingly, the existing Monroe Street Bridge's early beginning was quite controversial. A headline article in the January 27, 1912, edition of the *Spokane Daily Chronicle* claimed Spokane City engineers, during a visit to Cleveland, Ohio, had "outright physically stolen" the plans to Cleveland's "Rocky River" bridge. This article further advised that the City of Spokane was going to be sued for $15,000 for infringement of copyrighted plans. The director of the Engineering Department for Cuyahoga County, Ohio, stated: "The Rocky River bridge plans were taken bodily by Spokane's engineers and used practically as they were drawn, except that one foot was added to the main span so that the claim of the biggest bridge in the world could be made." The Monroe Street Bridge has a span of 281 feet, which, at the time, made it the longest concrete span in the world. The Rocky River Bridge in Cleveland had a 280-foot span.

Eighty-eight years from the date of this allegation, Tony Bamonte contacted Bill Dobish, a tenured bridge engineer with Cuyahoga County in Cleveland, Ohio. Mr. Dobish was well informed on the Rocky River Bridge. He stated that it was built in 1908 and was a concrete-arch structure. In 1978 it was removed because it was beginning to fall apart. There was a marina directly below the bridge and large chunks of concrete were falling on the boats. Mr. Dobish provided Bamonte with a complete set (16 pages) of the 1908 plans for their Rocky River Bridge. The similarity in the plans for this bridge appears to corroborate the 1912 allegations by the director of Cuyahoga County Engineer's Office.

The Rocky River Bridge plans, which were designed in 1908 and revised in 1909, were for a 280-foot concrete-arch bridge and are remarkably representative of the present Monroe Street Bridge. The 1907 edition of the *Encyclopedia Britannica* illustrates and describes ten different styles of bridges, including arched bridges. However, none of them were concrete. Consequently, it appears the Cuyahoga County Bridge, at 280 feet may have been the longest concrete span in the world – until the Monroe Street Bridge was built to span 281 feet.

Spokane has always been proud of the Monroe Street Bridge. Shortly after it was completed, two separate issues of postcards with differing views appeared. The first of these postcards was a southeasterly view with a narrative stating: "Part of Busy Spokane, The Lower Falls and the New Monroe Street Bridge, The Longest Concrete Span in the World." The second postcard was an easterly view, with a narrative stating: "New Monroe Street Bridge, Spokane, Washington, Largest Concrete Span in the World."

Although the renowned Spokane architect Kirtland Cutter is frequently credited with having designed the Monroe Street Bridge, his firm only designed the handrails and four small lookout pavilions placed over the main structural piers of the bridge. That, too, was controversial. The city fathers originally believed Cutter was donating his services for these designs. However, he sent the City of Spokane a bill for $2,500.

The Louis Davenport/Richard Porter home, located at the present site of Sacred Heart Hospital, built in 1911 by Davenports and sold to Porters the following year.

(Photo courtesy Bill Stewart.)

Spokane Interstate Fair, circa 1915. *(Photo EWSHS L93-17.68)*

Standard Fuel and Ice delivery wagons in front of the James Monaghan house, 217 East Boone, circa 1913. The Moties lived at 308 East Boone. *(Photo EWSHS, L96-2.46)*

Looking east on Riverside from Howard in 1914. *(Photo courtesy Larry Elsom & Dean Ladd.)*

Chapter 2

The Concept, the Contest and the First Miss Spokane

When the original Miss Spokane contest was conceived, the intent was to select the face of an attractive young woman to represent the city of Spokane in an aggressive advertising campaign by the Spokane Advertising Club. The ad campaign was designed to draw attention to Spokane, with the ultimate goal of attracting more people and businesses to the city.

The woman chosen for her face was Marguerite Motie. Although the original intent was primarily to use her image in promotional materials, after Marguerite was chosen, the objective quickly evolved into much more. Marguerite was charming, warm and friendly, and suddenly the image to be used on advertising materials came to life – the concept of a Miss Spokane as an official representative, ambassador or hostess was born. This was a unique concept to have a woman serve in the capacity of an official representative of the city, and many other cities adopted the idea. However, the chosen motif of dressing Miss Spokane in Native American attire, representative of the region's rich native culture and history, remained unique to Spokane. Many of the Miss Spokanes were adopted into local tribes, which became involved on a personal level in the creation of the authentic ceremonial gowns worn by the official city hostesses. For the duration of the contest, which ended on January 1, 1977, the Indian dress was the enduring trademark.

This contest was never intended as a beauty queen contest, although as the following pages reveal, Spokane was well represented in that regard. Subsequent to Marguerite Motie and because of her example, the official city hostess was chosen for her eloquence, poise before an audience, intelligence and overall potential to represent the city in a mature and professional manner.

Marguerite Motie was not only the first Miss Spokane, but she also developed the role and set the lofty standards for the future Miss Spokanes to follow. Marguerite had a profound effect on people, who were charmed by her sincerity, and she became an integral part of the most intense advertising campaign Spokane has ever known. For that reason, a large portion of this book is devoted to her, the Motie family history and the advertising campaign that helped shape Spokane's early history and development. Due to the difficulties in contacting all former Miss Spokanes or a lack of response from some of those contacted, the history of the Miss Spokane contest is chronicled by a representative cross section of willing participants.

Miss Spokane Contest Originated in 1912 by the Spokane Advertising Club.

Marguerite Motie, Miss Spokane I	Officially 1912-1920, unofficially until 1939
Catherine Betts, Miss Spokane II	Officially 1937-1943, unofficially until 1947
Margel Peters, Miss Spokane III	1947-1948
Glenda Bergen, Miss Spokane IV	1948-1951
Marcia Gusman, Miss Spokane V	1951-1952

Commencing in 1953, the Spokane Chamber of Commerce, sponsor of the Miss Spokane Contest, established new guidelines whereby the official city hostess position would be held for the duration of one calendar year. The following is a complete list of the Miss Spokanes through 1976, when the contest was discontinued.

Connie Oldershaw, Miss Spokane VI	1953
Patricia Culhane, Miss Spokane VII	1954
Diane Rumberg, Miss Spokane VIII	1955
Toni Burch, Miss Spokane IX	1956
Suzanne Thompson, Miss Spokane X	1957
Patricia Kelly, Miss Spokane XI	1958
Shirley Eagle, Miss Spokane XII	1959
Maureen Ann Brown, Miss Spokane XIII	1960
Sally Ann Amick, Miss Spokane XIV	1961
Kathleen Smith, Miss Spokane XV	1962
Natalie Monte, Miss Spokane XVI	1963
Rosemary Harness, Miss Spokane XVII	1964
Sharron Sweeny, Miss Spokane XVIII	1965
Gaye LaRane Mooney, Miss Spokane XIX	1966
Terry Dawn Starr, Miss Spokane XX	1967
Genie Lynn Ellis, Miss Spokane XXI	1968
E. Vicki Miner, Miss Spokane XXII	1969
Leilani Ann Wickline, Miss Spokane XXIII	1970
Colleen McCarty, Miss Spokane XXIV	1971
Charlene Dupper, Miss Spokane XXV	1972
Kristin Kay Lowe, Miss Spokane XXVI	1973
Judith Likarish, Miss Spokane XXVII	1974
Pamela Caudill, Miss Spokane XXVIII	1975
Susan Laib, Miss Spokane XXIX	1976

Marguerite Motie
at age 18.

Preface: The significance of Marguerite Motie to the development and continuation of the Miss Spokane contest calls for a fairly comprehensive presentation of her role in Spokane's history. For that reason, this documentation about her life and times includes the following summary of her ancestry.

Marguerite Motie's brother-in-law, Roland Bayne (married to sister Emily), researched and wrote a family history. Delving into the family lineage, Bayne traced the bloodline to the family of the Marquis de Lafayette of American Revolutionary fame, whose full name was Marie Joseph Paul Yves Roch Gilbert du Motier, Marquis de Lafayette. With the difficulty in tracking back two or three centuries, he wasn't able to make a precise determination of the exact ancestry, but was able to conclude the bloodline did relate to the Lafayettes of French nobility.

Bayne explains, "One family researcher describes two branches of the family in the years prior to the birth of Lafayette. When the current titled branch had no male offspring or the other branch had a stronger personality, the title was switched over. As France was almost continually at war, the mortality of the upper class, such as our ancestors supposedly were, was great. There was probably a good deal of switching back and forth."

Lafayette's father was Michel Louis Christophe Roch Gilbert du Motier de Lafayette, his paternal grandfather was Edouard du Motier Lafayette, and Edouard's father was named Charles du Motier de Champetieres. The Motier family of which Marguerite was a descendant hailed from a Raoul Motier (probably a much-shortened version of his full name and title).

The search for the family forebears who first stepped foot on American soil was more conclusive. Joseph Motier, Marguerite's great great grandfather, was the earliest American ancestor. Upon arriving in this foreign land, the Motiers were faced with the frustration of people's inability to use the correct French pronunciation of their name. Roland Bayne described the following: "The surname MOTIE is properly MOTIER, the "r" having been dropped by Francis P. Motie [Marguerite's father]. The French pronunciation of the name is approximately Motehay, but the Iowans insisted on calling it Mo-teer or some similar mispronunciation, so Mo-tee seemed a reasonable compromise. Herein, the two spellings are used interchangeably [referencing the narrative to follow]." In spite of the above explanation of the pronunciation, according to Marguerite's daughter, Dorothy Capeloto, the pronunciation is closer to "Mo-chee" (emphasis on the first syllable).

The following pages are a condensed and edited narrative of Roland Bayne's Motie family history, written about 1960, beginning with the earliest American ancestry:

Joseph Motier came into the district around St. Louis either through Detroit from Montreal or Quebec and down the Illinois River, or up the Mississippi from New Orleans. Randall Parrish, in his book *Historic Illinois*, says that settlers of Kaskaskia, Illinois, largely came from New Orleans, while those at Cahokia came largely from Canada. Kaskaskia was founded about 1700 when the Mission of the Immaculate Conception was moved to the junction of the Kaskaskia and Mississippi rivers. This was originally a Jesuit mission and later became the center of the French development of this area.

After Illinois and the eastern half of the Mississippi Valley was ceded to England in 1763, many of the French moved across the river into Missouri. Ste. Genevieve, Missouri, was the first permanent settlement in Missouri, in 1735. According to their marriage certificate, Joseph Motier and Felicite Rollet were married on February 6, 1769 in Ste. Genevieve, Missouri. So, it would seem that Joseph came from France through New Orleans.

Joseph and Felicite were the parents of 14 children, several of whom apparently died in infancy, including three that were named Joseph. It seemed to be in order in those days to perpetuate the name by giving it to another child in case the earlier bearer died. [One of Joseph and Felicite's children] Francois and [his wife] Felicite Constant were the parents of eight children.

The sixth child and third son [of Francois and Felicite] was Joseph Motier, born March 17, 1819. Joseph married Louise Knott, but she apparently died soon after, leaving no children. Joseph then married Mary Maguire, of Davenport, Iowa. She was born December 25, 1829, and died November 10, 1896. The cause of her death was given in one of Francis Patrick Motie's insurance policies, as 'bronchitis, after an illness of about one week.' The same policy states that his father's mother (Felicite Constant Motier) died of old age at 94, and his mother's mother [Mary Maguire's mother] of old age at about 90. He had no information about his grandfathers. One policy states that his father Joseph's death on August 28, 1880 in Davenport, Iowa, was the result of 'exposure after an illness of about one month' and another states that the cause was 'rheumatism of the heart.'

Thirteen children were born to Joseph and Mary, three of which, two boys and one girl, died in infancy. The ten that survived were: Marguerite, married Michael Lynch; Louise, married William Fayle; Emily, who became Sister Mary Henrietta, B.V.M.; Josephine, who became Sister Mary Isadora, B.V.M.; Francis Patrick, married Anna Mattes; Ella, married Charles Ward; George, married Mary Keating; Henry, married Alice Ryan; Eleanore, married Edward Keating; and Mary married Joseph Gillooley.

Francis Patrick, who was the fifth child but the first son, was born in Davenport, Iowa, as were the younger children. It is not known where the older children were born, but presumably in Davenport as Mary Maguire was a native of that city. Francis attended college at Cape Girardeau, Missouri, and apparently made a good record there; among his effects was a medal and a couple of books awarded for excellence in his studies. His insurance policy showed that in 1873 or 1874 he had a slight attack of typhoid fever, but no other serious illnesses.

After leaving college, he went to Odebolt, Iowa, and opened the Red Front Grocery. Not long afterwards, he went into partnership with John Mattes, brother of Anna [his future wife], as Motie and Mattes, in a general merchandise business. This continued until 1906 when the store was completely destroyed by fire.

Anna Mattes had come to Odebolt from Lyons, now a part of Clinton, Iowa, to work in her brother's store. On January 10, 1883, she married Francis Patrick Motie. Eight daughters were born to them, all in Odebolt:

- •Vivian Marie, born November 15, 1883; married Gerald J. DeWolf, October 8, 1920; died Los Angeles, Calif., March 9, 1955
- •Emily Loretta, born September 29, 1885; married Roland L. Bayne, April 16, 1914
- •Frances Anna, born December 25, 1887; entered Sisters of Notre Dame de Namur, August 15, 1917 as Sister Miriam Joseph
- •Miriam Josephine, born January 11, 1891; married George K. Reeder, December 31, 1913
- •Ruth Grace Theresa, born January 16, 1893; married Stephen A. Regan, October 7, 1916
- •Eleanor Marguerite [**Miss Spokane**], born January 19, 1895; married Walter P. Shiel, February 14, 1920
- •Dorothy Catherine, born November 27, 1897; married Frank C. Strebe, July 14, 1928
- •Esther Louise, born August 11, 1900; married Howard Brashears, July 5, 1928; died Boise, Idaho, October 21, 1930

After the store burned at Odebolt, Mr. and Mrs. Motie took a trip to the West Coast. In 1907 they moved to Spokane, where Mr., Motie engaged in the real estate business with Austin Ready and John Barnes, as Barnes, Motie & Ready. In 1927, Mr. and Mrs. Motie and Dorothy moved to Los Angeles. He died there as the result of a paralytic stroke April 5, 1936. Mrs. Motie died in Los Angeles June 27, 1951.

A History of the Mattes Family
(Marguerite Motie's Mother's Family)
Written about 1960 by Roland Bayne

Roman Mattes, his wife Marie Moser Mattes, and their six children emigrated from Germany to America in 1855. Little or no information is available about their earlier lives.

Roman Mattes was born in Wurttemberg, Germany, November 11, 1820. Marie Moser was born, presumably also in Wurttemberg, July 2, 1823. Roman died September 2, 1904, and Marie on September 27, 1901.

The family had heard of Iowa, and after landing in New York, went directly there. They crossed the Mississippi River and settled in Comanche, a few miles south of Clinton, Iowa. Later, they moved to Lyons, which is now part of Clinton.

While en route on the ocean, their boat was becalmed one day in a kind of vacuum. The captain ordered every one on deck, but refused to allow them to go below to rescue two of their children who were asleep in the cabin: Wentzel, born in 1851, and Abel, born in 1853. Both children suffocated and were buried at sea.

Children born to the couple were:

- •Joseph, born March 19, 1844; died March 28, 1844.
- •Rose, born March 10, 1845; married John Ketterer; died May 17, 1879.
- •Prisca, born January 18, 1847; married Joseph Ketterer; died February 15, 1884.
- •Mary Frederica, born September 20, 1848; married Keyser; lived in Eureka, Calif.; died February 25, 1926.
- •Brigetta, born June 19, 1850; married Gus Stoessiger; died January 11, 1937.
- •Wentzel, born 1851; died 1855 (at sea).
- •Abel, born 1853; died 1855 (at sea).
- •Joseph, born October 1, 1855; married (1) Kate Shelly (2) Elizabeth Platt; died April 17, 1924.
- •Twin brothers, born October 1, 1855; died about October 15, 1855.
- •John, born February 8, 1857; married Mary Hartman; died July 1921.
- •Anna Benedicta, born March 22, 1860; married Francis P. Motie; died June 27, 1951 **[Parents of future Miss Spokane, Marguerite Motie.]**
- •William, born July 28, 1862; married Estelle; died September 9, 1906.
- •Emily, born September 26, 1864; married Frank Butler; died March 22, 1887

The first photo of Frank and Anna Motie's family, taken prior to the birth of Marguerite's two younger sisters. Marguerite is in the center. Clockwise from top: Vivian Motie (DeWolf), Frances Motie (later became Sister Miriam Joseph), Mrs. Anna Motie, Miriam Motie (Reeder) and Ruth Motie (Regan), Frank P. Motie, Emily Motie (Bayne), circa 1896.

(Photo courtesy Dorothy Bayne Marchi.)

The Motie girls, from left: Vivian, Emily, Frances, Miriam, Ruth, Marguerite, Dorothy and Esther, circa 1905.

Dorothy (left) and Esther Motie (right) standing in front of the Motie family's first home in Spokane, circa 1908. This was located at 308 East Boone Avenue. The Knights of Columbus Hall is now on this site. *(Photo courtesy Dorothy Marchi.)*

Construction of the Moties' new home at 614 West Thirteenth Avenue began in 1909. Prior to completion in 1910, it was blessed by their parish priest and a religious medal was imbedded in the plaster above the front door.

Moties' home for the majority of their time in Spokane. *(Photos courtesy Dorothy Marchi.)*

Marguerite Motie, at about age 15, is at the center of both photos. In 1912, the year Marguerite Motie became Miss Spokane, the entire county had about 1,400 motorized vehicles. Most of her early years were in the era of horse transportation.

(All photos courtesy Dorothy Marchi.)

Left: Marguerite, Emily and Ruth Motie with some unidentified friends. **Right:** Marguerite and Miriam Motie. Both photos were at the Motie home on west Thirteenth.

Left: Eating watermelon on the porch of the Moties' cabin at Twin Lakes, Idaho. Marguerite is center front and Walter Shiel is far right. **Right:** Marguerite with her mother, father and a friend during a housecleaning session.

A photo montage of Marguerite Motie during her teenage years.

(Photos courtesy Dorothy & Bob Capeloto.)

Marguerite and a friend washing the family car. *(Photos courtesy Dorothy Marchi.)*

Marguerite in back seat with her sister Ruth at the wheel.

Marguerite Motie in the front yard of the family home at 614 W. Thirteenth Avenue, circa 1909.

Marguerite with the city of Spokane as the backdrop. *(Photos courtesy Dorothy Marchi.)*

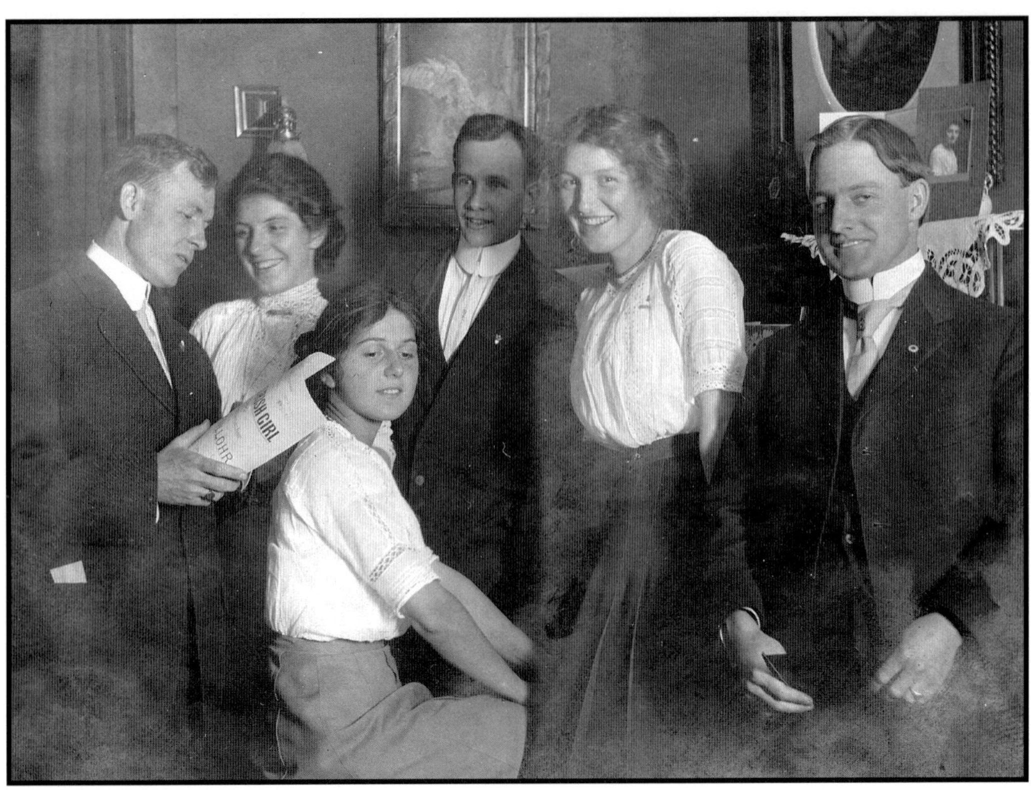

Marguerite (seated), sisters and friends in the family home at 614 W. Thirteenth.

(Photos courtesy Dorothy & John Marchi.)

Shampoo day at the Motie's summer cabin at Twin Lakes, Idaho.

Marguerite with her boyfriend, Walt Shiel, at Twin Lakes, circa 1911.

(Top photo courtesy Dorothy & Bob Capeloto. Bottom photo courtesy Dorothy Marchi.)

Marguerite (second from right) with three of her sisters at Twin Lakes, circa 1910.

Marguerite and more good times with her sisters at Twin Lakes, circa 1909.

(Top photo courtesy Dorothy Marchi. Bottom photo courtesy Dorothy & Bob Capeloto.)

Walter Shiel (left), Marguerite Motie (second left) and friends, circa 1910.

The Motie family during the girls' teenage years. Marguerite is third from the left in back row. *(Photos courtesy Dorothy Marchi.)*

Left to right: Ruth, Dorothy, Anna and Marguerite Motie and friends, circa 1910.

Dorothy and John Marchi, 1997. Dorothy, Marguerite Motie Shiel's niece, is the daughter of Roland and Emily Motie Bayne and was named after her Aunt Dorothy Motie Strebe. She taught the first and second grades at Grant School until she married John Marchi.

Marilyn and William Bayne, 1978. William Bayne is Roland and Emily Motie Bayne's son and Dorothy Marchi's brother. For many years, he was the office manager for Central Pre-Mix in Spokane. He was also one of the organizers of Spokane's Crime Check Program.

A History of the Motie Family

Written in 1985 by Dorothy Marchi.

(Unless otherwise noted, all photos in this section are courtesy of Dorothy and John Marchi.)

My mother was Emily, the second oldest of Frank and Anna Motie's eight daughters. Since we lived in the old family home, not a day went by without Mother referring to something or somebody from the past. The old home still stands at 614 W. Thirteenth Avenue in Spokane. Someday, I hope to go through it again and see just what has changed since Frank Motie built it in 1909 for $5,000.

Anna and Frank Motie lived in Odebolt, Iowa, where he had a grocery store. Anyway, they lived most of the time above the store and got along with what heat was generated from the store below. Some of the Iowa winters were pretty frigid. I heard many stories as I was growing up of how Emily and Vivian, who were babies, had to spend the whole day playing on the bed because the floors were so cold. The store burned one year and, although it was beyond help as far as opening again, there were many canned goods that were salvaged from the fire. The family moved to a small home and for many months used those canned goods themselves. They never knew what they were going to have for dinner, since the labels were either burned or soaked off from the water used to fight the fire. Many a time, a can of peaches was opened for breakfast and found to contain spinach or beans. Whatever was opened was used, as nothing could be wasted.

Frank and Anna Motie, circa 1911.

All eight girls were born in Odebolt. When the last one was still small, they migrated to Spokane, why I'll never know, unless it was because of cousins living in Davenport or Reardan.

The family settled in a house near St. Aloysius Church, which was located on the site of the present Knights of Columbus Hall. At first, the girls were thoroughly snubbed by many of the parents in the parish, as young "eligible" men were not too plentiful there. The idea of a family with at least four young daughters of marriageable age was just too much to bear. However, Frank had a beautiful bass voice and soon was welcomed into the parish choir and Anna was a hard-working woman who did more than her part at Altar Society functions. Her chicken pie was a real winner at the church dinners. It didn't take long before everyone found out that all the excitement was happening at the Motie house. All the girls were musical and the young people gathered there, with their parents soon joining them.

Frank worked at selling real estate and dabbled in investments, but he never again started a store or worked at a 9:00 to 5:00 job. He must have done fairly well, however, as early pictures show him to be well dressed in the latest fashions and Anna showing off her mink muff with her velvet-collared suit and modish hat. I still have the muff. As I was growing up, my mother let me hold it and stroke it and occasionally play dress-up with it in the house, but no one was ever allowed to take it outdoors. "We must save it – it's Mama's Japanese mink!" What did we save it for?

Frank was a tall, strong and very distinguished gentleman. Anna was a small, wiry woman, with boundless energy and the ability to do most anything she wanted to. She never stood on ceremony – if something needed doing she did it. A local cartoonist once drew pictures of the town's leading women. Anna was pictured with a hammer in one hand, a saw in the other and a mouth full of nails.

After they moved into their new house on Thirteenth Avenue in 1910, they had plenty of room for their growing family. The house had five bedrooms upstairs, with a large storeroom for linens, and a large sleeping porch big enough for three double beds. All the beds were used in the hot summer weather.

A full attic took up the third floor and was filled with trunks and boxes. As each girl married and left home, she always left part of her belongings packed away in the attic. Of course, the attic was always boiling hot in the summer and freezing in the winter, but Bill and I were occasionally allowed to play up there in bad weather. It wasn't too much fun; we knew the trunks were packed with treasures, but we weren't allowed to get into them. We could, however, have a big floor on which to roller skate or play miniature cars.

The house was huge, but even with ten people living there it had only one bathroom which was located on the second floor. No matter! Frank had a tiny lavatory built just off the kitchen, which was off-limits to everyone when he was in the house. That was HIS! No one, not even Anna, ever set foot in that room when PAPA was home. Can't say that I blame him, living with nine women. He did bathe in the room upstairs, as he had a special bathtub built to fit him. It was the usual style of the day, clawed feet and all, but was extra long so he could stretch out his legs. Needless to say, no one was allowed to put more than a couple of inches of water in it, as it just took too much to fill.

There were beautiful hardwood floors, which had to be waxed and polished twice a year. The woodwork was dark mahogany, which also had to be hand-rubbed, cleaned and polished twice a year. The accent was always on the "hand-rubbed," so we were never allowed to use polishing machines or cleaning solvents on it. How I hated housecleaning time after we moved into the house. We always had a cleaning woman who came for about three days and the house was turned inside out. The rugs were taken out in the back, thrown over the clothes line and whacked with carpet beaters,

Frank and Anna Motie

which were wire contraptions resembling tennis rackets. Curtains were regularly taken down and washed or cleaned, and the wallpaper was often gone over with damp cloths.

The house had huge rooms with sliding doors that could be opened so the occupants could have dancing parties, allowing the guests to dance all through the house. They could also be closed to give privacy. As the girls grew up and began to entertain "beaus," the doors would be partially (never all the way) closed as each girl staked out her room in the evening to entertain her "company." One couple could sit in the living room, one in the dining room, kitchen, library, small telephone room, hall, pantry and on the stairs. The ones on the stairs had to be very discreet and converse in low tones, as Mama and Papa were supposedly asleep upstairs, along with the younger sisters.

This didn't always work out! One time Miriam and George Reader were cozily getting acquainted in the dining room when, just as the atmosphere was becoming nicely romantic, a small voice belonging to Esther, who was about four at the time, piped up with "I've got some new panties." She had been hiding under the long cloth on the dining room table. She had evidently been missed when bedtime came or had sneaked down later. Needless to say, Miriam was wild and Esther was punished, but it sure caused some excitement.

Frank was deeply religious and Anna, while a convert to the Catholic faith, kept the family strictly on the straight and narrow path. Before the big house was completed, it was duly blessed by the parish priest and a medal, I'm not sure which one, was imbedded in the plaster above the front door. I suppose it's still there.

The Moties were very well known and were truly among the pillars of the town, though they were not wealthy. The girls were all very popular and had many friends. As they grew up, they all worked, most of them naturally turning to teaching.

The house was classed as a showplace, but was surpassed by the mansions down in Browne's Addition and on Seventh Avenue. It was not surrounded by huge lawns and gardens, but was at the very end of the Cable Addition streetcar line with nothing beyond it but pine trees.

The young men callers thought it was great, as the last streetcar on Saturday night would stop out in front of the house and give several toots on its whistle, waiting for all of them to say their good-byes and get safely on the "owl" car back to town. My father (Roland) and a couple of the others were all envied, as they could walk back down the hill to the YMCA on the corner of First and Lincoln where they had rooms; they could stay longer than the others. Even they could outstay their welcome, however. My mother (Emily) told of the time that Dad stayed quite late – about 12:30 a.m. – and when mother went up the stairs to bed, her father met her and said, "Emily, do you know what time it is?" She was 27 years old and "almost engaged," so she stood her ground and answered, "Yes, Papa, I do." He nodded to her and went off to bed without another word, but it really shook her up.

Grandpa Motie was a very kindly man, but he was straight and tall and rather quiet. We loved him but we didn't touch him, as he was not the type to cuddle. Vivian's daughters, Helen Godlewski and Frances Haley, will remember him better than I, as they lived with him in California. He was never around much in Spokane. Whenever I asked where Grandpa was, I would be told, "He's gone to Medicine Hat to look after his mining interests." Evidently he had investments in some mines and I assume they were in Medicine Hat, Alberta. At any rate, his family seemed to live all right on his income and, of course, as the girls began working, they all contributed toward the household expenses. He was strictly a no-nonsense person and believed firmly in law and order. A rule was a rule, and that was that. He never showed much emotion and never any affection toward Grandma, but everyone knew it was there, as his consideration for her came first. Her word was absolute law, after his, and if she gave an order, the girls had better jump to obey.

He expected everyone to do their part and for the household to run smoothly and so, of course, it did. When things got a little hectic, one sentence – "Go right now and help your mother" – brought an immediate response from whichever girl was nearby. He expected dinner to be on the table at a certain time and everyone to be there. When the family was called to the table, he took his place promptly. If some of the girls tarried upstairs and were late, he waited for Grandma to make one more call, then he stepped to the stairs and said, "Come this minute." They came in whatever state they were in – with wet hair, rumpled robe, or even in their slip with a hastily grabbed shawl. They ate dinner silently in disgrace, then were excused to go and "make yourself presentable." Consequently, it didn't happen often that they were caught that way.

Grandma was a sprightly, friendly little woman who bustled about – busy, busy, busy. She always had a story to tell the little ones as she worked and was always teaching as she went. Every story had a moral or some instruction, but we did love her. She whistled all the time, so we always knew where she was. When I was little, I loved to visit her as she had two large bins in her big kitchen – one filled with flour and one with sugar. She would let me scrub my hands well and wrap me in clean dish towels with lots of newspapers on the floor. Protected in that manner, she would then let me play in the flour bin. Her flour bin became my own private "sandbox" and more fun than anything. When I was five years old, the grandparents decided to move to California to be with Dodi and Miriam. At that time, my parents bought the big house and it became our home. Miriam was married and Dodi was working for the Richfield Oil Company. They thought their parents should get away from the big house and the harsh winters.

I don't remember much about Grandma and Grandpa Motie from then on, as we didn't see them very often, but when we did visit, Grandma was still whistling. It got to be an almost soundless whistle as she grew older, but whistle she did until she died.

Grandpa was in his 70s when he died from a stroke. Grandma lived well into her 90s, becoming very forgetful but still active. Their last few years, Vivian and her two girls lived with them. Poor Vivian almost went crazy trying to keep track of Grandma. Vivian got her started on a quilt once, thinking it would keep her busy and out of trouble for a few months. Grandma waited until Vivian went to the store, got out the sewing machine and put the quilt together in record time.

Vivian was the oldest of the eight girls, and from what I gathered, she took most of the brunt of the baby-sitting, housekeeping and other duties. I have heard my mother, Emily, say many times that she and Vivian had both raised their families before they ever got married. Their mother was so busy caring for the family that these two girls had to do more than their share of the work.

Vivian

I don't have many memories of Vivian as I didn't see that much of her, but I remember her as a quiet, warm, loving person. She devoted her life to the care of others. She and Emily were both finished with two years of "teachers college" when the family moved to Spokane, so they immediately went to work as teachers. Both taught at the old Grant School in the southeast part of town and I believe, but I'm not sure, that Vivian at one point was the principal of the school. Emily, I know, taught the primary grades.

Before they had been in Spokane for too many years, Vivian met and married Gerald DeWolf. They had two daughters, Frances and Helen. I remember him as a friendly uncle. Gerald had a small farm, where we used to go often. I always envied Frances and Helen because they had kittens and baby rabbits to play with.

Eventually this marriage dissolved. Vivian and her girls went to Los Angeles to live with grandmother, grandfather and Dorothy. Vivian kept the house running smoothly while caring for her girls, parents, and Dorothy and her husband.

Emily, my mother, was the second oldest of the eight girls. She and Vivian undertook most of the housekeeping and baby-sitting chores. They were both natural housekeepers and cooks, always seeming to enjoy their work.

Emily

Emily was raised in Odebolt and had finished her two years at the local teachers college when the family moved to Spokane. She had desperately wanted to be a nurse, but her folks said absolutely no. They felt the work was too hard for a girl and, no matter how hard she pleaded, she got nowhere – so teaching it was. When they moved, she immediately went to work at the Grant School teaching the first and second grades. In 1914 she married Roland Bayne, my father. That same year, they moved to Minneapolis, where my brother Bill was born. Following his birth, they moved back to Spokane, where I was born.

Mother and Dad met at a party where each had gone with another date. They continued to date others and always showed up at the various group activities with other dates, so everyone was amazed when they announced their engagement and forthcoming marriage.

Mother was an energetic, fun-loving person, always ready for a party, but still ran her life in an orderly way. When I was growing up, we always did things on a strict schedule. It used to drive me batty. Every picnic had to be planned beforehand and the housework done first. We washed on Monday, ironed on Tuesday, sewed and shopped on Wednesday, cleaned the upstairs on Thursday and the downstairs on Friday. Saturday was kept open in case Dad wanted to do something and, of course, Sunday was church day. The housework was always done by noon and then we could go to town or do something else in the afternoons. Her family always came first and she had a strong sense of duty.

She was a born manager and always kept her family clean, comfortable and well-fed. We were never rich and some years were quite poor, but she managed the house and family, and kept us out of debt with whatever allowance Dad could give her. He always gave her full credit and said that whatever we had was due to Mother's saving and planning.

When I was in about the sixth grade, he bought our first car for her as she had saved her pennies for a long time for it. She immediately learned to drive, although he didn't for a good many years. He just didn't care for it and didn't want to; he had to later, as he needed to drive to get around. It changed our life considerably, but what really changed it was when Bill turned 16 and was able to get his driver's license. Then we were able to drive to California and go a bit farther afield. I hated some of those trips as I always had to sit in the back seat because Mother wanted "a man" in the front next to her in case anyone started to accost us. As if anyone would dare! We regularly went to visit the family in Los Angeles every two years. It was a long trip by automobile.

Mother and Dad made a good team. He earned the living and she carefully ran the household. We found out many years later they had helped many young relatives and students out of financial difficulties.

Mother followed in the footsteps of her mother and was always teaching. Every story, every chore, had a reason or a moral. We did things because they had to be done, and we did them a certain way because that was the right way to do them. It was many years later, after I was grown and had a family of my own, before I felt comfortable washing on any day but Monday or leaving beds unmade for several hours. She lived to be 93 and was strong and healthy almost until the last.

Frances

Frances was the "devil" of the family. She was very musical and very talented, so when she finished high school she made her living giving piano lessons. I don't believe she had much of a voice, but she sure could play the piano. She had a regular job in the evenings and on weekends playing the piano at the local theater for the vaudeville shows and later for the "talkies" and the silent films. They always had a local pianist or organist who provided all the background music for the shows.

According to the others, Frances had a whole swarm of "beaus" around her all the time and was always getting up a party of some kind. She was good at practical jokes and fast with a retort and really enjoyed life. Consequently, everyone was simply astounded when she announced with no warning that she was joining the convent. They really didn't object to the move, but she had made all her plans without a word to anyone. She had investigated the various orders and made all the arrangements, simply announcing she was leaving on a certain date to go east and enter the Sisters of the Holy Name (not the same order as is in Spokane).

She was to be Sister Miriam Joseph and she went calmly about her departure plans while the excitement swirled around her. When girls entered the convent then, they had to take with them a whole list of supplies. My mother remembered helping Frances purchase yards of black cotton for underclothes, black stockings and a whole bolt of black serge for habits. She turned into a fascinating nun and was obviously happy with her choice.

Sister Miriam Joseph

She was based at several locations in California and we always went to visit her when we went down there. She always came to greet us with her skirts flying, her freckled nose crinkled and usually sunburned, and her black eyes dancing. She always had a story or joke to tell and all the nuns and students loved her. She taught music in the girls' convent schools until she died.

Ruth was the tallest of the girls; tall, big-boned and a real lady. She was gentle, gracious, and quiet in her movements and her voice. She had a beautiful voice and always sang in any choir that happened to be in the town where she was living. I believe she could have had a career in voice if she had had the training.

Ruth

She had lovely, long brownish-blonde hair, which she wore coiled on her neck until her children were grown and she decided she needed a "new" look. Then she cut it and wore it short until her son Morgan came home from the service after WWII. He told her that every night when he was so far from home, he imagined his mother sitting at her dressing table brushing her long hair. She immediately let it grow and never touched at again. I wonder if Morgan remembers.

Steve Regan was a perfect match for Ruth. He was tall, quiet and gentle in his movements.

Steve and Ruth moved to Salt Lake City, where they developed a good seed business. He and Ruth worked like slaves day and night for years. They hung on through thick and thin and eventually had a good business.

Then there was **Miriam**. If Frances was the devil of the family, then Miriam was surely the spitfire. She had reddish hair and a very quick temper. All you had to do to bring on a tongue-lashing was to say something about her red hair and then duck.

She always maintained it was brown. She was lively and a lot of fun.

Miriam

Miriam married a very nice, quiet and easygoing man named George Reeder. They had a happy marriage for many years, living in southern California. George was an engineer. When they moved to California, he was hired by Disney, where Dorothy worked. He was highly thought of there. He designed a camera that enabled them to take the series of cartoons as they passed rapidly in front of the camera lens. His invention made possible a lot of the Disney films.

Marguerite

Marguerite was the most well known of all the girls. Through her role as the first Miss Spokane, she became a prominent member of Spokane's history. She was barely 17 years old when friends entered her name and picture in the contest run by the Spokane Ad Club for the Miss Spokane contest. She won the contest for her beauty. However, her aptitude for meeting people and speaking at all kinds of public functions, both large and small soon proved to be a tremendous asset. She had a real talent for remembering names and could call people by name years after meeting them.

Her duties as Miss Spokane were very demanding. She gave a public address at most functions of the Spokane Ad Club, as well as at city-wide functions. She traveled as ambassador of Spokane all over the West Coast.

Dorothy (Dodi)

Dorothy was next to the youngest and the artist of the family. She was very like her mother in that she talked very softly and was always bustling around behind the scenes while the rest of the family were singing, arguing, or just carrying on in general.

Dorothy, or Dodi, as we all called her, was still in grade school when the family moved to Spokane. She went on to Lewis and Clark High School and then to the University of Washington for a year or two. She returned to Spokane with secretarial skills and worked for a time for the *Spokane Chronicle*. She then took off for California and a better job with the Richfield Oil Company, which at that time was a major oil company. She bought a small house and persuaded her parents to live with her to get away from the Spokane winters.

Marguerite Motie in the back seat during an early appearance as Miss Spokane.
(Photo courtesy Dorothy & Bob Capeloto.)

Marguerite, about 1916, during the time she attended the school of oratory at Northwestern University in Chicago for a year. Although she was already highly praised for her speaking abilities, she still sought to improve her skills and took a leave from her studies at the University of Washington to attend Northwestern.

(Photo courtesy Dorothy & Bob Capeloto.)

She had an old car (a great big "touring car," as they were called then) and one of my earliest memories is of leaning out the window and watching all of them leave for California. Dodi had driven up to get her folks. The old car was piled high with suitcases and household supplies, even having various pieces of baggage tied on the roof. They made it safely to Los Angeles and, eventually, Vivian joined them with her two girls. They stayed there for the rest of their lives.

Soon after this, Dodi met Frank Strebe while ice skating at an indoor rink in Los Angeles. Frank was an instructor there and it wasn't long before they were married. She and Frank seemed to be very happy and they got along well. Frank was an engineer with Richfield when they met. He subsequently went to work at Walt Disney Productions, where Dodi then worked.

Later, when Dodi's folks lived with them, Grandpa Motie had a stroke and was partially paralyzed. Frank proved to be an excellent and devoted nurse to him and a valued companion and helper to Grandma. Dodi and Frank later built a small bungalow at the back of their lot, which solved a lot of problems. It didn't have a kitchen, just a bed, sitting room and bath. Consequently, they ate all their meals with the family, but everyone still had their privacy.

Dodi was a real artist and worked for many years for Walt Disney. She dabbled in art and was always decorating everything she touched with little pictures. She was also quite a story teller and wrote many of the stories that appeared in Disney's comic books. We were always very impressed that she was on a first name basis with Walt Disney and knew his whole family. When I got married, she put together the picture of Snow White meeting her dream prince and had Walt sign it himself. I still have the picture.

Esther was the youngest of the girls. She resembled Marguerite a great deal, as they both had the very dark hair and eyes. After she finished school, she joined Frances as a pianist in the local theatre, but didn't work very long before moving to Boise. There she met and married Howard Brashears or "Beanie," as he was known.

Esther

Esther and her new husband came to Spokane on their honeymoon. Sadly, they were not married very long before she died from injuries received in an automobile accident. She was only thirty years old.

Esther and her new husband, Howard Brashears, circa 1928

Esther Motie in the 1920s.

Dorothy "Dodi" Motie in the 1920s.

Emily Motie on a picnic with friends, circa 1920. Inset is also Emily.

Marguerite Motie, The First Miss Spokane

Officially 1912 to 1920, unofficially until 1939

Marguerite Motie, 1912
(Photo courtesy Dorothy & John Marchi.)

Marguerite Motie's life was going to change considerably during the early part of April in 1912. At the age of 17 and barely out of high school, she was about to mature into the most celebrated and popular woman in Spokane's entire history. In a recent interview, her daughter, Dorothy Capeloto, said, "Everyone loved Mother."

Already admired and well known in Spokane's Cannon Hill area, Marguerite was a tall, dark beauty with poise beyond her years. She radiated a genuine sincerity and kindness toward others. Before Marguerite graduated in June 1911 from Lewis and

South Central High School, corner of Howard Street and Fourth Avenue (on the site of the present Lewis and Clark High School.). It was known for its red brick tower and clock that faithfully struck on the hour. This photo was taken in June of 1910, when it mysteriously caught fire during summer vacation and burned to the ground. Until Lewis and Clark was built, the students from this school attended North Central High School. (*Photo courtesy Spokane Public Library.*)

Clark High School, she was voted the most popular girl in her class. (South Central High School, where she had been attending, was renamed Lewis and Clark after the building burned in 1910.) She was intelligent, talented and athletic, but her outstanding achievement was her oratory skills.

Born in Odebolt, Iowa, on January 19, 1895, Marguerite moved to Spokane in 1907 with her father Frank, mother Anna and seven sisters. Upon arriving in Spokane, the family settled in a house at 308 East Boone, now the site of the Knights of Columbus Hall near St. Aloysius Church. With nine women in his family and one bathroom in their home, early morning starts were often challenging at the Motie home. Frank became involved in the real estate profession, eventually becoming a partner in the firm of Barnes, Motie & Ready. Their office was located at 811 West Sprague.

Marguerite lived in the Gonzaga neighborhood until 1910. During those years, one of her neighbors was the young "Bing" Crosby, whose family lived about two blocks

South Central High School varsity basketball team. Marguerite, who was a fine athlete, is in the middle row, second from right.

1911 South Central (Lewis and Clark) class officers. Marguerite was the secretary.

away. By the time Marguerite moved to Spokane's South Hill, Bing was about seven years old. Even at that young age, he was already becoming known in the neighborhood – being fondly remembered by Marguerite and many of her friends as somewhat of a little "brat." In 1909 the family began construction of a new home at 614 West Thirteenth Avenue on Spokane's South Hill.

When the Motie family arrived in Spokane in 1907, the population was about 65,000. Spokane had only one high school, which had been built in 1890, called Spokane High School. In 1908 North Central High School was built and Spokane High School took on the name South Central High School. When South Central burned in 1910, all of Spokane's high school students attended North Central until 1912, when the new Lewis and Clark High School was built on the old South Central site.

Spokane Seeks a Symbol

By 1912 a large group of Spokane's businessmen had officially united together as the Spokane Ad Club. Hoping to increase the city's population for the benefit of their businesses, their main objective was to initiate a public relations program that would capture nationwide attention. To that end, they held a drawing-and-design contest, open to the entire Inland Empire. They hoped to capture some type of symbol that would be representative of the Inland Northwest. Their intent for this symbol was revealed in the January 17, 1912, edition of the *Spokane Daily Chronicle*, following an interview with R.E. Bigelow, president of the Spokane Ad Club:

> Many of the leading countries in the world are represented in sketches and illustrations by figures that bespeak something of what these countries are. The United States is represented by Miss Columbia, a heroic figure that typifies this country. Canada has its sturdy figure, a woman in stocking cap and mittens. England has its Britania [*sic*], a warlike figure with a proud, determined face. All these designs are significant, and they are typical of the countries represented. What we are going to do by means of this contest is to give Spokane a figure that will be equally typical.

Another description of what this design should depict appeared in the January 23, 1912, edition of the *Spokesman-Review*. This statement was attributed to Miss Halliene Hall and again reflected the Ad Club's intentions for Spokane's symbol:

> My idea of Miss Spokane is that she should be a figure that would express something more than life, activity and progress. She should be the embodiment of soul and thought and beauty, and the expression of these characteristics would perforce, embrace power . . . No one need feel shy about portraying a woman of the days gone by, for it would be ridiculous to have a figure too entirely modern. What is needed is a woman expressing thought and soul, no matter in what age she may be represented.

The article that officially announced the contest, which appeared in the January 17, 1912, edition of the *Spokane Daily Chronicle*, read as follows:

> **WANTED – "MISS SPOKANE," AD CLUB PLANS CONTEST**, Prizes Offered for Drawings and Descriptions of Figure Typical of Spirit, Enterprise, Wealth and Charms of Metropolis of Inland Empire – Conditions of the Miss Spokane Contest: Contest is open to all – artists and laymen alike. Sketches and designs may be submitted by those entering, or a written description of the candidate's ideas of the figure may be submitted. The contest will open Thursday morning. Communications are to be addressed to R.E. Bigelow, president Spokane Ad Club, in care of Wentworth's Clothing Store.

The Spokane Ad Club offered the winner of this contest $25 in gold coins. This and the honor of selecting Spokane's official design proved to be an adequate incentive. The response was excellent – numerous artists and art students in the Spokane area took part. The contest called for a conceptual drawing of an ideal face and figure clad in an appropriate costume representative of the entire Inland Northwest. The rules of the contest asked for a design, not only artistic, but built around a concept typifying Spokane. It also asked for a written description outlining the keynotes or predominant characteristics of each drawing submitted.

A public statement in a 1912 local Spokane paper by Mrs. B.L. Gordon, a well-known art patron and society woman, sums up a segment of the community's attitude: "Without a doubt this movement is having a most beneficial effect toward encouraging art in Spokane. Recently there has been aroused a new era in appreciation of art and music in Spokane, and the Miss Spokane contest is going a long way toward making Spokane up to date in this important particular."

The Selection Process

Nine judges were selected by the Ad Club and included the following: Halliene Hall, art enthusiast and society woman; Adolph Well, artist and merchant; August Wolf, secretary of the publicity committee for the Spokane Chamber of Commerce; Spokane Mayor William J. Hindley; W.D. Vincent, cashier for the Old National Bank; William C. Morris, cartoonist for the *Spokesman-Review*; R. Lewis Rutter, vice president and secretary of the Spokane and Eastern Trust Company and president of Western Union Life Insurance Company; Alex Green, advertising manager for the Crescent; and Gordon C. Corbaley, the manager of the real estate department for the Arthur D. Jones & Co. and also a trustee of the Chamber of Commerce.

By February 12, 1912, when this contest officially closed, 105 drawings and scores of written suggestions had been submitted. From the inception, this contest had attracted enormous attention, appearing almost daily on the front pages of the local newspaper. The Ad Club made arrangements with Louis Davenport for the use of the Hall of the Doges in the Davenport Hotel for the purpose of displaying all the designs submitted. This was the most beautiful and fitting facility in Spokane for this exhibition. There was room enough to display every entry, which the judges would examine and deliberate upon.

The following day, the difficulty of picking a winner was announced in the newspapers. The *Spokane Daily Chronicle* reported:

> "MISS SPOKANE" ARTISTS ASKED FOR NEW IDEAS, Seven Best Drawings Picked and Designers Will Seek to Improve Work. After deliberating for more than three hours this morning the board of judges of the Miss Spokane contest threw up their hands, and announced they were unable to reach a decision. Splendid ideas were numerous in the drawings, but the judges were unable to pick out any one as head and shoulders above the rest.

The contest would continue for an additional three weeks, giving the seven finalists time to fine-tune and resubmit their drawings. During that time, the *Spokane Daily Chronicle* began publishing each of these winning sketches on a daily basis. The Ad Club also put on a one-day public display of these finalists' entries in the east banquet room of Davenport's Restaurant.

On March 7, 1912, the winning entry, drawn by Eleanor Gaddis, was a combination of two sketches of an Indian maiden. The first sketch portrayed a maiden with outstretched arms; the second depicted this same girl with a jug of flowing water under her left arm and sowing grain with her right. The Ad Club members were enthusiastic about the results. Of interest, on March 13, 1912, just after the close of the contest, the Ad Club auctioned off Eleanor Gaddis's drawing. Intense bidding ended with J.H. Overhauser, heir of the Overhauser Candy Company, receiving the drawing for $130.

The Fairest Young Woman is Chosen

This winning sketch would soon be brought to life. The following day, on March 8, 1912, the Spokane Ad Club initiated a photo contest seeking the face of a young woman that would typify Spokane. The face of the contest's winner was to be superimposed on Eleanor Gaddis's winning drawing. The *Spokane Daily Chronicle* article announcing the contest contained the following:

> Beauty alone will not win this contest. There should be something in the face of the girl selected for the honor of representing the city that will tell without words something for which Spokane stands or hopes to become. Whether that something is determination, the expression of progressiveness, hope or any other quality, only the pictures submitted will tell.

The next day, the paper added: "The features, of course, must show strength and beauty, and neither quality alone will be sufficient." No prize, monetary or otherwise, was offered other than the honor of being chosen.

The cutoff date for the Miss Spokane photo contest was March 28, 1912, by which time 138 photographs had been submitted to the Ad Club. This response was quite significant considering each contestant was to submit front-view and profile photos, preferably with long hair prepared in braids. All but three or four entrants posed in braids. There was no interview process, but many of the contestants were already well known in the community. Of all the entrants, only one was part Native American. Vera Mann, the daughter of Judge and Mrs. Samuel A. Mann of 503 East Nineteenth Avenue, claimed to be able to trace her family tree back to Pocahontas. The official photographer was Charles Libby, Sr., who had a studio in the Granite Building.

For this final contest six judges were chosen: C.E. Hickman, commercial superintendent for the Pacific Telephone and Telegraph Company; Herbert Kippen with Western Car Advertisement Company; Gus W. Roche, advertising manager of the *Spokane Daily Chronicle*; F.H. Lloyd, Hayward Larkin Advertising Company; and Alex Green, advertising manager of the Crescent Store. The judges were purposely selected for their talents in the advertising and promotional field. Interestingly, no women were asked to be judges.

Marguerite Motie's photos, in which she wore a lacy white dress, long braids and a headband, won the honor. The Ad Club was overwhelmingly impressed by her image and, on March 29, 1912, chose her as the winning entrant. Soon after the contest ended, perhaps much to Marguerite's credit, the Ad Club decided to have Miss Spokane "come to life" and, as the "fairest young woman" in the city, Marguerite would represent Spokane as its official hostess. Her image would typify Spokane and be used in all publicity matters and her likeness would be Spokane's emblem.

Marguerite Assumes the Role

Shortly after Marguerite's selection as Miss Spokane, her mother and sisters made a pattern for her official gown, which was almost identical to that of the winning sketch by Eleanor Gaddis. Bodeneck & Jacobs, dressmakers in Spokane who made the official gown from sheepskin, completed the design. A sunburst on the breast of her dress was of yellow velvet, covered with thousands of small glass beads. The remainder of her costume consisted of a triple strand of Indian beads and a beaded sash-belt and moccasins. When this was completed, her braided hair was ornamented with flowers. She now took on the look the Ad Club had desired and sought to obtain. Charles Libby again took her photos. This time, however, it was a different type of photo session; he was taking pictures of Miss Spokane for the world to see.

On April 8, 1912, the Ad Club honored Marguerite as queen of their first annual jubilee held in conjunction with a popular play, *Miss Nobody From Starland,* at the Auditorium Theater. This appearance was Marguerite's debut as the city's new Miss Spokane. Her first official appearance as Miss Spokane, on April 13, 1912, was at a baseball game for charity between the Spokane Indians of the Northwestern League and a team picked from eight companies of the 25th Infantry Regiment stationed at Fort George Wright. When she tossed the first ball over the plate, six maids of honor, who were also dressed in Native American costumes, attended her. These women had also been selected from photographs they submitted to the Ad Club for

These are newspaper copies of the photographs submitted of Marguerite Motie to the Spokane Ad Club in 1912. The decision to select her as Miss Spokane was made as a result. (*News clipping courtesy Dorothy & Bob Capeloto.*)

the contest. They were: Carol Rutter, Blanche Kemp, Marjorie Lindsley, Ruth Oppenheimer, Margaret Jensen and Rachael Hutchinson. For several years, members of this group accompanied Marguerite Motie as maids of honor during various functions. Although even the maids of honor were dressed in Native American attire, no actual Indians were ever represented in the contest.

Over the next eight years, Marguerite Motie was at the center of the most intense and active promotional campaign the Inland Northwest has ever witnessed. Her photograph even appeared on many letterheads of area businesses. She received both national and worldwide attention. During the period of its inception and application, the creation of Miss Spokane was considered a brilliant concept, lauded and copied by other cities. It was a success in numerous ways, mostly as an excellent means of introduction to Spokane.

Marguerite Motie was originally chosen because of her comeliness, but it was her charm, poise and ability as a speaker that stood out. She was truly Spokane's first ambassador and a noteworthy player in its early history. She attended and spoke at almost every important Spokane function – typically as the featured attraction. She often traveled and represented Spokane throughout the United States. Postcards and brochures were printed with her likeness. In 1917 a beautiful, twin-engine passenger steamship was built on Lake Coeur d'Alene and named the *Miss Spokane*. During July of 1917, the *Miss Spokane* made her trial run, with Marguerite Motie as its honored guest. On June 5, 1919, she christened the first airplane of the Northwest Aircraft Company in Spokane. This aircraft was also named *Miss Spokane*. Buttons, medals, statues, fountains, spoons, candy, perfume and even a license-plate bracket were made in or with her image. A huge, beautiful stained-glass likeness of her was also created, which hung in the entryway of the Cheney Cowles Museum for many years. There were poems about Miss Spokane and even two popular songs came out about her: *Hello Miss Spokane* and *There Never was a Girlie Like You*. She was venerated in almost every conceivable way.

In 1920 she married her high school sweetheart, Walter Shiel, and soon moved to Seattle. However, she was occasionally called back to Spokane to officiate at major functions. After starting her family, her children sometimes accompanied her, which was a true indication of Marguerite's dedication to her role. During the Depression years, as the nation struggled to survive, the role of Miss Spokane nearly fell into obscurity. However, the contest was revived in 1939 when the second Miss Spokane in this contest, Catherine Betts (Williams), was selected. Marguerite, of course, was given a special invitation to participate in the installation ceremonies. Within a decade, the guidelines were changed, requiring the annual selection of a new Miss Spokane to serve as the city's official hostess. An annual selection was made until the contest was terminated on January 1, 1977.

Marguerite Motie dressed in the official Miss Spokane Indian costume. She was typically Spokane's center attraction and an outstanding crowd pleaser.

Marguerite Motie with the key to Spokane. The official flag for the City of Spokane is on the left. *(Photos courtesy Dorothy & Bob Capeloto.)*

GREETS ROOSEVELT

Princess Spokane Introduces Colonel to Women at Auditorium Theater.

"Typifying as I do the spiit of Spokane and the Inland Empire, I most cordially welcome you to our great section of the northwest," stated Princess Spokane, as she met Colonel Roosevelt at the meeting for women at the Auditorium this afternoon.

"Miss Spokane, I am so glad to see you. This is a real occasion," stated Colonel Roosevelt, as Princess Spokane led the distinguished speaker to his chair.

The colonel drew a real matinee at the Auditorium this afternoon. The big theater was filled to the topmost seat an hour and a half before the Colonel was due to appear. Over 2000 women were turned away from the doors by 2 o'clock and the stage entrance of the theater was the scene of a lively shouldering of feminity, eager to get a look at Colonel Roosevelt as he entered the theater.

The jam was so great that the committee on arrangements at 2 o'clock secured the American theater for an overflow meeting and Colonel Roosevelt addressed a capacity audience in that house following the meeting at the Auditorium.

The doors of the Auditorium theater were closed at 1:15 p. m., an hour and 15 minutes before Roosevelt was scheduled to commence his address. Already every seat in the house, and every foot of standing space was jammed with women. The street outside began to mass solidly before 2 o'clock with the belated throng which could not enter.

Princess Spokane (Miss Marguerite Motie.)

Theodore Roosevelt, president of the United States from 1901 to 1909, visited Spokane in 1903, 1911 and 1912. During his visit on September 9, 1912, he was greeted by Miss Spokane Marguerite Motie. Copy from *Spokane Daily Chronicle.*

Auditorium Building and Theater

Miss Spokane and one of her maids of honor during a horse racing event at Playfair Race Track, circa 1913. *(All photos this and facing page courtesy Dorothy & Bob Capeloto.)*

Miss Spokane with three of her maids of honor in the dignitary box at Playfair Race Track, circa 1913.

A motorcade of dignitaries on Riverside, east of Monroe, in front of the Review Building, Graves Music, Grandma's Kitchen and the Vogue, preparing for the trip to Mt. Spokane for its dedication and name change. Governor Marion Hay, Marguerite Motie and Francis Cook, who owned Mt. Spokane at the time, are in the back seat of the lead car. *(All photos this and following page courtesy Dorothy & Bob Capeloto.)*

On August, 23, 1912, Washington State Governor Marion Hay accompanied by Miss Spokane Marguerite Motie, Francis Cook, Mayor William J. Hindley and a motorcade of other dignitaries, proceeded to the peak of Mt. Carlton (formerly Mt.Baldy) for a formal name change to Mt. Spokane. During that time, many of the large cities in the west claimed mountains (such as Denver's Pike's Peak, Portland's Mt. Hood, Bellingham's Mt. Baker and Seattle's Mt. Rainier). Spokane, too, wanted to claim a mountain.

Francis Cook had purchased the top of the mountain in 1910 and with his son Silas built the road to the summit, paving it with crushed granite and shale. In 1912 the 11-mile climb of 5-percent grade was claimed to be the longest auto grade in the world.

Others present during this dedication were: Spokane Mayor W.J. Hindley; Robert Insinger, president of the Chamber of Commerce; R.E. Bigelow, president of the Spokane Ad Club; A.F. Rogers, president of the Rotary Club; Mrs. Carrie Hathaway, representative of the State and Inland Historical Societies; Thaddeus Lane, president of the Home Telephone Company; R.W. Roberts of the *Spokesman-Review*; H.A. Pierce of the *Chronicle*; Frank Guilbert, president of the Good Roads Association and the Inland Auto Club; Aubrey L. White, president of the City Park Board; H.L. Bleecker, vice president of the Washington Water Power Company; Arthur D. Jones; Harl J. Cook, event organizer; and several members of Francis Cook's family.

Gov. Hay seated behind driver.

Gov. Hay and Marguerite Motie.

Preparing Spokane's official flag.

Gov. Hay and Marguerite Motie.

Left: Mayor Hindley, Marguerite Motie, Francis Cook and Governor Hay.

The raising of the American and Spokane City flags at the summit of Mt. Spokane by Washington State Governor Marion Hay and Miss Spokane Marguerite Motie. In an unexpected gesture at the end of the ceremony, Governor Hay christened Miss Motie "Princess Spokane" as he sprinkled her with a few drops of crystal water from nearby Skyline Spring. He then kissed the hand of Spokane's new "princess."

Miss Spokane Marguerite Motie in San Francisco during the 1915 Panama Pacific Universal Exposition. *(All Photos through page 97 Courtesy of Dorothy & Bob Capeloto.)*

Miss Spokane and her court during the 1915 Panama Pacific Exposition.

Miss Spokane at the Vancouver, Washington, Pageant, 1914.

Marguerite Motie and the Spokane Ad Club with Little Miss Portland at the Portland, Oregon, 1915 Rose Festival. During the festival, Marguerite rode at the head of the Rose Parade in the largest car to be found in Portland.

SPOKANE AD CLUB DELEGATES TO BE LOCAL GUESTS

Left to right—R. E. Bigelow, H. S. Wagner, T. M. E. Keane, Bert Hilborn, Dr. H. C. Lambach, L. E. Shears, Miss Spokane (Miss Marg rite Motie), Miss Para Dalton, assistant secretary; E. R. Anderson, Dr. J. B. Anderson, C. O. Peterson, F. H. Lloyd, M. Whittin ham, W. S. McEachern and Howard S. Clemmer, president, in foreground at left.

Headed for the national convention of Ad clubs to be held in Los Angeles, May 27, 28 and 29, a delegation from the Spokane Ad club will arrive in Portland this morning for a day's visit as guests of the Portland Ad club.

Portland's delegation will join the folks from the inland empire here and the two parties will leave for sunny California tonight in a special r.

The Spokane delegation is due to arrive at 8:30 o'clock this morning and a full day has been mapped out for them. They will be taken for an automobile ride through the city and out over the highways this afternoon with a dinner at the Commercial club at 5:30 o'clock following the ride.

The two delegations will leave for San Francisco at 8:15 o'clock, where the Portland Ad clubbers will take part in the celebration of Spokane day at the Panama-Pacific exposition as the guests of the Spokane Ad club.

Heading the delegation from Spokane is Howard S. Clemmer, president of the club, but the whole party is escorting Miss Spokane (Miss Marguerite Motie). Included in the number are W. S. McEachern, Dr. J. B. Anderson, C. O. Peterson, R. E. Bigelow, T. M. E. Keane, Dr. H. V. Lambach, H. S. Wagner, F. H. Lloyd, Whittingham, L. E. Shears, Bert H born, E. R. Anderson and Miss P Dalton, assistant secretary of club.

Portlanders who will make the t are Dr. R. H. Emerson, chairman, a Mrs. Emerson; Louis Hamig, G. Schmidt, Walter Evans and wife, J W. Vogan and wife, W. B. Senos and wife and sister, and Bruce Rowan and wife.

Miss Spokane during the Spokane Ad Club's visit to Portland in 1915.

Marguerite (Motie) Shiel in 1939 with Catherine Betts, Marguerite's successor, who was chosen by the Spokane Ad Club as their second official Miss Spokane.

The Davenports' Miss Spokane Album

In 1916 Louis Davenport and his wife Verus presented Marguerite Motie with a large, personalized leather-bound photo album, inscribed with: "In appreciation of Miss Spokane by the Davenports." A sample of the photographs, courtesy of Dorothy and Bob Capeloto, follow the narrative on the Davenport Hotel.

Louis Davenport

The Davenport Hotel was Spokane's premium hotel, hosting the majority of Spokane's most important events and often world-famous people. During her tenure as Miss Spokane, many of the numerous functions Marguerite attended were at the Davenport Hotel. Events where she made appearances were always well attended. Consequently, the Davenports considered her among their friends and regular associates.

Because of the Davenport Hotel's significance to Spokane and the Miss Spokane contests and events, beginning with Marguerite Motie's tenure, a little background history on Mr. Davenport and his legendary hotel seemed warranted.

Louis M. Davenport led Spokane in the hospitality business, which began with his arrival at Spokane Falls in 1889. His first restaurant was called Davenport's Waffle Foundry, located in the 200 block of west Sprague Avenue. It was a modest business that quickly gathered an enthusiastic following. Davenport's business was destroyed, along with the business center of the city, during the Great Fire of 1889. He wasted no time in establishing a new restaurant on the opposite corner. Within a brief period, he was able to move back across the street and again enjoy a lucrative business. The *Spokane District Directory* for 1890 lists Davenport's facility as: "Davenport, Louie M. restaurant, 207-209 W. Sprague; tel 491."

The fire that destroyed his establishment also created the environment leading to his classification as one of Spokane's major businessmen. At that time, the massive rebuilding projects associated with the reconstruction of the city would have enabled almost any area business to thrive. The Inland Northwest was experiencing an industrial awakening and Spokane was booming. During these times, it would not have been necessary to concentrate on quality. The demand for food and lodging was great, and Davenport was in the midst with his experience and ambition. Although restaurants soon became abundant to fill the need, he became the top competitor.

Born in 1868 at Pawnee City, Nebraska, Louis Davenport was the son of a businessman. In 1876 the family moved to San Francisco, where he spent most of his childhood. Those years in San Francisco gave Davenport a zest for the more sophisticated trimmings of life. Coupled with his excellent business ability, great attention to detail and determination, he soon became very successful in his chosen vocation.

From the inception of Davenport's career, his endeavors were marked with quality. The 1906 *Raymer's Dictionary of Spokane* (self described as *"An Encylopaedic-Dictionary of the State of Washington, U.S.A., in general and the City of Spokane in particular."*) listed his business in the following language:

> Davenport's – The best illustration of Spokane enterprise is Davenport's restaurant, which is one of the most unique and nearly perfect restaurants in America. It covers a block and represents an outlay of a little over a quarter of a million dollars. Davenport's is not only beautiful, but scrupulously clean. The retiring rooms are elegant, in marble and tile and between the serving rooms and kitchen there are immense plate glass windows so the customers can get a look at the kitchen. The style of the architecture is early Mission, but inside there are Flemish, German, French and Marie Antoinette rooms. There is also a lunch counter and buffet.

By 1912 Davenport's business was an enormous success. He had created a valuable reputation and was now ready to embark on the largest venture in his career. The front page of the July 25, 1912, *Spokane Press* headlined the story:

> **COWLES, HILLS, DAVENPORT, HEAVILY INTERESTED IN NEW $2,000,000 HOTEL – FINE STRUCTURE TO BE ERECTED ON SITE OF DAVENPORT RESTAURANT – SPOKANE MILLIONAIRE ADDS TO INVESTMENTS.**
>
> W.H. Cowles, multimillionaire newspaper man and real estate holder of Spokane; James J. Hill and Louis Hill, railroad magnates, and L.M. Davenport, restaurant man, are reputed to be the heaviest stockholders in the company which announced late yesterday afternoon that a $2,000,000 hotel would be immediately erected in Spokane on the block bounded by Post and Lincoln Street, and First and Sprague Avenues.
>
> That the institution will be completed within ten months is the announcement made by Mr. Cowles today.
>
> Notice has been given to occupants of other buildings in the block where the Davenport restaurant now stands that they must vacate within 60 days, provision in the leases having been so inserted.
>
> Several days ago Mr. Cutter of the firm of Malmgren & Cutter, which is preparing the plans, stated when asked for information regarding the proposed hotel, that Mr. Cowles was interested, and had directed that no information should be given out. A lessee of one of the buildings which must be vacated stated today that Mr. James J. Hill and his son Louis were among those vitally interested. The plans provide for a very handsome structure, which when completed will rank among the finest in the northwest.

Obviously, Davenport's business aptitude and good reputation had influenced two of the area's most financially powerful men, and many other large investors, to back his venture enthusiastically. What happened as a result of this partnership proved to be one of Spokane's most celebrated successes.

The Davenport Hotel opened in 1914 at a total cost of $3 million, which was a million dollars over the projected cost. It was a masterpiece of the times. With the new addition and Davenport's genius-level promotional campaigns, his hotel and restaurant were becoming internationally famous.

When Louis Davenport died in 1951, a lengthy newspaper article described his success and popularity as follows:

> . . . Hotel men from America and foreign lands visited the hotel in an effort to discover the secret that brought so much fame to the Davenport hotel. The Waldorf Astoria's famed Oscar Maitre d'hotel, who recently died was one of these. He spent two weeks at the hotel making a study. Whether these men found the secret, most were agreed that it was Mr. Davenport's genius to do the unusual – that combined with his passion for beauty and the perfection of service. His motto was, do more for the customer than he expects.
>
> In particular, travelers, who were guests of the hotel took away stories of the ornamental columns of fish which graced the old Italian Gardens; the wall of fish in the Coffee shop; tropical birds that filled the lobby with their song; the fountain that was always abloom with flowers; the great fireplace where logs burned continuously for 31 years, under Mr. Davenport's regime, and the grandfather clock, never allowed to run down.
>
> . . . The hotel's opening was unique in the history of hotel operation and made Mr. Davenport a luminary in the world of innkeepers.
>
> The evening of the gala affair, the hundreds of guests inspecting the hotel were amazed to discover Indians in full regalia of white buckskin and feathered headdresses wandering through the public rooms. Members of the Blackfeet tribe from Glacier park, they were guests of the hotel and lived in tepees which they pitched on the roof. The president of the Great Northern and a lifelong friend of Mr. Davenport brought the Indians over from the park in a special train, in honor of the opening.
>
> **Fame Spread**
>
> Guests found still another surprise when they danced in the Marie Antoinette ballroom. An Indian band supplied the music. Browning, Mont., sent its unusual musicians to the opening by way of honoring its builder. The unique opening spread the hotel's fame far and wide and presaged Mr. Davenport's genius in making it a Mecca which brought people from all over the world to its doors. Royalty, Presidents, generals, statesmen and the great of opera, stage and screen enjoyed its hospitality.
>
> Beginning with President Taft, all succeeding Presidents have either stayed at the hotel or enjoyed its hospitality in short visits. President Taft was a guest several times and one of the hotel's most enthusiastic boosters. He used to tell Mr. Davenport, "This is home, the best hotel I was ever in." William McKinley was a guest of the Davenport restaurant before the hotel was built.

Herbert Hoover, a frequent quest, was a great booster for the hotel and since his first visit sent a Christmas card to Mr. Davenport almost every year. Another illustrious guest was Will Rogers. He called the hotel "the best spot to stay outside of my Oklahoma home."

In the illustrious parade of guests were such glamorous personages as the great Sarah Bernhardt, famed French actress; Pavlowa [*sic*], the Russian ballet artist; Ethel Barrymore of stage and screen, and the great Schumann Heink. Mary Pickford stayed at the hotel for two weeks at one time and Douglas Fairbanks was its guest.

Queen Visits

Queen Marie of Rumania [*sic*] with her two children, Prince Niki and Princess Illeana, were entertained at the Davenport while en route to Maryhill, where the queen dedicated the Maryhill museum. Other royalty whom Mr. Davenport entertained at his hotel were Crown Prince Olaf and Princess Martha of Norway.

Col. Charles Lindberg stayed at the hotel in the days when he was America's only hero and was receiving his nationwide ovation. The late General Pershing enjoyed the hotel's hospitality and so did General Marshall, before he attained his high estate. Mr. Davenport showed his unusual gifts as "mine host" when the hotel entertained Marshal Ferdinand Foch, when he visited Spokane on his tour of the United States after World War I. Mr. Davenport had the Marie Antoinette ballroom transformed into an apple orchard for the banquet given in the marshal's honor. As the great soldier dined he merely had to reach into the branches of the tree above him and pick an apple.

In his appreciation for beauty, Mr. Davenport built the Davenport Easters into a flower festival that brought people from far-distant points each year to enjoy them. The lobby and dining rooms were filled, literally, with thousands of blooms. The great tubs of rhododendrons, laden with blooms 12 inches across, were kept, from year to year, in greenhouses and put on display in the hotel for the Easter festival.

2400 Guests Served

Mr. Davenport's genius for organization was shown in his handling of large banquets. The biggest one given at the hotel was when he turned the lobby into a banquet room, the first time, for the annual dinner of the Chamber of Commerce. Almost 2400 guests were served. However, in stand-up dinner service, the hotel has served 2852 diners.

Although no medal was bestowed on Mr. Davenport for his wartime service to the military, the military would have been happy in seeing him so honored. Wartime activities in and around Spokane forced the hotel man to take much of the town's brunt in providing hospitality to the hundreds of army, navy and air corps men who had to be given shelter. Weekends the hotel gave every inch of space to accommodating servicemen. At nights, every chair and davenport in the lobby would be occupied by servicemen and several hundred would sleep on the floor of the mezzanine. Accounts of the Davenport hospitality to the military reached to Paris, where the Stars and Stripes, army newspaper, eulogized Mr. Davenport for his generous hospitality to servicemen . . .

Amelia Earhart was another famous guest of the Davenport Hotel. A front-page headline, corroborating her stay in Spokane, appeared in the *Spokane Press* on January 31, 1933:

AMELIA EARHART "TAKES OFF" DESPITE BLINDING SNOWSTORM, GIRL FLYER IS FACING ROUGH TRIP, Noted Aviatrix Is Typical Feminist, Interview Reveals; The Northwest Airways party, with Amelia Earhart Putnam as their guest, left the Davenport hotel at 2:30 p.m. Tuesday, bound for Felts Field, where the big Ford tri-motor plane in which they are flying was being prepared to go up in a snow storm. Colonel L.T. Britten, vice president of the airways company, said that the party would fly on to Pasco this afternoon if it were at all possible. An official at the Mamer Transport Company, Felts Field, said at 2:30, "weather is terrible here. It looks like the Earhart party is preparing to fly, but I doubt if they will get far."

Davenport sold his hotel to William Edris, president of the Olympic Hotel in Seattle, in 1945. Louis Davenport died on July 28, 1951, in his suite at the Davenport Hotel where the Davenports had maintained an apartment since the hotel opened. Verus Davenport, his wife of 45 years, maintained her residence there until her death in 1967.

In addition to their home in the Davenport Hotel, the Davenports owned other residences in the area, including one of Spokane's most palatial mansions, located at 34 West Eighth. In order to help finance construction of the Davenport Hotel, the Davenports traded Mr. and Mrs. Richard Porter for their home on Sumner, with Porters paying a monetary difference. They later built Flowerfield, a 459-acre estate on the Little Spokane River, now the site of St. George's School.

Other interests Davenport pursued were: director of the Spokane and Eastern Trust Company, the Washington Water Power Company, the Western Life Insurance Company, and vice president of the Ryan & Newton Company. He was a member of the Masons, Elks, Spokane Club, Spokane Country and Spokane Amateur Athletic clubs. He was also a longtime member of the Spokane Park Board. He played a key role in the campaign to purchase the land on which the Galena Army Air Force Base was built (now the site of Fairchild Air Force Base). The purchase of this land was instrumental in establishing the Air Force in Spokane. He was a director of the Old National Bank, vice president and director of the Old National Bank Building and vice president and director of the Old National Corporation. In 1950 Washington State College awarded him a certificate of merit for his contribution to the state.

Davenport Hotel 1915. This is an actual photograph of the Davenport Hotel with the people and cars on the street sketched in. The autos against the curb are real.
(This and following photos are from the Davenport Album, courtesy of Dorothy and Bob Capeloto.)

The Davenport Restaurant in 1909, photographed prior to the hotel's construction. The buildings to the right (west) were demolished in 1912 to make way for Davenport's new $3 million hotel, which adjoined the restaurant. The Hall of the Doges and the Davenport's apartment were on the second floor of the restaurant.

One of the many functions in the Marie Antoinette Room of the Davenport Hotel.

The Davenport Restaurant interior decorated for a function in 1912. At the time, the Davenport was Spokane's most elegant restaurant and the location for many important functions.

A typical social event at Davenport's facility, circa 1912.

Festive decorations adorned the Marie Antoinette Room of the Davenport Hotel for one of the many celebrations held there.

Dignitaries attending an event in the Marie Antoinette Room in 1915.

The Italian Gardens were reflective of the Italian Renaissance. Two large crystal columns, serving as aquariums, were located at the entrance to this room. The area was filled with numerous living plants and flowers. The focal point was a fountain.

A Maypole dance in the Davenport Lobby in 1915.

Socialites attending a ball in the Hall of the Doges at the Davenport. This room was located just off the hotel's mezzanine and was Spokane's most popular place for weddings and other social functions. Its name was suggestive of the palaces of the Italian doges of medieval times. A doge was a leader, specifically the chief magistrate, in old Venice and Genoa, Italy. In Venice the doge was originally chosen by the vote of the people, held office for life and was regarded as the civil, military and ecclesiastical chief. A doge had almost unlimited power.

Marguerite Motie, front row second to the left, after receiving an award.

This photo was taken in 1916, during an exchange between members of the Blackfoot Indian Tribe from Glacier National Park, Marguerite Motie and some of Spokane's dignitaries. *(Photo courtesy Dorothy & Bob Capeloto.)*

In 1914, when Louis Davenport opened his new Davenport Hotel with a gala affair (as previously described in a newspaper quote), James Hill, president of the Great Northern Railroad and Davenport's personal friend, arranged a special event for the occasion. Hill invited some members of the Blackfoot Indian Tribe from Glacier National Park, commissioning a special railroad car to transport them to Spokane. As guests of the hotel, they pitched their tepees on the roof where they stayed for the duration of this event. While at the hotel, the Blackfeet mingled with the crowd, dressed in full native regalia of white buckskin and feathered headdresses. This proved to be one of the most impressive events of the opening and was considered an honored experience by those in attendance.

This was Marguerite Motie's first meeting with members of the Blackfoot Tribe and it blossomed into a lifelong mutual admiration. Two years later, in a show of friendship, twenty Indian braves from Glacier National Park acted as her personal escorts on her special train en route to an event in California. During this time, they adopted her into their tribe, giving her the name "Itsatapiaka," which means: "She is an Indian girl." At that time, Marguerite Motie was the only white woman to have received that honor.

A meeting on November 29, 1921, at the Davenport Hotel to honor French General Ferdinand Foch during his visit to Spokane. Marguerite Motie was asked to officially greet him as the representative of Spokane. Both are seen here shaking hands. Although Marguerite was married and living in Seattle by now, she was occasionally requested to attend important Spokane functions such as this.

General Ferdinand Foch was the French general who commanded all the Allied Armies, including the American forces, on the Western front during the final campaign of World War I. As such, he led a series of counteroffensives resulting in the final victory that brought about the end to the war.

Present at this event were some of the era's most prominent men from Spokane, Washington State and the nation. A partial list (some of who are in the picture above) includes: Col. Frank Parker, Leo Duffy, Col. John D. Markey, Col. Francis E. Drake, Spokane Mayor Charles A. Fleming, General James Drain, C.D. Cunningham, General Desticker, Washington Governor Louis F. Hart, Hanford McNider, Robert Insinger, Lt. Gov. W.J. Coyle, Col. G.S. Albert, Major de Mierry, George A. Phillips, E.D. Potvin, M.B. Connolly, Alan Toplet, Frank P. Motie, Miles Cahill, W.S. Gilbert, Waldo G. Paine, E.K. Erwin, E.P. Chapin, Harry Heylman, Frank T. McCollough, A.B. Fosseen, H.T. Anthony, Arthur D. Jones, Charles Dilio, G.H. Ellis, Lester M. Livengood, W.P. Hopkins, Roy R. Gill, Walter Hogan, Dr. H.L. Moorehouse, George H. Keith, B.Gard Ewing, H.M. Blakely, Harry Olive, Major Bidds, C. Herbert Moore, William Beardsmore, Dr. C.O. Liner, Grant Ware, C.L. King, Thomas Keene, Al Ware, and Dr. C.E. Grove.

Some of these family names are still prominent in Spokane today.

Louis Davenport and Miss Spokane greeted the vice president of the Northern Pacific Railroad and Thaddeus S. Lane, president of the Inland Automobile Association, with the "Great Big Baked Potato" celebration at the base of the Northern Pacific Railroad Bridge in 1916. This was in conjunction with the Pathfinders Promotion Trips. The photos show the crowd making its was down the river bank.

Miss Spokane's Early Thespian Ties

The technology for making silent movies was developed in 1895, the year Marguerite Motie was born, and the first movie in the United States was shown in New York City the following year. In 1907 the first film company arrived in Los Angeles, California, and by 1910 there were approximately 13,000 theatres in the United States that offered viewings of "moving pictures."

The 1906 *Raymer's Dictionary of Spokane* lists seven theaters in Spokane: two opera houses, three vaudeville theaters and two variety theaters. At the time, the variety theaters were dedicated to showing the new silent movies. The 1911 *Blue Book* directory for Spokane lists 18 theaters, 12 of which were dedicated to showing silent moving pictures. These early movies typically consisted of three reels and were approximately 30 minutes long. A pianist, who was able to view the movie and improvise music according to the scenes, normally accompanied these films. As mentioned in Chapter 2, two of Marguerite Motie's sisters, Frances and Esther, did this kind of work in Spokane.

By 1915 the tremendous financial potential of silent screen movies was being realized. Many independent movie picture companies began opening at locations throughout the United States and Spokane was no exception. Marguerite Motie and the Spokane Ad Club played a significant role in inspiring a movie studio to locate in Spokane.

Marguerite was among many of Spokane's early supporters of the arts. Even in her grade school years, she held an interest in acting, often performing in school plays. After being chosen as Miss Spokane, Marguerite found herself at the center of the largest Spokane advertising campaign in its history; thousands of Spokane promotional brochures with her photo were circulated throughout the Inland Northwest and the United States. These efforts, along with Marguerite's enthusiasm as a thespian, attracted some prominent entertainers to Spokane. One such attraction came in the form of Tyrone Power II.

Tyrone Power II

Frederick Tyrone Power II was one of the nation's leading actors, a noted tragedian and Shakespearean actor. He was a well-respected star of the theater, playing

Tyrone Power III

classical and contemporary roles, later gaining considerable fame in the silent movies. He was born in 1869 to a family of entertainers and died in 1931. His grandfather, Tyrone "the Elder," (1795-1841) was a famous stage comedian in Wales. Tyrone's father, Harold, was not successful as an actor but gained fame as a concert pianist. His son, Tyrone Power III, also followed in the family's footsteps, becoming a Hollywood superstar and the most well-known member of the family.

Tyrone Power Comes to Spokane

On August 19, 1917, Power arrived at the Great Northern depot on Trent Avenue (now Spokane Falls Boulevard), and was greeted by Marguerite Motie and representatives of the Spokane Ad Club. Later that evening, he was honored with a dinner in the Marie Antoinette Room of the Davenport Hotel.

An official welcome was extended to Tyrone Power today by Miss Spokane. The noted actor will be in the city for several days studying the motion picture possibilities of Spokane's scenic panorama.

August 20, 1917, *Spokane Daily Chronicle* news clipping of Miss Spokane Marguerite Motie welcoming Tyrone Power II to Spokane.

Following a six-day survey of Spokane's scenic possibilities, Power made the decision to establish a movie studio in Spokane. He had earlier commented on the beauty of the area, remarking on its perfect setting for a motion picture studio. The site he picked was Minnehaha Park, a scenic area north of present-day Havana Street and Euclid Avenue, which the City of Spokane had acquired in 1909. Members of the Spokane Park Board, eager for the chance to attract a movie studio to the area, quickly signed a lease providing the entire Minnehaha Park area for this venture. In early August 1917, preliminary incorporation papers were signed for a moving picture production studio to be established at Spokane with capitalization of $500,000.

On August 24, 1917, the Spokane newspapers announced that the new corporation would be called the Washington Motion Picture Corporation. Tyrone Power had signed a three-year retainer with the company. The studio itself was to be a reproduction of the famous Universal City Studios in Los Angeles, California. The most interesting news was yet to come. On Monday, August 27, 1917, the *Spokane Press* carried the following article:

Spokane to Have Huge Picture Project

A brand new industry, backed by millions of dollars and with the world for its market, is coming to town. This city is to become famous as the home of a tradition-breaking religious revolution.

Spokane is to become the center of a continent-wide motion picture syndicate, financed, operated and owned exclusively by 125,000 churches in the United States and Canada.

A "Holy City" is to rise and be devoted to the production of plays depicting stories from the Bible. The film sermons will be used in thousands of churches all over the world, and will take the place of the present evening preachment.

Millions of dollars are to be spent here within the next five years by California-jaded producers who will flock to the city with fresh scenic beauties and untapped pictorial possibilities. This is the exclusive announcement made through the Press today of C. J. Ward of San Francisco, manager of the Tyrone Power Motion Picture corporation.

New Church Warfare

"Fight the movies with the movies" is the slogan of the thousands of modern churchmen, who since the pictures became popular have watched the church crowds slowly dwindle and the throngs at the movies grow by leaps and bounds.

To bring the crowds back to the churches to stir a world wide religious revival such as the earth has never known, thousands of churches are to join hands to put the precious story of the salvation of mankind upon the film – the universal language of mankind.

Photo Old Stories

And so the famous story of John the Baptist is to be reenacted in the Dry Lands around Grand Coulee; the tale of St. Paul's to be fashioned upon the background of the Inland Empires lakes, mountains and rivers; the simple beautiful stories of the Bible will again leap into being within auto ride of Spokane.

Just as soon as Tyrone Power's commercial producing company is underway the formation of the religious syndicate, which will handle and produce the pictures will take place. Not one cent of local capital will be required, the entire capitalization being contributed by leagues of churches. The syndicate will not operate for profit, but will be a cooperative affair, releasing its pictures only for churches and barring any attempt to commercialize the undertaking.

No More Revivals

The day of the religious revivalist, as he now is known, is past, Mr. Ward declares. The new revival will be one in which conversion by pictures will play the star part. Several churches in a city, instead of banding together to finance a series of revival meeting, will band together and secure a series of Biblical pictures put out by the Spokane Corporation.

Not only long features of five and six reels will be made, but short one-reel films with stories for Sunday schools and children's gatherings, will be featured.

Two of the world's most famous women stars, now under contract in California, will be brought here in association with Mr. Power for the production of his pictures.

The First Movie Filmed in Spokane

On May 5, 1918, the *Spokane Press* announced that work had begun on Spokane's first motion picture. Tyrone Power, the leading man, had arrived the night before and the first scenes were to be filmed on the Little Spokane River that day.

Although the Washington Motion Picture Corporation succeeded in erecting a significant studio at Minnehaha Park and at least one of Power's silent movies was filmed there, his venture failed; funds from investors in New York never materialized and, unable to secure the capital in Spokane, Power gave up and returned to his home in Cincinnati, Ohio. Following his departure, the impressive studio sat vacant. Over the next few years, several other movie companies made unsuccessful attempts at establishing businesses there. However, through the efforts of Miss Spokane and the Ad Club, the studio had been built and did attract some attention in Hollywood.

Big Name Movie Actress Comes to Spokane

Nell Shipman, a well-known silent screen actress, arrived in Spokane with her cast and crew in the early spring of 1922. She described their accommodations in the following manner: "The Cast lived at Louis Davenport's lovely hotel and ate high on the hog. I marched in and out of an expensive suite in my leather coat, carrying my briefcase, playing Madame Producer to the hilt but scared cold-silly inside. Could *The Grub Stake* [the feature film she was producing and starring in] carry the load?" One of Nell's first challenges was raising money for the production and to tailor the Minnehaha studio to her needs. Within a short time, they raised $180,000 to film *The Grub Stake*. She immediately hired a team of carpenters to begin working on the required changes and the accommodations for her zoo of animal actors she had brought with her. The carpenters were Paul Peters and two of his sons, Lloyd and Ray. Both sons had a desire to be movie actors and worked for Nell as carpenters and actors for the duration of her stay in the Inland Northwest. Filming began immediately, with some of the first scenes being shot during March of 1922 near Tiger, Ione and upper Lake Thomas in Pend Oreille County. Other scenes were shot at the Minnehaha studio and on Mt. Spokane.

Later that year, Shipman moved her production company and zoo to the northern end of Priest Lake, where the Peters clan built a studio and movie camp called Lionhead Lodge. Nell and her hearty group of moviemakers remained active there until 1925.

Nell Shipman

A History of Spokane's First Professional Entertainment

Spokane's first professional entertainment was provided in 1880 by John Maguire, a thespian from Butte, Montana. Maguire was engaged in the theatrical profession as an actor, manager, builder and theater owner. Prior to moving to Montana, Maguire had been the manager of the Newmarket Theater in Portland, Oregon. The Newmarket was owned by Captain Ankeny, father of Senator Levi Ankeny, for whom Ankeny's Restaurant in Spokane's Ridpath Hotel was named.

Maguire's first appearance in Spokane was a one-man show. He was celebrated throughout the western United States as a monologist and his act was a money-maker. In an article appearing in the August 11, 1903, edition of the *Spokane Press,* Maguire recalled the event during a visit to Spokane 23 years later:

> It was held over a drug store situated diagonally across from what was known before the big fire as the California Hotel. "It was a Saturday night. I opened to an audience of about 100 people at $1 per," said the pioneer actor. "The conditions under which I acted were not the best, the low roof forcing me to remain in nearly one position for fear of bumping my head. However, they gave me a great hand and I was well satisfied. The next day, Sunday, the lawn in front of the hotel was like a country market. There were hundreds of gaily bedecked Indians…trading with the whites, and the picturesque scene in front of the hostelry is one that has ever remained in my mind in connection with my initial appearance in this city."

At the time of Maguire's engagement, Spokane's population was around 300. One third of the populace attended, each paying an admission price of one dollar. It was easy to conclude that the general public in Spokane was eager for entertainment.

By 1881 a part-time actor by the name of Harry Hayward settled in Spokane. In 1883, seeing the potential for success in the entertainment business, he booked *The Bohemian Girl*, a popular opera of the times. He was suddenly faced with a dilemma – Spokane didn't have a playhouse. Prior to the arrival of the opera's actors, Hayward leased a warehouse on the corner of Riverside Avenue and Post Street and converted it into Spokane's first official playhouse. In his book *Spokane and the Inland Empire*, N.W. Durham quotes a portion of the account about this event from a local newspaper: "The audience paid two dollars each for reserved seats on gang plows and farm implements. Nail kegs in the rear were a trifle cheaper. It was a fifteen hundred dollar house altogether." From then on, Hayward devoted his vocational ambitions entirely to Spokane's theater business, managing most of the early theaters, including Joy's Opera House, the Falls City Opera House and the Auditorium Theater.

SPOKANE AD CLUB

WEEKLY BULLETIN

Devoted to the Best Interests of the Community and the Spokane Ad Club in Particular

Vol. XII. No. 132 SPOKANE, WASHINGTON May 21, 1919

MISS SPOKANE WEEK

AT THE

WOODWARD THEATRE

"JERRY"

FEATURING

MISS HAZEL WHITMORE as "Jerry"

and

MISS MARGUERITE MOTIE (Miss Spokane) as "Joan"

WITH ALL THE WOODWARD PLAYERS

Week Beginning May 25th, 1919

Every Evening—Curtain 8:30.
Matinees Sunday, Wednesday and Saturday, 2:30 P. M.
Reserved seats must be called for 24 hours in advance.

Miss Motie as Miss Spokane has always graciously done her share in the favorable promotion of Spokane. Let's do our part in this testimonial to her spirit and efforts of the past in giving her the opportunity to develop her talent for dramatic art.

The Spokane Ad Club has always featured Miss Spokane. Let's show our appreciation and pride in her by making Miss Spokane week a week of standing room only,

This photo, which appeared in the Saturday September 13, 1919, edition of the *Spokane Chronicle,* was captioned as follows: "Miss Marguerite Motie (Miss Spokane) is now a permanent member of the Woodward players, and has adopted the stage as her profession, at least for this season. She has been capably playing roles that are usually assigned to players of much more experience. Next week will find her in a light comedy role in *Fair and Warmer*." The ad on the right was from the Spokane Ad Club's weekly bulletin promoting Marguerite Motie's first performance with the Woodward Theatre.

The following article from the May 12, 1919, edition of the *Spokane Press* gives a glimpse of the enthusiasm surrounding Marguerite's presence on stage:

> **Miss Spokane to Go on Stage Here**, Miss Marguerite Motie whose picture as "Miss Spokane," in native costume, was instrumental in bringing the Woodward Stock company to this city, is to join the Woodward company for one week, beginning May 25, it was announced Monday.
>
> Miss Motie will play the role of Joan in the play, *Jerry*. Miss Hazel Whitmore, leading woman, and Miss Motie will be co-stars for the week.
>
> Backing Miss Motie in her first public appearance on the stage will be the Ad Club, Chamber of Commerce and other civic organizations. Manager Woodward's offer to Miss Motie came after he saw her work in *Cousin Kate*, which was staged by the Woman's College Alumnae association at North Central high school recently.
>
> Miss Motie, as "Miss Spokane," has been given perhaps more publicity than any other American woman. Her picture has gone all over the world.
>
> Woodward, at Denver, happened to pick up a Spokane folder, bearing her picture, and was so impressed with the invitation . . . that he investigated, and later moved his company here.

Spokane's Greatest Advertising Campaign

From the inception of Marguerite's reign and with the Spokane Ad Club's management, she became the centerpiece for the majority of Spokane's promotional advertising projects, both public and private. She was in great demand in the entire Inland Northwest.

Among the first and most successful promotional materials were brochures with her likeness and an informational narrative. Often these brochures contained scenic photos of the area being promoted. Hundreds of other innovative uses capitalized on the Miss Spokane logo, a sampling of which are illustrated in the following pages. The often-used slogan, "Miss Spokane Welcomes You," and the accompanying photograph of Marguerite became one of the best known "advertising signatures" in the country.

MISS SPOKANE INVITES YOU TO THE LAND OF MOUNTAIN LAKES

SPOKANE

Invites you to come and visit her; to travel along the National Park highways into the heart of the Summer Play Ground of America—that you, too, may play and take unto yourself some of the joy that Nature has spread there.

YOU ARE INVITED

not alone in a spirit of play, but also that you may see a people at work building in the richest empire in our country, an empire passing the pioneer days and beginning the swing toward the richness of full development.

In the work of such a people in such a country there is much for you to see and, perhaps, an OPPORTUNITY for you.

Whether you come singly, or with those with whom you dwell, or as a part of a gathering for a convention, we bid you come, and we will make you

WELCOME

SHAW & BORDEN CO. 147323

Mountain Trout Will Give You Battle in the Waters of the Spokane Country.

"Standing on the slippery rock, I selected a spot where the water bubbled over a boulder deep in the river bed, a miniature waterfall singing a song of challenge and of invitation. I dropped the fly fairly in the center of the broken water, and there came that wonderful thrill along the rod that marks the strike, and makes the body tingle and the heart thump. Over my left shoulder the towering office buildings of Spokane smiled on my endeavors and seemed to inquire, 'Any luck'?"—
LOG OF THE SUNSET TRAIL.

DO YOU know of a city that has fishing in its front door yard? Do you know of a spot where you can walk off a paved street to the banks of a river; where fishing is guaranteed, with a million young fry planted in its waters each season?

What a boast to make: "I caught the big fellow within five minutes' walk of my hotel."

Fishing in the front yard is only one of the many things that make Spokane distinctive, unusual. If you pass this way, you must not miss this city.

Buy that 1915 Exposition ticket so that you may ride along the northern route

VIA SPOKANE

For Information Book of Attractions
Write to Travel Service Bureau, Spokane.

Examples of the many waterways in and around Spokane being promoted.

Songs written and dedicated to Miss Spokane.

In 1912 the Spokane Ad Club declared *Hello Miss Spokane* the official song of Spokane.

Words to *Hello Miss Spokane* written by Frank Finney, author of *Sunny Old Spokane,* and published by the Spokane Ad Club and dedicated to Miss Marguerite Motie.

Words to *There Never Was a Girlie Like you* Words and music written by Harry L. Stone, also the writer of *My Golden Dream, Every Season In The Year, I Want a Wife*, etc.

Hello Miss Spokane

There's a maiden fair, yes wondrous fair
As fair as the winds e'er caressed – And she was born
one sunny morn In the grandest town in the great Northwest
There are busy mills 'neath the purple hills
What a prosperous story they tell
When that town you see, you just take it from me
You'll throw up your hat and yell:
Hello Miss Spokane – For you, fond hearts are pining
And the dear old town where you were born, Where the sun is
ever shining, Where the nodding grain on the golden plain
Bid a welcome to each man – They'll be glad to meet you,
they'll be proud to greet you with a Hello Miss Spokane.

Oh, your sturdy pines, your wondrous mines
Are rated with all of the best– Your apples sweet, your golden
wheat, They have crowned you queen of the great Northwest
You're the busy bee of home industry
You're the best town on this earth today
And the falls all call "live in peace one and all"
And take off your hat and say:
Hello Miss Spokane – For you, fond hearts are pining
And the dear old town where you were born, Where the sun is
ever shining, Where the nodding grain on the golden plain
Bid a welcome to each man – They'll be glad to meet you
They'll be proud to greet you with a Hello Miss Spokane.

There Never Was A Girlie Like You

My poor brain is in a whirl, Over just one little girl,
She's a dainty little miss with two, big smiling eyes;
In my dreams we meet each night, Neath the moon's pale silv'ry light,
There in love land's garden, is my queen of paradise.
There's sunshine in your smile dear and love-light in your eyes
Other things about you that I just idolize,
I know a place dear where we can go and spoon,
Where we can talk of a future honeymoon;
Build a home in love-land like other sweethearts do,
Just a place where we can bill and coo,
Ever since this world began and someone named you Miss Spokane,
There never was a girlie like you.

And someday in future time, May I hope to call her mine,
Build a little bungalow for two or three or four; –
Settle down in simple life, Throw away the key of strife,
Fill each day with sunshine could a girlie ask for more.
There's sunshine in your smile dear and love-light in your eyes
Other things about you that I just idolize,
I know a place dear where we can go and spoon,
Where we can talk of a future honeymoon;
Build a home in love-land like other sweethearts do,
Just a place where we can bill and coo,
Ever since this world began and someone named you Miss Spokane,
There never was a girlie like you.

"Princess Spokan"

This is the *Official Photo* of *"Miss Spokan"* the *Crowned Princess* around whom a beautiful Indian legend has been woven, and clothed her in picturesque Indian garb, in keeping with the Indian name *"Spokan,"* which translated, means *"a Child of the Sun"* (a little flower of sunshine).

Miss Marguerite Motie is the young woman who has been chosen by the residents of Spokane as the personal embodiment of the city, that (in a brief space of years) has grown to be the center of the far famed Inland Empire, rich in products of the soil—grain, fruits, timber, mineral, stock, etc.

The city over which *"Princess Spokan"* reigns is second largest in the State of Washington, the gateway to the northwest; it ranks forty-eight among the one hundred principal cities of the U. S., with a population of over one hundred thousand.

SPOKANE is the HUB of a *Wonderful Empire*, just in the beginning of progress; it calls for your help.—"With best wishes," *The Princess Invites YOU* to COME TO SPOKANE!

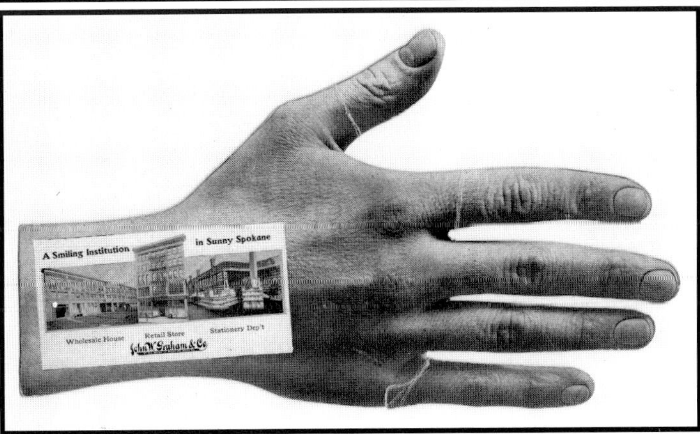

Above: The original official photo of Miss Spokane with a short promotional explanation. **Left**: Photographic reproductions of Miss Spokane's hand with her photo and promotional information. The front of the wrist has the inscription: "Miss Spokane extends her glad hand to you. Compliments Spokane Ad Club and John W. Graham & Co." On the back of the wrist is a group of pictures showing three views of the John W. Graham buildings. Ten thousand of the hand promotionals were printed and distributed.

A photo and caption of the steamer *Miss Spokane*, which appeared in Volume I of *History of Idaho, The Gem of the Mountains* by James H. Hawley (published in 1920).

The steamer *Miss Spokane* at Harrison, Idaho, circa 1919. Insets are Marguerite Motie on board during two separate occasions, including the christening.

(Photo of Harrison and the steamer Miss Spokane from the Museum of North Idaho. Photos of Marguerite Motie courtesy Dorothy & Bob Capeloto.)

In her book *Steamboats in the Timber,* published in 1952, Ruby El Hult describes the history of the steamer *Miss Spokane.* In the following quote, she refers to J.C. White, who was the father of the freshwater steamboating in the Coeur d'Alene area and the man responsible for making Lake Coeur d'Alene the scene of more freshwater steamboating than any lake west of the Great Lakes. In Hult's words:

> . . . White conceived the idea of building the beautiful, fast, passenger yacht, *Miss Spokane.* White had recently visited New York City and had very much admired the big passenger boats in the harbor; and he dreamed of seeing such a boat on his own Idaho lake. So in an effort to recapture some of the business lost to the *Harrison,* [a popular steamboat on the lake], and to lure people away from the Milwaukee trains, the *Miss Spokane* was constructed – a harbor-type boat, designed by an Eastern man, powered with twin gas engines and twin propellers.
>
> It was a magnificent gesture. She was a long white boat, very "ritzy," costing $45,000. White, who had always had strong leanings in the direction of Spokane where he had important connections and where he had thrown many an expensive party, selected the name. Spokane citizens were pleased, but Coeur d'Alene residents were piqued at the honor going to the rival city.
>
> In July, 1917, with Electric Line and Northern Pacific officials as guest, with lovely Miss Marguerite Motie representing "Miss Spokane," the boat made her trial run. Everyone on board exclaimed over her luxurious appointments. A few weeks later, however, after the boat had gone into regular use on the lake, Red Collar Line officials began to realize that almost everything about the *Miss Spokane* was wrong. The gas engines were expensive to operate, and the propellers sucked up logs and were constantly being damaged. She had only two engines whereas the New York Harbor boats had three, had only half as much speed backwards as forwards, and was, therefore, impossible to handle on the river. And, built like a seagoing vessel, she was too high for the low docks around the lake.
>
> Nor did the big boat lure any great number of passengers away from the *Harrison* or the Milwaukee railroad. Travelers more and more craved speed. They did not care to change from a fast train to a slow boat no matter how scenic the boat trip was. Since there was not enough straight passenger traffic on the lake to keep the *Miss Spokane* busy, and since she was not designed as a freight boat, she was soon losing money. Even her sleek appearance was against her, for lumberjacks and farmers felt out of place on her fancy decks.
>
> The Red Collar Line had a "white elephant" on its hands. The *Miss Spokane* ran regularly only one season and was tied up and her machinery sold. White sued the designer but did not win the case. For a few years the big hull was used as a floating dance hall, towed behind steamers on moonlight excursions and harvest moon excursions. At last she was abandoned altogether. With windows gone, with paint peeling, she sat year after year on the Coeur d'Alene waterfront . . . The stripped hull of the Miss Spokane was destroyed on the lake in 1914 – burned to make a spectacular but sad display at the Fourth-of-July celebration that year.

Spokane's Greatest Ad Campaign Takes to the Air

One of Spokane's first locally-constructed aircraft was also christened the *Miss Spokane.* The following article appeared in the *Spokane Chronicle* on June 14, 1919:

NAMESAKE OF MISS SPOKANE SOARS ALOFT
Christened With Flowers, It Flies Over Heads of Cheering Hundreds

Dedicated to the beginning of a great industry, the first Spokane made airplane was christened Miss Spokane by Miss Marguerite Motie, the original Miss Spokane, before a large crowd at Parkwater aviation field this afternoon.

The airship was given its appellation when Miss Motie cast into its whirling propeller a beautiful bouquet of sweet peas, red roses, canterbury bells and fern leaves.

Lieutenant Clyde Pynborn [Pangborn], the aviator, then flung off into a graceful exhibition of the machine's maneuvering power, passing the spectators each time so near the ground that they could plainly distinguish the workings of the machine.

Miss Motie was dressed in a beautiful costume of black and white. She wore a white crepe de chine dress, white pumps and gloves and a black broad brimmed hat. She carried a monstrous bouquet of gorgeous red peonies, after she had thrown the smaller bouquet into the propeller.

"I shall be as proud of christening this airship as any honor that will come to me," said Miss Motie in a short talk. She was introduced by President George A. Phillips of the Spokane Ad Club, who declared she was representative of the spirit and enterprise of Spokane.

On the platform with Miss Motie and Mr. Phillips were R.C. Steeple, Lloyd Gandy and Charles Merriman, representing the Northwest Aircraft corporation, owners of the aeroplane.

"This is the beginning of what we hope will be a great industry in a short time," said Mr. Gandy addressing the crowd of more than 500 people. "This industry is now like the automobile business of 20 years ago. We hope to make Spokane one of the flying manufacturing centers of the country."

Although this article claims the aircraft was the first "Spokane made airplane," a man by the name of Arthur Arneson had built a monoplane in his garage at 218 South Brown Street about 1914. Prior to that, Arneson had also built three other airplanes. In his book, *The Spokane Aviation Story* (published in 1982), James McGoldrick quotes a newspaper clipping that stated Arneson's other attempts to build aircraft were "more or less successful." To that statement, McGoldrick added the following commentary: "He apparently survived them."

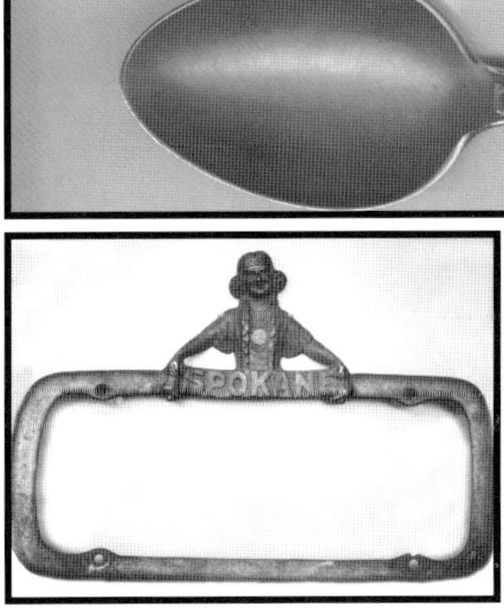

A small sampling of Miss Spokane memorabilia produced during the Miss Spokane promotional campaign. The photo at the lower left is an automobile license plate bracket using Miss Spokane's image. Among other things were Miss Spokane Chocolates by Overhauser Candy Company and a Miss Spokane perfume.

THE ANDERSONIAN

SENT OUT EVERY LITTLE WHILE FROM ANDERSON'S PRINT SHOP
FOUR HUNDRED and SIXTEEN J ST., SACRAMENTO, CALIFORNIA

Volume IX. JUNE, 1913 Number 2

MISS SPOKANE
(Miss Marguerite Motie)

This 1913 front cover reproduction of a California publication, which featured Marguerite Motie, is an example of the widespread popularity she enjoyed as Miss Spokane. The publication, called *The Andersonian,* announced its unique publication schedule beneath its masthead: "Sent Out Every Little While . . . "

Spokane "Ad" Men Visit Exposition Site

Gorgeous Flag of Living Asters Planted

News clipping of the Ad Club, Miss Spokane and R.E. Bigelow, club president, on the Washington site of the 1915 Panama Pacific Expo in San Francisco. Their promotion included countless pies baked from Washington apples, which Marguerite distributed. The free pies drew a crowd of 25,000. After the Expo, Marguerite and the Ad Club visited Los Angeles, winning trophies for being the most active club in the association and employing the most effective approach with the Miss Spokane ad campaign.

Marguerite (Motie) Shiel **Walter P. Shiel**

Remembrances of My Parents,
Marguerite and Walter Shiel
Written in July 2000 by Dorothy "Dodie" Shiel Capeloto.
(All photos in this chapter are courtesy of Dorothy and Bob Capeloto.)

Mother and Dad met as students at South Central High School. Their school building burned down in 1910 and, until a new south side school was built (and named Lewis and Clark), the South Central students attended North Central. Both were active participants in school life. Mother was the secretary of the senior class and played on the girls' basketball team. Dad was successful at both football and track. They graduated in June 1911.

Upon graduation from high school, Mother and Dad both entered the University of Washington in Seattle, from which they both graduated – Mother in drama and Dad in law. Mother became a member of Gamma Phi Beta sorority and Dad a member of Phi Gamma Delta fraternity.

Mother carried out her duties as Miss Spokane while in school. During her university years, to further her public speaking abilities, she spent one year in a special oratory program at Northwestern University in Chicago. She achieved the honor role while there. On her way to Northwestern, she visited Miss Chicago and received a wonderful welcome from that city.

While at the University, Dad achieved prominence in both campus activities and football. He played fullback and was chosen captain of the team in 1915. He was a renowned member of the famous Gil Dobie team that had many consecutive unbeaten seasons. In 1916 he served as president of the YMCA chapter on campus. In 1917 he was elected president of the University of Washington Student Body. He was also a member of the Oval Club and Fir Tree honoraries.

After graduation, Dad was chosen to attend an accelerated course at Annapolis for second lieutenants. He was on destroyer duty in World War I.

Mother and Dad were married in Spokane on February 14, 1920. They settled in Seattle and lived their married lives in Laurelhurst, a neighborhood in northeast Seattle. They had three children: Mary Ann, born June 23, 1922; Walter Jr., born September 9, 1924; and me (Dorothy) on December 22, 1928. My sister and I and our husbands also raised our families in Laurelhurst. Walt Jr. lived in Seattle and then in San Francisco for many years, where he passed away in December of 1991.

Dad was a very successful salmon broker in Seattle. He first worked with Kelly Clarke Inc. and then started his own firm, Walter P. Shiel & Co. During the Kelly Clarke years, my parents took many trips to Hawaii on the beautiful ocean liner *Lurline*. I clearly remember their arrival and departure bedecked with flower leis.

Mother and Dad were well known in Seattle, where they were quite active socially. Both served as board members for several private clubs. Mother was recognized and acclaimed for her book reviews. She also volunteered for several charitable organizations and worked diligently for Children's Orthopedic Hospital, now Children's Hospital & Medical Center.

For a number of years after their marriage, Mother continued to serve as Miss Spokane, returning to officiate when needed. In 1939, when she passed the honor to the second Miss Spokane, Catherine Betts, a series of special events were held for mother and Catherine. It was pretty amazing for me, as a child of 11, to see my mother being so acclaimed. Our family truly enjoyed these festivities.

Mother and Dad enjoyed the close proximity of my sister Mary Ann and me and our families. Mary Ann and Carl Neu's family included their three children, Carl Jr.

("Cappy"), Tom and Christine ("Christie"). They had the joy of living next door to Mother and Dad ("Nana" and "Gramps") on Lake Washington.

Cappy Neu and his wife Sally, with their children Sam and Max, live in Seattle, as do Tom and his children Kelly and Peter. Christie Caldwell and her husband Jim live in Ventura, California, with their sons Jeff and Chad.

My husband Bob and I raised three sons just two blocks from Nana and Gramps and the Neus. Our sons Mark and Paul are living in Laurelhurst with their families. Mark and Maribeth have two children, Claire and Ben. Paul and Shelly are the parents of Alexandra ("Alex") and Tony. Our middle son, Jay, lives in downtown Seattle. Since 1977, Bob and I have lived in Mother and Dad's house, which they built in 1952. This is a special home. Our family continues the Laurelhurst tradition.

As of 1997, I am the only survivor of my birth family. Dad died in October 1962, at 69 years of age. Mother was with us until March of 1982, when she died at the age of 87. My sister Mary Ann passed away on February 14, 1997, and her husband Carl followed in May 1999.

Bob and I are enjoying the same pleasure of living close to our children and grandchildren as did Mother and Dad. We also consider Mary Ann and Carl's children and their families as our own.

Mother and Dad were special and talented people who are deeply missed by their families and friends. They had very loving relationships with all their grandchildren and were always thoughtful and caring toward others.

Marguerite, third from left, on the South Central girls' basketball team, circa 1909.

Walter Shiel,
age 1

Walter Shiel,
Age 4

Walter Shiel during a University of Washington Huskies football game, where he played fullback and was the team captain. During his college years, he was also the UW Student Body president and president of the campus chapter of the YMCA.

Walter Shiel (right) and Marguerite Motie (second from right) on campus. Shiel graduated with a law degree and was selected for a Phi Alpha Delta law honorary.

During his years at the University of Washington, Walter Shiel was one of the most prominent athletes in Northwestern football. He played four seasons with the University of Washington Eleven, was captain of the team in 1914, and was considered one of the most effective ground gainers of the squad.

Walter graduated in 1911 as one of the greatest football stars in Lewis and Clark High School's gridiron history and regarded by his coaches to be among the best defensive men who ever played high school football. He also won letters in track and baseball and was a member of the basketball team. He is remembered as one of the track team's greatest weight men.

The bridal party at the wedding of Marguerite Motie and Walter Shiel on February 14, 1920. The wedding took place at the home of the bride's parents, Frank and Anna Motie, at 613 West Thirteenth Avenue. From left: Walter's brother Howard Shiel, best man; Walter and Marguerite; Marguerite's sister, Esther Motie, bridesmaid; and Marguerite's nephew (Emily's son) William Bayne, ring bearer. At the time Lieutenant Shiel was an officer stationed on the destroyer *U.S.S. McDougal* out of San Diego.

(Photo EWSHS, L87-1.17491-20)

Walter Shiel served as a lieutenant in the Navy for three years, much of that time on a destroyer in the Baltic Sea. Upon his return to the States, he was stationed at San Diego. Shortly before his discharge, he was transferred to Puget Sound.

Left: Marguerite and her first born, Mary Ann.
Right: Walt Jr.
Bottom: A news clipping of Marguerite and her two daughters, Mary Ann and Dodie, while in Spokane for the coronation of the second Miss Spokane, Catherine Betts. The 1914 date on the news caption is incorrect. She became Miss Spokane in 1912.

First "Miss Spokane" Participates in Cavalcade

Guests of the city this week are Mrs. Walter Shiel, Seattle, and her daughters, Miss Mary Ann Shiel (left) and Miss Dorothy Shiel. Mrs. Shiel, formerly Miss Marguerite Motie, has been Miss Spokane since 1914. She came to Spokane to participate in the coronation of Miss Catherine Betts as Miss Spokane at the Columbia Cavalcade Tuesday evening.

From left: Mary Ann, Marguerite, Walt Jr. and Walt Sr., circa 1930.

In a boat on Lake Washington. From left: Barnett girl, Mary Ann Shiel (Neu), Barnett boy, Howard Shiel Jr., Patty Shiel (Harrison), Walt Shiel Jr., Dorothy "Dodie" Shiel (Capeloto).

Walt Shiel Jr., with a string of fish, and Walt Sr. (inset) both loved to fish and spent many hours together in that sport.

Upper left: Walter Shiel Sr. with his son Walt Jr. in 1953. **Upper right:** Marguerite and Walter holding up his "Big W" blanket from the University of Washington with four stars indicating he played on a varsity team for four years. **Lower:** Marguerite and Walter in April 1941, during a trip to Honolulu.

Walt, Marguerite and their friend, George Gunn, fishing in Florida.

Mary Ann (Shiel) Neu, circa 1958

Carl Neu, circa 1958

Carl and Mary Ann (Shiel) Neu (seated) and their children (standing, from left) Carl H. "Cappy" Neu Jr., Christie (Caldwell) Neu and Tom Neu.

Bob and Dorothy "Dodie" Capeloto on the porch of their home in Seattle. Bob and Dorothy live in Marguerite and Walt's former home on the shore of Lake Washington. Dodie is their last living child. *(Bamonte photo taken in 1999.)*

Dorothy and Bob Capeloto's children (photos taken in the mid-1990s):
Top: Youngest son, Paul Capeloto, and his wife Shelly.
Lower left: Middle son, Jay Capeloto.
Lower right: Oldest son, Mark Capeloto, and his wife Maribeth.

Marguerite and Walter Shiel. Walter was born in Eugene, Oregon, on July 6, 1893, and died in Seattle in 1962. Marguerite was born in Odebolt, Iowa, on January 19, 1895, and died in Seattle in 1982. Both are buried at Acacia Cemetery in Seattle. The Shiels had been happily married for 42 years at the time of Walter's death.

Chapter 3

Spokane's Official City Hostesses, 1939 - 1976

Catherine Betts

Miss Spokane, 1939 to 1943 (unofficially until 1947)

Catherine Betts, the second Miss Spokane, 1939
By this time, the contest originated by the Spokane Ad Club in 1912 was sponsored by the Spokane Chamber of Commerce.

(All photos in this chapter courtesy of Cay Betts Williams.)

The legacy of Miss Spokane was about to be renewed following a 19-year lapse in the (official) position. By 1939 Spokane and the nation had suffered through some hard economic times since the first Miss Spokane had been selected. The first of these occurred between 1920 and 1921. Then, with the stock market crash of 1929, the worst depression in United States history began.

By 1939 the outlook was more optimistic. Washington was about to celebrate its 50th anniversary of statehood and Spokane intended to participate. It was time to select a new Miss Spokane. With her marriage in 1920, Marguerite Motie's official role as Miss Spokane had ceased. However, for a number of years, she continued to be called back to appear at various functions. During the 1930s, as the nation struggled through the Depression and recovery period, she had not been called upon, nor had any attempt been made by the Spokane Advertising Club or the Chamber of Commerce to select a new Miss Spokane. Marguerite was still Spokane's favorite sweetheart, but it was time for a new Miss Spokane. Whoever she might be, the new Miss Spokane would have to be a special woman – she had some big shoes to fill!

Catherine "Cay" Betts, the special woman chosen to fill those shoes, came into the world at St. Luke's Hospital in Spokane on March 18, 1917. Cay was the daughter of Ray and Mercieta Betts and granddaughter of early Spokane pioneers, Mr. and Mrs. Chauncey Betts and Mr. and Mrs. Charles Liftchild. As a little girl, she admired both Marguerite and the role of Miss Spokane, and had witnessed Marguerite's visits to Spokane on a number of occasions. Cay was proud of Spokane and loved everything about her hometown where she was born and raised.

After graduating from Lewis and Clark High School, Cay went on to college at the University of Washington and joined the Kappa Kappa Gamma sorority. She majored in drama and minored in literature. When her father died suddenly during her junior year in 1938, she took a temporary leave from school and returned to Spokane to help her mother with funeral arrangements and her father's fuel oil business. Bett's Oil Company had been founded in 1906 by Cay's grandfather, Chauncey Betts, a pioneer in the fuel oil business, who had died the previous year. Cay's mother, with no prior business experience, found herself in charge of the company. She managed very well, even during the war years of shortages and rationing, and Cay became Spokane's first heating oil saleswoman. In 1945 Mercieta turned the reins over to her son, Cay's brother Ray. (Ray is still involved with the business, which has evolved over the years to meet the changing energy demands, but he has since put his son Clark Betts and stepson Lee Letsch at the helm.)

Among the ways Mercieta had sought to educate herself about running a business was to join a business club. The Chamber of Commerce, which was taking over the role of the Spokane Ad Club in promoting the Miss Spokane contest, was reviving the contest and encouraging the various Spokane clubs to sponsor candidates. Cay was a natural candidate and the possibility of becoming the next Miss Spokane was among the highest honors of her life. Cay made it her goal to do her best to capture that claim. Her efforts and talents soon paid off.

Catherine Betts Assumes Her New Role

On July 30, 1939, Catherine Betts was chosen from a field of about 50 contestants to be Spokane's official greeter, hostess and ambassador of goodwill. Although the selection of the first Miss Spokane had been solely on the basis of a photograph, it was immediately evident how important public speaking skills were in the position, a talent at which Marguerite Motie excelled. For this new contest, judges representing leading Spokane organizations interviewed the candidates to select a young woman with the poise, grace and maturity to handle the role. The main selection criteria was based on the woman's speaking ability.

Cay was installed on August 1, 1939, at the opening ceremonies of the Columbia Cavalcade at the Spokane Fairgrounds. This was Spokane's official celebration of the 50th anniversary of Washington's statehood and of Spokane's Great Fire. Another honor was bestowed on Cay that evening. Marguerite Motie Shiel had traveled from her home in Seattle to pass her title to the new Miss Spokane. The *Spokesman-Review* reported the following day:

> "I name you Miss Spokane," Mrs. Shiel said to Miss Betts, her voice faltering just a trifle as she gave the charge to her successor. "I am happy to come back to Spokane," she said, in replying to Mayor Frank G. Sutherlin's introduction of her. She had heard herself praised for the charm and graciousness with which she had imbued her role. She heard reviewed briefly the trips she had made, of the famous personages who had come to Spokane and been officially welcomed by her . . .

One of Cay's first exciting honors was greeting New York Governor Thomas E. Dewey, who was in Spokane during his campaign for president of the United States. Cay accompanied him to the newly-constructed Grand Coulee Dam in a car driven by Henry Kaiser, founder of Kaiser Aluminum and inventor of the Kaiser car.

One week later in February 1940, she attended the annual Banff Winter Carnival in Canada and was elected as its queen for the 1941 festivities. The judging for this contest, open to both United States and Canadian citizens, was based on sportsmanship, personality and winter sports attire. An article in the February 14, 1940, edition of the *Calgary Herald* described the goodwill Cay generated between the two countries:

> **Charm Proves Outstanding Quality of Spokane Girl, Carnival Queen Candidate**
> Miss Catherine Betts, the only candidate from across the line for the honor of being Queen of the Banff Winter Carnival for 1941, was chosen "Miss Spokane," because of her charm, intelligence and beauty, and after meeting Miss Betts one understands the reason why.
>
> Accompanied by Miss Mary Ruth Barnes, attractive 17-year-old figure skating champion, and Mrs. Grace Kirkpatrick, official chaperone and representative of the Spokane Chamber of Commerce, Miss Betts arrived in Calgary last night. Her party planned to leave early this morning for Banff, there to enjoy a short rest before the strenuous festival program of the four-day carnival commences.

The biggest and most rewarding challenge Cay faced during her tenure was following the Japanese bombing of Pearl Harbor on December 7, 1941, bringing the United States into World War II. Cay was well into her tenure as Miss Spokane at the time and was employed at Galena Army Air Corps Depot, working for Special Services. Galena, renamed Fairchild Air Force Base in 1951, was located at the site of a Great Northern Railroad station that was a grain stop for farmers. It opened in 1941 mainly as a repair depot for planes involved in the war, and many civilians were employed there in various capacities. Cay's job in Special Services was heavily involved in public relations. This was a perfect job, as her supervisors allowed her whatever time necessary for her Miss Spokane duties. Her immediate supervisor at the time was Perry Lafferty, who later became the producer of the Danny Kaye Show. Cay worked with him on three to four radio shows a week. For the duration of World War II, a majority of Cay's role as Miss Spokane was devoted to the war effort, primarily helping to support the thousands of servicemen stationed in the Spokane area, most far away from home and their loved ones. Her work involved making them feel at home and appreciated.

Cay belonged to a group of women called the "Flying Squadron," whose main purpose was to schedule and conduct entertainment events for servicemen stationed in Spokane. This energetic group selected that name because they seemed to "fly" from place to place, organizing events. Dances and other social events were the preferred entertainment. The Spokane Women's Club, located on the northeast corner of Ninth Avenue and Walnut Street, was a favorite and popular location, especially since they were given free access to that facility. Some of the top tunes during this era were: *Sentimental Journey* by Les Brown and Doris Day; *Buttons and Bows* and *Lavender Blue* by Dinah Shore; *Ballerina* by Buddy Clark; *I've Got My Love to Keep Me Warm* by Les Brown; and *It's Only a Paper Moon* by the Benny Goodman Orchestra.

During this same busy time in 1941, Cay met her future husband, Thomas Williams, a Walla Walla architect and farmer. They were married in 1943 and moved to Walla Walla. Like her predecessor, Cay was also called back to officiate as Miss Spokane after her marriage. In 1947 the third Miss Spokane was selected and Cay was relieved of her duties. She then devoted her time to raising two sons, Tom born in 1947 and Ray in 1951. Today Cay and her sons run a cattle ranch on land previously owned by the Hudson's Bay Company. Located on their property is a plaque with the following inscription: "This plaque commemorates the Hudson's Bay Company Farm 1821-1856 where 500 head of horses and 100 cattle were run. The farm was bounded by the Snake River on the north, Blue Mountains on the east, Umatilla River on the south, and the Columbia River on the west."

Cay's time spent as Miss Spokane was the busiest period in her life. The following photographs and captions highlight many of her exciting contacts and events.

Right: On December 23, 1939, Cay Betts, Miss Spokane II, was seen in this news clipping officially greeting Chief Thunder Cloud, Hollywood's leading Indian actor and the hero of the recently released picture *Geronimo.* Thunder Cloud came to Spokane to promote his new movie. During his stay, he pitched his tepee on the roof of the Davenport Hotel.

As part of this promotion, Spokane was "given back" to the Indians. Mayor Frank Sutherlin, in a ceremony held in his office, handed Chief Thunder Cloud a four-foot-long proclamation and declared that since the city of Spokane was once the domain of the American Indian and because it was Christmas, the city should be given back to the Indians in the person of Chief Thunder Cloud.

Left: A 1940 publicity shot of Miss Spokane Cay Betts with Janet Campbell, promoting the upcoming Lilac Festival. Janet also accompanied Cay when she served as the queen of the 25th Annual Winter Carnival in Banff, Canada, in 1941. The vehicle they were using was a DeSoto convertible, which was priced at around $900 to $1,100 at the time.

Right: A 1941 *Spokane Chronicle* news clipping showing Miss Spokane Cay Betts and her attendants during Cay's four-day reign as queen of the 25th Annual Banff Winter Carnival in Alberta, Canada. Cay is seated (center), with Caroline Leuthold on the left and Janet Campbell on the right. Standing in the back, from left: Nora Clifton, Janet Martin, Connie Crommelin, Frances Stanton and Patricia Bartlett. The Spokane group was sponsored by the publicity-tourist bureau of the Spokane Chamber of Commerce, the Retail Trade Bureau and the Inland Empire Early Birds Breakfast Club. Raymond P. Kelly, local Chamber president, and his wife joined the party at Banff to participate in the final two days of festivities.

Left: Cay, overlooking the city of Spokane from Cliff Drive, was posed in her official Miss Spokane costume. Through the efforts of Chappie (Mrs. J.W.) Dunning, Cay's costume was custom made by members of the Spokane and Coeur d'Alene Indian tribes. Mrs. Dunning, who was also instrumental in providing costumes for other future Miss Spokanes, grew up in Santa Fe, New Mexico, where her father headed the Indian research for the Smithsonian Institution. She developed a great interest in the native cultures and especially in their artwork. An artist herself, she worked as an illustrator for the *Portland Oregonian* and was hired by Louis Davenport to come to Spokane to do some artwork for the Davenport Hotel. While in Spokane, she met her husband, pioneer dentist J.W. Dunning. Upon learning that the local Indians had no place to sell their beautiful crafts in Spokane, Chappie opened the Indian Art Shop on West Sprague. She later set up a tepee in her yard at 1412 South Grand where the Indian women could make and sell their crafts. There, Dunning supervised the creation of Cay's white buckskin costume. A sunburst of orange beads was embroidered on the bodice. She wore a necklace of blue beads with ties of ermine, a white buckskin headdress with "Spokane" painted on it and braids wrapped in beaver tails. The shell and bead earrings she wore were a gift from the Indians to one of the first white children born in this area.

Parade dignitaries passing in front of the King Edward Hotel in Banff during the parade at the opening of the 25th Annual Winter Carnival in 1941. Queen Cay Betts and Mayor Andy Davison of Calgary, Alberta, were the official parade openers.

Queen Cay with her mother Mercieta and two Cub Scouts assigned to her during the festivities.

Miss Spokane Cay Betts at the Banff Winter Carnival on the throne of the popular Canadian playground's Ice Castle, where she was crowned queen of the carnival. The throne was lined with a buffalo robe to protect her from direct contact with the ice. Constable Waterhouse of the Royal Canadian Mounted Police is to the left. In the background are chiefs from the Stoney Indian Tribe in full regalia.

During the Banff festivities, the queen and her court had special transportation like this sleigh. From left: Janet Martin, Doreen Rounds (one of Cay's Banff hostesses) and Connie Crommelin. The Cub Scouts with Cay were her constant companions.

Left: Cay had many talents and, in this candid shot taken by a friend, she could have passed as a professional model. One of Cay's talents was writing. For about a year after returning to Spokane following her father's death, in addition to working at Betts Oil Company, she wrote a weekly column for the *Spokesman-Review.* The column was a long-running feature entitled "Shop With Sue."

Below: James Hilton, author of *Lost Horizons*, *Goodby Mr. Chips* and *Random Harvest,* is on the left signing copies of his latest books in John W. Graham's book department in 1941. Hilton was in the United States raising money for "Bundles for Britain" to help with their war efforts. Cay's brother, Ray Betts, is on the far right. *(Photo taken by Mr. Parker, a professional photographer with the Spokesman-Review.)* **Above right:** Prior to the book signing, Cay had welcomed Hilton to Spokane at a luncheon in his honor.

In December of 1941, Miss Spokane was sent to Los Angeles to present Bing Crosby with *Thanks Bing*, a book containing 20,000 signatures of appreciation for Crosby's continuous efforts to publicize Spokane. The purpose of this meeting was to let Bing know how important he was to Spokane.

Cay Betts and Bing Crosby

While in Hollywood, Cay was escorted on a round of studio and night club visits by song writer Jimmy Van Heusen. On the film set where the presentation was made, Cay also met Bing's father H.L Crosby Sr. and his brother Larry; Crosby's prop manager, Jimmy Cottrell, a former middleweight fighter; musician Del Porter; Marion Birke, music company secretary; 1936 Olympic swimmer Mary Lou Petty Skok; and singer Margaret Lenhart, all formerly of Spokane. Cay also got to meet Bob Hope, a lifelong friend of Bing's, who dropped by while she was there. An added thrill was getting to watch some filming of the popular movie, *White Christmas*. (When the movie was released the following year, it won an Oscar for the best song of 1942.) During Cay's California visit, Pearl Harbor was bombed and the United States entered WWII.

Left: An Associated Press wirephoto news clipping of Cay Betts and Bing Crosby looking over the big *Thanks Bing* book.

During Bing's long musical career, he always had a fondness for Spokane, his old hometown. This was demonstrated by the donation of his entire memorabilia collection and all of his Gold Records to Gonzaga University and the numerous contacts he maintained with Spokane residents. He also had a summer home at Hayden Lake, Idaho.

Cay and friends at Manito Park, posing in front of what is now the Joel Ferris Perennial Gardens. From left: Janet Campbell (later Mrs. Oliver Treyz), Cay Betts (Williams), Connie Crommelin (now Mrs. W.W. Richardson living in Vero Beach, Florida), Janet Martin (now Mrs. Bruce Allan of Vancouver, B.C.), and Pat Bartlett (now Mrs. George Bulkley of Winnetka).

Left: Cay Betts in front of the rock underpass near the present Rose Garden at Manito Park. **Above:** Arnt Ofstad, Spokane Ski Club Class A champion in 1941, practicing for a slalom championship ski meet on Mt. Spokane. Ofstad, who was one of the top skiers in the area, was Cay's ski instructor.

An Associated Press wirephoto of Miss Spokane Cay Betts greeting First Lady Eleanor Roosevelt during a War Bond rally in Seattle, Washington, on April 3, 1943.

A news clipping of the "Flying Squadron," organized to aid in entertainment of boys of the Second Air Force in Spokane during WWII. From left: Mary McCabe, Martha Whitehouse, Janet Anthony, Sue Fry, Shirley Abrams, Virginia Rogers, Miss Spokane Catherine Betts, chairman; Ruth Buscho, Elizabeth DuBois and Doris Dyer. This was just one of many patriotic efforts to support the war effort.

Cay, as a baby, with her mother, Mercieta, at their home at Seventh Avenue and Brown Street, where she lived with her mother, father and her mother's parents, the Charles Liftchilds (and later, her brother Ray). The Liftchilds had commissioned Kirtland Cutter to design this house. Later, the family moved to a home near Manito Park, where Cay and her brother attended Roosevelt Grade School. Her favorite home while in Spokane was at 319 West Sumner, the former home of architect Charles Malmgren, Kirtland Cutter's partner. It was a quick trip over Cliff Drive, down some stairs and a pathway to Lewis and Clark High School.

News clipping montage following Cay's selection as Miss Spokane showing some of her favorite activities. These were taken at the family home on Sumner Avenue.

Cay and Tom Williams on their wedding day, August 28, 1943.

Top: Tom Jr. (left) sharing his dinner with their dog Miss Brown and Ray having fun with his dog Barry. **Middle left:** Cay and Tom Williams with sons Tom Jr. (called "Toby" as a child) and Ray. **Middle right:** From left, Ray, Cay and Tom Jr. at Cay's home in Walla Walla. **Bottom:** Mercieta Betts snorkeling with Dr. Harold Lamberton in Hawaii in 1988 at age 100. She attributed her longevity (she lived to be 108) to "swimming and eating chocolate." In 1985 she was named Pioneer Woman of the Year by the Eastern Washington State Historical Society.

Margel Peters

Miss Spokane 1947

Margel Peters (center), the third Miss Spokane in the original Miss Spokane contest. She is joined by Glenda Bergen, the fourth Miss Spokane (left) and Cay Betts, the second Miss Spokane, with son Tom. *(Photo courtesy Cay Betts Williams.)*

On May 22, 1947, Margel Elaine Peters was crowned by Mayor Arthur R. Meehan as the third Miss Spokane to represent the city in an official hostess position. The Spokane Advertising Club, Chamber of Commerce and the *Spokane Daily Chronicle* were the sponsors of that year's contest.

Margel, the 23-year-old daughter of Mr. and Mrs. Frank H. Peters, lived at 1828 West Ninth Avenue. She was born in Priest River, Idaho, and graduated from Metaline Falls High School. She attended Holy Names College in Spokane for two years. She was a talented singer with an excellent soprano voice and was well known throughout the city for her musical ability. She was a soloist with the choir at the Westminster Congregational Church and with the Serenaders, a young people's choral group.

Margel's Miss Spokane costume was an authentic Native American white buckskin dress which had belonged to the Spokane Indian Tribe. Her first duty as Miss Spokane was to attend the Apple Blossom Festival at Wenatchee, Washington. From the 60 participating princesses, Margel was chosen as the assistant queen of the festival.

The Contest's Trademark: the Indian Ceremonial Dress

The first two Miss Spokanes chosen as the official city hostess, Marguerite Motie and Catherine Betts, wore Indian dresses that were unique in their designs and custom made (see pages 71-72 and 135 respectively), and both were allowed to keep their dresses. Marguerite's dress is now in the possession of the Northwest Museum of Arts and Culture (formerly Cheney Cowles Museum). With Miss Spokane III, Margel Peters, a new tradition was established. Margel donned a white buckskin dress of historical significance and, like a mantle being passed, it was handed over to the each new Miss Spokane. Each woman's moccasins were custom made and hers to keep. The following article, which appeared in the *Spokane Daily Chronicle* on April 18, 1947, described the new official dress and its significance:

> **Costume for Miss Spokane Has Interesting Background:** Miss Spokane's official costume . . . is an authentic costume of the Spokane Indians.
>
> The dress to be worn by the new Miss Spokane . . . was made for Mattie Boyd, wife of the late Sam Boyd, last of the Spokane chiefs. In addition to the multi-colored beaded design on the neckline and shoulders, the costume will have some of the rare "fur" beads, old beads used by the Indians for trading [from the Hudson's Bay Company in the early 1800s] . . .
>
> Susan Michele [Michaels] of the Spokane tribe, who was raised here . . . but now is on the Coeur d'Alene reservation, made the dress for the Spokane chief's wife about 15 or 20 years ago, according to Mrs. J.W. Dunning of Spokane, who made arrangements for the purchase of the costume. Susan is one of the "finest of the old beaders and has established quite a reputation for her work," Mrs. Dunning said. Lizzie Ford, daughter of Chief Sam Boyd, is making the beaded headband . . . a narrow band of white with Spokane lettered in blue beads . . .

Before the year was over, a controversy swirled around the issue of wearing the Indian dress versus more contemporary attire. Some complained the dress was not flattering, while others argued that the tradition, unique to Spokane, of the official city hostess in Indian dress honored the area's native heritage. The *Spokane Daily Chronicle*, stating that the controversy was "warming up to the red-hot stage," even conducted a poll soliciting the public's opinion. After much debate, a decision was made to retain the Indian dress, but the controversy continued to surface periodically. For appearances in which the Indian dress was not deemed appropriate, clothing fitting the occasion was worn, but the Indian dress remained the official Miss Spokane attire until the contest ceased in 1977.

In 1957 a second official dress, first worn by Suzanne Thompson, was designed by Ella McCarty of the Spokane Tribe. Additional firsthand information about the dresses is scattered throughout the next 90 pages in the Miss Spokanes' personal accounts, and there are numerous photographs showing the two designs. Like a badge of honor, the dresses were worn with pride and dignity.

Glenda Bergen

Miss Spokane 1948-1951

Glenda Bergen, 1948

(All photos in this section are courtesy of Glenda Bergen Thompson.)

Born in Spokane on August 31, 1925, Glenda was adopted as an infant by Eva and George Bergen. George was a locomotive engineer for the Great Northern Railroad and Eva was a homemaker. Raised as an only child by the Bergens, Glenda's childhood was filled with love.

Glenda's grew up in Hillyard in a small bungalow at 4711 North Cook Street. She attended Regal Grade School and John Rogers High School. By the time Glenda graduated from Rogers in 1943, she had achieved the reputation of being an outstanding student, attaining the third highest scholastic rating in her class of 179. While at Rogers, Glenda was also a drum majorette, song leader, active in the Girl's League, lieutenant in charge of the girls' Victory Corps, was chosen for the National Honor Society and came in second in a contest for the "Spring Sports Queen."

Among Glenda's fondest early memories were the summers of 1939-1941, which she spent with her Aunt Emma and Uncle Ralph Henrichs on their homestead near Granite Creek on Lake Pend Oreille. Three of her male cousins, two to five years her junior, were also visiting at the log house built by their uncle. These visits were spent fishing, riding the family horse, picnicking and doing farm chores.

Following her high school graduation, Glenda entered Washington State College (now WSU) in Pullman. At WSC she was elected president of the freshman class and the same year was selected as queen of the 319th Air Force Ball. She became secretary of her class during her junior year and was a member of the executive council of her senior class. She also began acting in the college drama department. During Glenda's senior year, she was elected to the "Big Five," an honor given the most outstanding girls in college. Glenda graduated with a Phi Beta Kappa key and a Phi Kappa Phi national honorary, Alpha Kappa Delta (sociology honorary) of which she was president and Psi Chi (psychology honorary). She was also a member of the college-day and orientation committees.

When Glenda won the title of Miss Spokane, the *Spokesman-Review* announced her selection in the March 3, 1948, edition with the following comment:

> **GLENDA BERGEN '48 MISS SPOKANE, G.N. Engineer's Daughter Noted for Many Achievements** – Here she is, the city's new Miss Spokane, Glenda Jean Bergen, a vivacious brunette who looks as if she were made to play the part of an Indian maid. . . . The city's new Miss Spokane overflows with the exuberance of youth and invites friendliness. She typifies everything that is wholesome. She wears her almost black hair in a long bob. . . . It was fun to watch her almost black eyes as she told her story, for they expressed such complete happiness.

Following Glenda's initial appointment as Miss Spokane, she was asked by the Chamber of Commerce to continue for two more years. During her three-year reign as Miss Spokane, the highlight for her was meeting President Harry Truman, his wife Bess and daughter Margaret on two separate occasions while they were in Spokane.

Among Glenda's many interests were horses and she loved to ride when she had the opportunity, as revealed in a August 2, 1948, *Spokane Chronicle* article entitled; "**GLENDA HAS A GALLOP**." This article went on to say:

> When Miss Spokane (Glenda Bergen) agreed to ride in the parade at the Joseph, Ore., rodeo yesterday, officials began looking around for the usual convertible automobile.

> "Oh, I can ride on a horse like the rest of the others," Glenda assured them. So they brought out a light brown mare, and Miss Spokane climbed in the saddle and joined in the march.
>
> Then when it came time for the individual introduction of celebrities, Glenda urged her horse into a gallop and swept pass [*sic*] the reviewing stand with a salute to the applauding crowd.
>
> "We had no idea she could ride," said P.J. Limacher, chairman of the committee in charge of Miss Spokane's arrangements. "She rode as well as the featured performers in their introduction."

Although Glenda loves horses, according to a letter she wrote to the authors of this publication, her earlier horsemanship experience was less than her performance indicated during this ride. However, after they moved to Carmichael, California, in 1969, she became the leader of her daughter's 4-H equestrienne group, which she said was a lot of fun. In her letter dated July 13, 2000, Glenda stated:

> I want to clarify my interest and really limited experience with horses. I never owned one, but enjoyed riding with friends when there were opportunities, usually at a stable which rented them out on an hourly basis. While I was at WSC, my friends and I would occasionally ride at the stables there. . . . Pete Limacher, in his statement in the *Spokane Chronicle* was very generous in his praise of my riding at the Joseph, Oregon, rodeo. I am amazed that I didn't fall off my horse, "Minnie Pearl," as she galloped madly across the arena. It's pretty hard to stay aboard wearing moccasins and a buckskin dress, but I hung on and pretended it was a breeze.

In 1950 Glenda met her future husband, Bill Thompson. Bill was stationed at Fairchild Air Force Base and had a friend who was married to one of Glenda's girlfriends. These mutual friends invited Glenda and Bill to dinner. Shortly after, they began dating, fell in love and married on February 25, 1951. Although their wedding invitations read "Captain," the Air Force bestowed a special present just before the wedding, so it was Major Thompson who said "I do" to Glenda.

Bill has also had an exciting career. He spent 29 years in the military. His first years were as a pilot for both B-17s and B-29s. His job took their family to numerous places throughout the world. He eventually attained the rank of colonel and became commander of the 821st Civil Engineering Squadron at Ellsworth Air Force Base in South Dakota. When Bill retired in 1969, he became a sixth-grade teacher at Del Dayo Elementary School in Carmichael, California, from 1970 to 1986. Following that, he was a substitute teacher for grades K-12 for another three years.

At age 44, after raising her six children, Glenda met her blood siblings for the first time. Her half-brother, Don Steele, lives in Apple Valley, California, and her half-sister, Virginia Allen, lives in Kettle Falls, Washington. Although Glenda left Spokane over 48 years ago, she has fond memories of Spokane and those wonderful years she spent with her kind and loving family, friends and neighbors.

Glenda Bergen
Growing up in Spokane

1925 1928 1933

1934 1938 1941

H.S. graduation, 1943 College graduation, 1947 Miss Spokane, 1948

The Bergen home at 4711 North Cook Avenue in Spokane's Hillyard neighborhood. This bungalow was built in 1928.

Left: The Bergen family in downtown Spokane in 1938. From left: Glenda, mother Eva and father George. **Right**: Glenda's first photo, which appeared in the March 3, 1948, edition of the *Spokesman-Review,* following her selection as Miss Spokane.

Glenda and friends at Loon Lake in 1933. From left: Marian (Leavett) Pfeffer, Mary Edith McCarty, Roland Kay Ecker (cousin), 3, unidentified, and Glenda, 8.

Glenda, age 13, with her cousin, Roland Ecker, (left) and at a cabin the family rented for the weekend at Hope, Idaho, in 1947.

Left: Glenda with some of her Alpha Gamma Delta sorority sisters during a horseback riding excursion, circa 1947. From left: Beverly Berry, Glenda, Helen Nervig and Marilyn Cone. **Right**: In 1946 Glenda was one of six students in Washington selected to go to New York City with the College Summer Service group, where she worked with children in Brooklyn's poorest district. She is shown here with some fellow students, from left, Myra Vandersall, Suzanne Pope, Glenda, Betty Stewart.

Left: Joseph Drumheller, president of the Spokane Chamber of Commerce, crowning Glenda Bergen as Miss Spokane during a ceremony held at the Civic Building. **Right**: The largest crowd of the 1950 baseball season turned out to see Bing Crosby and his sons in action during a benefit ball game between Crosby's Hayden Hellcats and the Empire Furniture Legion team. Glenda threw the first pitch of the game.

Glenda Bergen, the fourth Miss Spokane, in 1948. Inset photo is of her future husband, William Thompson, taken in 1943 while attending West Point in New York. Bill was a B-17 and B-29 pilot in the military. He retired after 29 years of service.

President Harry Truman and his wife Bess on the train's observation platform during his 1948 campaign tour. Glenda is presenting Mrs. Truman with a bouquet of lilacs.

Glenda greeting New York governor, Thomas Dewey, during his 1948 campaign tour.

Glenda on the Spokane Indian Reservation in 1948 dressed in her official Miss Spokane attire, an authentic Indian ceremonial dress, which had originally been made for Mattie Boyd, wife of the Spokane chief, Sam Boyd (see page 146). This dress weighed 12 pounds. (*Photo by Dick Lewis.*) Inset is Glenda with a doll collection representing the first four Miss Spokanes created by Mrs. H.B. Bearden.

Edgar Bergen (no relation) and Glenda with Charlie McCarthy, the nationally famous puppet, on April 29, 1948, during the annual Apple Blossom Festival in Wenatchee, Washington.

Glenda with her mother and father, 1949, (left) and on the Spokane Indian Reservation.

Glenda on the Miss Spokane float during the Spokane Lilac Festival in May 1949. Upon being crowned Miss Spokane, she was also named the queen of the 1948 Lilac Festival.

Left: During an All-Indian Fair ceremony on the Spokane Indian Reservation in September 1950, Alex Sherwood, tribal council chairman of the Spokane Indians, placed a headband on Glenda and adopted her into the tribe. **Right**: During the same fair, from left (women with headdresses only), Christine Peouse, Lucille Boyd, Alice Raymond, Glenda Bergen, Donna Moomaw, Agnes Lott and Margaret Brown.

This photo was taken at Gonzaga University on May 11, 1950, at a ceremony in which officials from Gonzaga presented President Harry S. Truman with a citation of merit. This was during Truman's second visit to Spokane. During this goodwill tour of the Inland Northwest, the Trumans visited Grand Coulee Dam, Walla Walla and Cheney in Washington and Hayden Lake and Potlatch in Idaho. Glenda, who is seated between Bess and Margaret Truman, accompanied the party to Grand Coulee.

The flight crew of the 98th bomb group standing in front of a B-29 bomber at Fairchild Air Force Base in 1951. This particular plane, named the *Miss Spokane,* flew 50 bombing missions while in service during the Korean War. Glenda Bergen was the model for the painting on the plane's fuselage.

Members of the crew, back row from left, are: Capt. E.L. Johnson, 3106 Woodlawn Ave., Spokane; Lt. Robert L. Shaffer, N. 5612 Alberta St., Spokane; Capt. James F. Michalski, S. 826 Oak St., Spokane; Capt. Michael Evanco, 1216 W. 11th Avenue, Spokane; and S./Sgt. Sigismund Zuzelski, Spokane. Front row, from left: S/Sgt. George E. Egan, Southbridge, Mass.; T/Sgt. Arless O. Jones, 2408 W. Pacific Avenue, Spokane; S/Sgt. Claude D. Day, 2918 W. 8th Avenue, Spokane; S/Sgt. Curtis L. Rice, Pocatello, Idaho; and Sgt. Donald E., Garrison, Anderson S.C.

Left: Glenda and Bill Thompson in March 1994. **Right**: Glenda with her mother and the Thompson's six children, Christmas 1965, Ellsworth AFB, South Dakota.

The Thompson family: Bill, 44, holding Robert, 3, Glenda, 39, Sally, 11, David, 9, Jack, 13, Mary, 6; George, 10. Photo taken in Spokane, August 1965.

Glenda and Bill Thompson on April 12, 2000.
The Thompsons were married 49 years
and counting at the time of this photo.

Marcia Gusman

Miss Spokane 1951

Marcia Gusman, 1951

(All photos in this section are courtesy of Marcia Gusman Bigelow.)

Born in Lewiston, Idaho, in 1928, Marcia moved to Spokane with her parents, Alexander H. "Joe" and Bertha (Brammer) Gusman, in 1939. Her father was founder and owner of Inland Truck and Diesel Company. Sadly, he passed away before seeing his daughter become Miss Spokane.

During her tenure as Miss Spokane, Marcia lived at 2405 West Second Avenue with her mother and sisters, Celeste and Sally. She attended Washington State College, where she majored in English and speech.

Marcia worked for a short time as a dental assistant before taking the job of copy chief and account executive in an advertising agency. Later, she became part owner of a modeling school and agency.

In 1953 Marcia married Lieutenant Robert Bigelow, who was stationed at Fairchild Air Force Base. They have four children: Mark, Tracey, Scott and Rick.

Remembrances of My Miss Spokane Days

Written in 2000 by Marcia (Gusman) Bigelow

Just a few days after my selection, a photographer from the paper took Jim McConville and me up to the Spokane House Hotel for a photo overlooking the city. Mr. McConville said he was a chief of the Nez Perce in Lewiston, so the photographer asked if the tribe could adopt me and give me an Indian name. I was given the name, which I believe was spelled "Pocht," meaning "Little Sunflower."

When I was given the costume, there were instructions on how to weave my own hair into the braids, which were then to be wrapped with beaver fur strips and topped with a circle of abalone shell. This was all fine and good, but my hair was very short, and it took a lot of bobby pins and hairpins (it was too early for super glue) to keep me together. (By the way, I was the last Miss Spokane required to wear the braids.)

The town of Bridgeport was opening a new bridge and asked that I attend. It was soon after my selection so there had been little hair growth. The day started very early and included a parade, many photo sessions, ceremonies and interviews. By the time I was able to get to a mirror, one braid was swinging from a skinny tendril of hair – sort of resembling a man swinging from a noose.

I hold one other memory very dear just to remind myself to never become self-impressed. It had been over a year since my selection – a year filled with my picture in the paper at least once a month, some full-page spreads, a well publicized trip to California and my picture in *Life Magazine*. One day I had given a speech at North Central High School, but had to stop at my doctor's office on my way back to work. I carried the costume with me in a large hat box, which was very fashionable at the time. When my doctor saw it, he asked me what it was. I replied that it was the Miss Spokane costume. He then asked me what I was doing with it. I told him I was Miss Spokane and he asked, "What happened to the other girl?" That brought me down to earth fast.

Naturally, the attention I received as Miss Spokane on the trip to California was impressive and at times intoxicating, but the people who really spoke to me were the ones I most remember. On the train to San Francisco, there was a waiter in the diner who was especially attentive (of course he had been prompted by the manager of the Portland office of the railroad, and since I always appeared in the buckskin dress, it was hard to miss me). At dinner we chatted and he told me he was anxious to get home because it was his wedding anniversary. He also asked if I would give him an autograph for his daughter. Of course I gave him the autograph, and since several dignitaries had given me corsages, which were inappropriate on the dress, I gave him an orchid for his wife. When we returned home, I received a thank you note from his wife and daughter. For several years we exchanged Christmas cards.

While in Los Angeles, the brother of the famous comic, Milton Berle, was assigned to show me around the television studios. It was then I received my first exposure to lecherous Hollywood men with a resounding pat and pinch on my behind. Jerk! But even better, on the train to Salt Lake City, my sister and I were chatting with two nice gentlemen when one of them offered us jobs working as strippers in his chain of clubs!

My mother accompanied me on the trip to Los Angeles, as there wasn't an escort provided by the Chamber of Commerce, and I really needed her at times. But one of the things that really upset her was the fact that so many people would call me a "squaw" during the trip. She was aware of the connotation of the word held by the Native Americans and their objections to its use. It is interesting to me that there is a current controversy in regard to lakes and creeks having that name.

The trip to Wellpinit for the annual Pow Wow was very interesting but I wish I had been better prepared by knowing whom I would be meeting and what was really expected of me. Mrs. J.W. Dunning, who was the experienced go-between with the Indians, told me later that I should have been very honored when they let me hold the drumsticks and hit the drum. Women were never allowed to touch those things.

Mrs. Dunning introduced me to the most influential women of the tribe, who took me under their wings and treated me like a queen. They taught me some newfangled ways of adapting the clothing. They had broken with tradition years ago by not bothering to tie the abalone shells on their braid with horse hide thongs – they just made earrings out of the shell. (Mrs. Dunning checked my dress frequently and would never have allowed that.) They also allowed me to put on the most exquisitely beaded cape and to hold a beautiful beaded buckskin rifle cover.

Later in the evening, I was asked to participate in the "owl dance." This really surprised and scared me. I didn't know what the steps were, and since a nice young man was to be my partner, I didn't want to trip over him. It ended up being a very slow step-together-step dance, but it was fun. Just recently, I learned that it is a sort of "Sadie Hawkins" dance – the women ask the men to dance.

My "fifteen minutes of fame" lasted almost 18 months, which were filled with exceptional memories.

The Gusman home at 2405 West Second Avenue in Spokane's Browne's Addition, circa 1940. Inset are Marcia's mother and father, Bertha and Joe Gusman.

Inland Truck and Diesel Company, Joe Gusman's business, 25 East Third Avenue.

A convention Marcia's father Joe attended at the Davenport Hotel, circa 1940.

Marcia and her mother, Bertha, inside the family home at 2405 West Second.

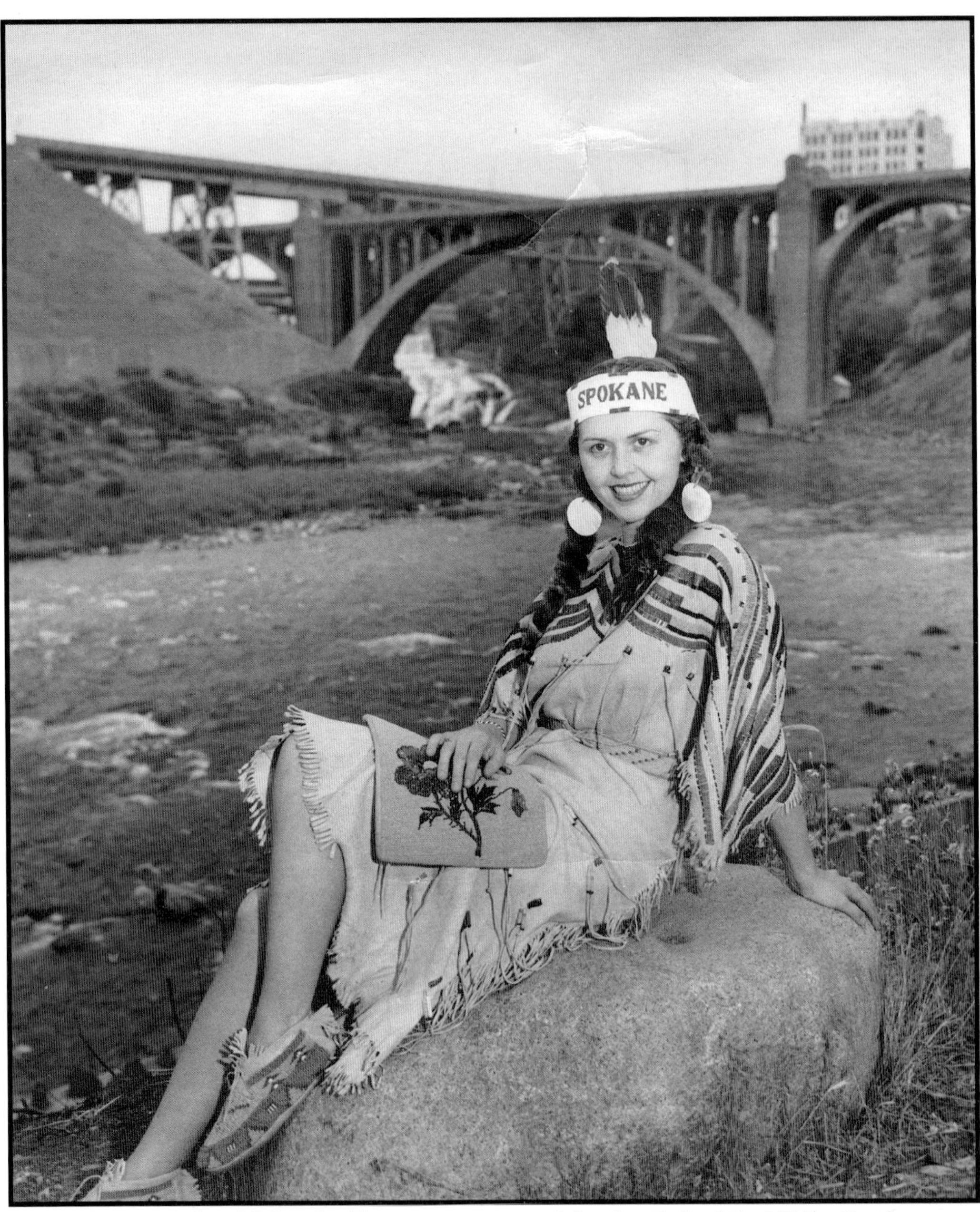

This photograph of Marcia Gusman appeared in the July 15, 1951, *Spokesman-Review* with the following caption:

> Spokane's new first lady, Marcia Joan Gusman, poses in the traditional costume of the Spokane Indian tribe in a symbolic setting. The talented 23-year-old brunette will be the fifth Miss Spokane to represent the city as official hostess. A graduate of Lewis and Clark High School and Washington State College, Marcia Joan has a college background of dramatic art, radio and music. Her duties as Miss Spokane will be to appear at civic functions and to be on call whenever needed to greet distinguished guests of the city. She succeeds Mrs. William M. Thompson, the former Glenda Jean Bergen.

Marcia with two adorable Indian girls, who were assigned as her escorts during a Pow Wow she attended as Miss Spokane in 1952 at Wellpinit on the Spokane Indian Reservation. In this photo, Marcia is wearing the cape mentioned in her narrative and cuffs loaned to her. The handbag was a gift from the Spokane Indian women. Symbols and designs woven into this kind of bag generally told a story, so each bag was unique. The reverse side of the bag is visible in the photo on the following page.

It was a rare honor for the male tribal members to allow Marcia to beat this drum, which belonged to a visiting tribe from Montana. Pete Beaverhead is at the drum on the left and Chuck Cox, son of Etta Adams Cox (below), is standing behind him.

One of Marcia's highlights at the 1952 Wellpinit Pow Wow was the kindness and consideration shown her by the Indian women. The women with Marcia (center) are, from left, Winifred Sherwood, Annie Brown, Etta Adams Cox and Margaret Brown.

According to Marcia, Californians never did understand that Miss Spokane was a hostess, not a beauty queen. Her term was a constant face-off with bathing beauties. In this photo, Marcia is seen placing a "head-covering of sorts" on "Miss Sunshine."

Marcia presenting Hopalong Cassidy (William Boyd) with a bouquet of red feathers and her most adoring look. Hollywood was one of the stops during Marcia's week-long goodwill tour of the major western cities. During this visit, she attended one of Bing Crosby's shows, where he introduced her to the audience.

Marcia and the chief of the Washington State Patrol, James A. Pryde of Olympia, at the annual police benefit ball at Natatorium Park in 1951, where they led the grand march. With formal attire, Marcia wore a rhinestone headband with a silver feather

A promotional photo taken for a car dealership at Manito Park in 1951.

Marcia with Shirley Flowers, Seattle's Seafair queen, at the Columbia Basin Water Festival in Pasco, Washington, in 1951.

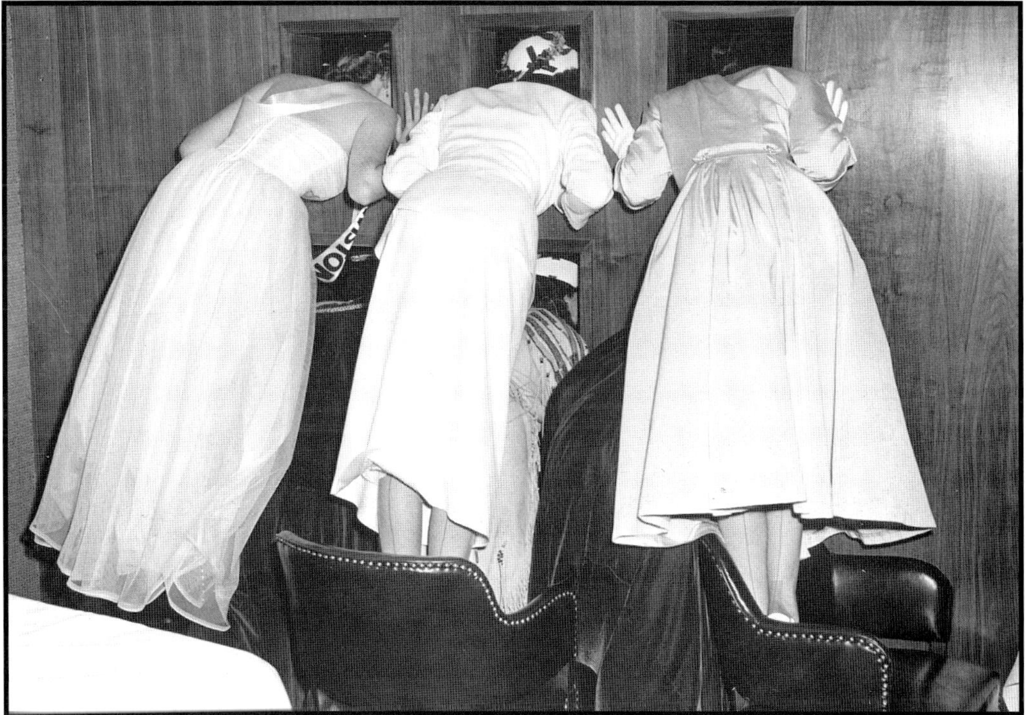

Top: From left: Carol Braun, Portland Rose Festival; Carol Haas, Lilac Festival; Carol Bird, Lewiston Roundup; Jackie McDonald, Seattle Seafair; Marcia Gusman, Miss Spokane; and Barbara Wickham, Miss Pasco. This photo was taken to celebrate the opening of the Ridpath Hotel following a major remodel. **Bottom:** Obviously there was some collusion going on between two photographers.

Miss Spokane riding in a 1951 Cadillac convertible during the Lilac Parade.

Marcia (second from right) with her mother Bertha (second from left) and sisters Sally Butterworth Levitch (left) and Celeste Gusman, circa 1948.

Marcia and her husband, Robert Bigelow, with their four children, from left: Mark and Tracey (standing) and Rick and Scott (seated), circa 1962.

Robert and Marcia (in back) with their children, from left: Rick, Tracey, Mark and Scott. At the time of this photo in 1997, Traccy had just returned from Berlin, where she had worked for eight years, and Mark was visiting from Norway, where he has lived since 1986. Proud mother Marcia included a note with the photo that read: "Happily, I can tell you that they have all become responsible, contributing members of society."

Suzanne Thompson

Miss Spokane 1957

Suzanne Thompson, the tenth official city hostess, in the "Spokane Welcomes You" pose, with the city of Spokane in the background.

(Unless otherwise noted, all photos in this section are courtesy of Suzanne Thompson Adams.)

On November 27, 1956, Suzanne E. Thompson was at work as the home service director for the Spokane Natural Gas Company, when Jack Gwyer, chairman of the Miss Spokane Contest Committee, walked into her office at 10:30 a.m. He was accompanied by photographers and other members of the Spokane Chamber of Commerce, who had just made the decision to name Suzanne as Miss Spokane, the official hostess for the city.

On January 1, 1957, Suzanne became the official tenth Miss Spokane. Her term was packed with over 70 official appearances.

The daughter of Ted A.L. and Emilou (Daubert) Thompson, Suzanne was born in Spokane and raised at 2311 East Seventeenth.. Her father was the Spokane general agent for Western Life Insurance Company. Suzanne was a graduate of Lewis and Clark High School, where she had won a number of honors, one of which was the statewide Knights of Pythias "Abraham Lincoln" speech contest. She also had the leading role in a school play, was president of an all-city girls' talent club called Dasidrian, and head of the Lewis and Clark Girls Federation.

Suzanne graduated from Washington State College in June of 1957, with a Bachelor of Arts degree in Home Economics. During her college years she was a member of Spurs, sophomore women's honorary and in her junior year she served on the WSC Board of Control. As a senior, she was president of her Pi Beta Phi Sorority and a member of the Mortar Board. She was named Outstanding Senior in 1956.

Suzanne's year as Miss Spokane is best described in her own words, which she wrote for this publication, as follows:

My year as Miss Spokane

Written in January 2000 by Suzanne (Thompson) Adams.

The city of Spokane gave me a very special gift when its leaders selected me to be Miss Spokane X for the year of 1957. There were many marvelous people who helped me in so many ways that year. The Chamber of Commerce gave wonderful support and provided escorts for all of my appearances. That meant picking me up and staying through the event and then getting me back to my job or my home, depending on the hour of the day or night. (How I would love to see the calendar of that year in my life.) Luther Essick helped me learn some Indian sign language, which I used in my welcoming talks to groups. Ella McCarty helped me learn the beautiful symbolism of the new costume she had made, which I was the first Miss Spokane to wear. I tried to share what she had taught me with all of our city's visitors. Frank Parker was ever present in his quiet professional way photographing the events.

Many important and famous people visited Spokane that year and it was my privilege to meet and visit with them. Eleanor Roosevelt was a delightful luncheon companion on one occasion. Senators Henry Jackson and J.W. Fulbright also visited Spokane in 1957. I had a college roommate who attended WSU as a Fulbright Scholar and so was doubly interested in greeting Senator and Mrs. Fulbright. The Lennon Sisters were fun to greet, as was Ted Mack of the *Amateur Hour* – and so many others.

A highlight of the year was my christening of Fairchild Air Force Base's B-52 the

City of Spokane. To be adopted by the Spokane Indian Tribe was another very special event in my life that year. I still enjoy getting out the lovely beaded bag and the eagle feather with a leather piece attached that says "Quent-Mah, Suzanne Thompson, Spokane Tribe." Everywhere I went there were children. They were all so interested in Miss Spokane and wanted to feel the elegant leather costume and touch the beadwork and the ermine. I enjoyed the children so much and found them absolutely enchanting!

And then the year was over! It was a whirlwind year – delightful and memorable in every way. My mother, Emilou Daubert Thompson, was unfailing in her support from the beginning of the contest to my final appearance. She helped in so may countless ways – lending a critical ear, always giving encouragement, providing nutritious meals, reminding me to get adequate rest, and sometimes chauffeuring me to appearances.

In April of 1958 I became engaged to Lt. j.g. Gordon E. Adams, who also was born and raised in Spokane and was a graduate of Lewis and Clark High School and the University of Idaho. We married in July that year and lived in Brunswick, Maine, where he was serving as a pilot in the U. S. Naval Air Corps. In 1959 we moved to Walla Walla, Washington, where he joined his brother in business. I worked as a recruiter for Kinman Business University during our first year in Walla Walla. In 1960 our daughter Elizabeth was born, followed by Peter, our first son, in 1963, and our youngest child, Daniel, in 1968.

As the children were entering school each one would ask if he or she could take some of my Miss Spokane treasures to school with them for "Show and Tell." I would learn later from the teacher that they would begin the presentation with "When Mommy was an Indian . . ." Their classmates always seemed to enjoy this "Show and Tell."

Our years raising our family were wonderful, busy and interesting years. I worked as a volunteer all those years – for the PTA, our church and various other philanthropic organizations, serving as president of the Junior Club of Walla Walla, The PTA Council, the Northwest Gifted Child Association and Chapter BI of PEO. I also taught sewing and tailoring and worked as a home sewing consultant. In 1983, urged by my father, Ted Thompson, I became a registered investment representative for Metropolitan Mortgage and Securities Company, Inc. of Spokane. My husband and I continue to work as investment representatives with Metropolitan Investment Securities, an endeavor we find challenging and rewarding.

Elizabeth graduated from Cottey College and from Washington State University. She is married to Dan Armstrong and lives in Beaverton, Oregon, where she is an investment representative with Metropolitan Investment Securities. They have a young son Brian, our second grandchild. Before Elizabeth graduated from WSU, I was privileged to be selected as a WSU "Mom of the Year" in 1982.

Peter graduated from the University of Portland and earned an MBA at Northwestern University. He and his wife, Jean Tang, live with our first grandchild, Madeleine, in Portland, Oregon, where Peter works in marketing as a product line manager for Intel Corporation.

Daniel graduated from Northwestern University and earned a Master's Degree in Biomedical Engineering at Tulane University. He and his wife, Teresa Timons, live in Milton, Florida, where he is a flight instructor with the U. S. Naval Air Corps.

This brings us up to the year 2000. I am grateful for this book project, which provided the inspiration for me to look back and remember.

A news clipping of Suzanne Thompson from a montage of her photos published in the *Spokesman-Review* in 1957. The headline for the story was "Suzanne's Album – from Baby Steps to Miss Spokane." The caption under this photo was: "PROPHETIC of the honor to come as Miss Spokane was this pose of Sue in Indian headdress at the age of 3. Sue recalls her childhood enjoyment of costumes." This is reminiscent of the "Miss Spokane Welcomes You" pose used in various advertisements and promotional pieces.

Elizabeth Adams and Suzanne Adams.

SUZANNE ADAMS, ONE OF FIVE WSU "MOM'S OF THE YEAR"

Elizabeth Adams' mother Suzanne Thompson Adams, of Walla Walla, was named one of WSU's five "Mom's of the Year" during Mothers Weekend activities on the WSU campus May 1-3. Mrs. Adams was nominated by Kappa Delta with the final selection made by a student committee on the basis of her involvement at WSU as a student and community activities since her graduation in 1956.

As a student Mrs. Adams graduated in Home Economics. She was a member of Spurs, Mortar Board, president of Pi Beta Phi Sorority, and was an Outstanding Senior in 1956. Mrs. Adams has three children, including Elizabeth a senior in Business Administration. Mrs. Adams has been active in the Northwest Gifted Child Association, Pi Beta Phi Alumni Assoc. and the American Home Economics Assoc. As a member of the Walla Walla Parent Teacher Student Assoc., she served as Council President.

Elizabeth, who graduated in June, spent her first two years at Cottey College at Nevada, Missouri. She has been an outstanding member of Sigma Tau Chapter. For the past two summers and again this summer she has been a secretary in the office of Representative Tom Foley in Washington, D.C.

Above: Suzanne was named one of five WSU "Mom's of the Year." The above article appeared in the 1982 issue of the Washington State University *Alumnae News*. This event happened during Mothers' Weekend activities on WSU's campus on May 1-3, 1982.

Left: Christening Fairchild Air Force Base's B-52, the *City of Spokane*, on May 19, 1957, the opening event for the Armed Forces Day-Lilac Festival. Even with the inclement weather, a crowd of 15,000 turned out for the event.

Suzanne Thompson during the opening session of the 19th Annual Intermountain Logging Conference held in Spokane in 1957. With her are the Lennon sisters, a nationally renowned four-sister singing act; the Lennons' father; Spokane's mayor, Willard "Duke" Taft; and the president of the Intermountain Logging Conference, Burton Schmidt.

Left: The Lennon Sisters as they appear today. Forty-three years after meeting Miss Spokane, they are still active and appearing regularly on stage in Branson, Missouri. *(Publicity photo from the Lennon Sisters' Internet site.)*

Left: Suzanne Thompson and Nathan H. Gellert Jr., president of the Spokane Natural Gas Company, Just minutes after Suzanne was informed she had just been selected as the tenth official Miss Spokane. **Right**: Suzanne, on the job as home service director for the Spokane Natural Gas Company, pointing out the features of a modern built-in gas oven on display in the gas company's showroom. In September 1957, Suzanne left this job to become the employment manager for Kinman Business University, where she was in charge of the school placement office and supervision of Kinman's student housing accommodations.

Suzanne's wedding at the Cathedral of St. John the Evangelist in Spokane on July 12, 1958. From left: Suzanne's brother, Dan Thompson, Suzanne and her parents, Ted and Emilou Thompson.

Suzanne Thompson and Gordon Adams on their wedding day, July 12, 1958.

The Adams family on Thanksgiving 1999. Back row, from left: Peter Adams, Daniel Adams, Teresa Timons Adams, Dan Armstrong. Seated, from left: Jean Tang Adams, Suzanne with Madeleine, Gordon with Brian, Elizabeth Adams Armstrong.

Patricia Kelly

Miss Spokane 1958

Patricia Kelly, Miss Spokane XI, and members of the Spokane Chamber of Commerce greet the arrival of the newly reorganized Spokane Indians Baseball Team when the Brooklyn Dodgers organization decided to move their AAA farm team to Spokane to become part of the historic Pacific Coast League in 1958.

(All photos in this section are courtesy of Patsy Kelly Eggers.)

Recognized by her warm smile and equally warm personality, Patricia "Patsy" Kelly has truly been among Spokane's most gracious hostesses. Her life as Miss Spokane was filled with many honors. Her tenure can best be recalled by her association with the opening of Spokane's Maple Street Bridge. On July 1, 1958, Governor Albert Rosellini and Patsy Kelly, Miss Spokane XI, officiated at the ribbon cutting ceremony. As they each cut through the ribbon blocking the entrance to the bridge, over 4,000 spectators looked on. During the first 24 hours following its opening, 8,735 vehicles crossed the bridge, each paying their ten-cent toll. This much needed bridge signalled a new era to downtown Spokane transportation, both for convenience and traffic congestion. With a 40 miles-per-hour speed limit assigned, it also became, prior to the building of the east-west freeway, the fastest allowable means of transportation within the immediate downtown radius.

Patsy's family roots in Spokane go back to the late 1880s, when things were booming, but at a much slower pace. During Patsy's grandfather's early Spokane years, the city was without speed limits for cars up until 1902 (the maximum speed limit for horses in downtown Spokane, at the time, was six miles-per-hour). In 1902 new traffic ordinances were passed to apply to autos. These new limits were set at four miles-per-hour for crossing street intersections, eight miles-per-hour between intersecting streets within the city's fire limits, and 12 miles-per-hour outside the fire limits. Patsy Kelly's ancestors would have never imagined the Spokane of 1958.

Although the first jet-powered flight was in 1939, Patsy's tenure as Miss Spokane occurred during some of the most significant advances in speed and technology the world had experienced up to this time. Just months prior to Patsy's tenure, the first jet flew around the world and the Russians launched the first artificial earth satellite. In 1958 the United States launched its first satellite, the Explorer I. That same year NASA became operational and made its first launch and the first radio broadcast was made from space. Patsy Kelly was Spokane's official city hostess during some of the most exciting technological times and she experienced a touch of that excitement. The following is a short summation of Patsy's reflections about her life:

Miss Spokane 1958

Written in April 1999 (with update in 2000) by Patsy (Kelly) Eggers.

In my life, the honor of being Miss Spokane is second only to my marriage and my family. My grandfather, Albert A. Kelly, settled in Spokane in 1889 and founded the Kelly Gardens on East Sprague Avenue. Grandpa was a very active citizen in Spokane's early days. He served several sessions in the legislature in the early 1900s, as did my father, Albert Kelly Jr., in the 1930s. My mother, Emmaleta (Sims) Kelly, was the daughter of Dr. Richard and Gertrude Sims. She was actually born in Anaconda, Montana, because her mother went back to her hometown to have the baby. They soon returned to Spokane, where my mother lived until her death in 1984. I truly felt I was a daughter of Spokane and was thrilled to represent it as Spokane's official hostess.

I am from a family of seven. My father passed away when I was five and the baby, Larry, was three months old! My mom went straight to work and became a "single parent" long before the trend was set as it is today. She worked so hard to keep us all fed, clothed and housed, but did it with a great deal of style and grace. She was an exceptional woman and such a force in my life. She was as thrilled as I was with the Miss Spokane experience.

I was very proud to wear the magnificent Indian costume. In 1959 someone wrote a letter to the editor complaining about the costume. I answered that letter, explaining the story of the costume and the pride Spokane should have in it. My letter was featured on the editorial page.

In 1961 I married Arthur Eggers and moved to Walla Walla where Art served as Walla Walla County's prosecuting attorney for twenty-five years and where we raised our three children, David, Sarah and Matthew. I was active in Junior Club and served one year as its president. In 1975 I founded my own business, a retail fresh seafood market and gourmet restaurant, which I ran until 1985.

Art retired in 1986 and we moved to Seattle. At that time, I went to work for a line of fine cookware, Scanpan USA, Inc., and served as national director of Marketing Services. My duties included traveling the entire United States, working with major department stores and their buyers to present the product in the best possible light and teach sales associates the qualities of the product. A couple of years ago, I semiretired from that position, cutting down drastically on the traveling, although I still work their major shows in Chicago, San Francisco and New Orleans.

The pace has slowed giving me time to enjoy hobbies and our children's lives. David, 35, is a corporate jet pilot and manages Aeroflight Executive Flight Services here in Seattle. Sarah, 33, is a flight attendant with Continental Airlines. She married Troy Stevens in May of 1998 and presented us with our first grandchild, Tate Arthur Stevens, on October 6, 1999. They live in Houston. Matthew, 30, is the perennial student still working towards his degree in physics and lives here in Seattle.

Miss Spokane Patsy Kelly sitting between an army and a navy officer during the 1958 Lilac Festival-Armed Forces Day Parade in downtown Spokane.

Patsy Kelly being prepared for a jet ride.

On May 1, 1958, courtesy of the United States Air Force, Patsy Kelly experienced her first jet airplane ride. The event was covered in the *Spokane Daily Chronicle* with the following article:

> **Miss Spokane Sees Her City From Fast Jet** – She couldn't wear high heels. She couldn't go barefoot either. So Miss Spokane (Patsy Kelly) ended up with boots. And she may have shaken in them a bit as she saw Spokane upside down.
>
> The occasion was the first jet ride for Miss Kelly, who flew with 1st Lt. William R. Fillingham of Geiger Air Force Base during the Armed Forces Day open house program Sunday.
>
> She swapped street clothes for a helmet and flying coveralls. Told she couldn't wear her high heeled shoes, she said she'd go barefoot, but the air force issued her a pair of flight boots "in case you have to walk back."
>
> She flew for 45 minutes over points including Grand Coulee Dam and Mount Spokane. She was also twirled through some brief acrobatics during which she saw Spokane upside down or looking downward through the jet canopy.
>
> The perky brunette called the ride in the two-place trainer jet "fabulous." She expressed the hope of flying in a jet again. Miss Kelly said her 18 year-old-brother, Larry, was as thrilled as

she was as her jet taxied in front of the open-house crowd and she waved to the spectators.

A "bar" which the pilot told her to try during the flight she discovered was the control stick and it brought about a few unusual aerial gyrations while she controlled the plane briefly.

Miss Spokane and four other women were guest passengers in Geiger jets during the last week.

Patsy Kelly at the Spokane Lilac Parade with Colonel Edward A. Perry, the acting commander of the 92nd Bomb Wing, from Fairchild Air Force Base.

Miss Spokane with a group from the Volunteers of America on February 22, 1958.

The Eggers family celebrating Art's 76th birthday in 1995, from left, Matthew Eggers; Troy and Sarah (Eggers) Stevens; Art and Patsy Eggers; David Eggers and David's friend Lisa.

Sarah's wedding in 1998. From left: Matthew, Art, Sarah, Patsy and David.

Patsy and Art Eggers in 1999.

Shirley Louise Eagle

Miss Spokane 1959

Shirley Louise Eagle, 1959

(All photos in this section are courtesy of Shirley Eagle Deranleau.)

Shirley Eagle was born in Spokane on January 4, 1940, the daughter of Don and June Helen (Gaines) Eagle. She has one sister, Joyce (Eagle) Dimond, who lives in Englewood, Colorado. Her father was a well-known and respected musician and entertainer in the Spokane area. Shirley was born in Spokane, but when she was two years old, her father's music career took them to Hollywood for nine years. After returning to Spokane, Shirley attended Holmes Elementary, Havermale Junior High and graduated from North Central High School in 1957. At

North Central she was secretary of the Three Fives singing group; vice president of the Talent Club; corresponding secretary of Dasidrian, an all-city girls' talent club; treasurer of the Avant Junior Toastmistress Club; and on the scholastic honor roll.

On December 16, 1958, eighteen-year-old Shirley Eagle received the news she had been chosen to be Miss Spokane XII. She was working at her desk in the Sears, Roebuck and Co. credit department, when she was visited by Miss Spokane XI, Patricia "Patsy" Kelly; Chamber of Commerce president, Joseph Kipper; radio and television newsmen and a photographer. Shirley hadn't expected to win the contest and the news filled her with such excitement and emotion that the remainder of her day's work production was lost to the event.

Even before she became Miss Spokane, Shirley held an exciting life-style. At the time of her selection, she was taking voice lessons and had taken part in Children's Theater productions for two seasons. She was a soloist in her church's choir and taught a Sunday school class. She also sang in a girls' trio for lodges, luncheon and church meetings.

Following her selection as Miss Spokane, Shirley delayed her official city hostess duties for five weeks due to a pre-scheduled vacation to Hawaii. During that time, Patsy Kelly filled in for her. However, the Chamber of Commerce took advantage of a public relations opportunity and scheduled meetings in Hawaii. They prepared letters of introduction to three prominent individuals: Governor William Quinn, of the Territory of Hawaii, from Washington Governor Albert D. Rosellini; Honolulu Mayor Neal S. Blaisdell from Spokane Mayor F. Gaines Sutherlin; and to Henry J. Kaiser, world-renowned industrialist and former Spokanite, from J.W. Kipper, Chamber president. Arrangements were also made to send a number of containers of Washington State apples for Shirley to present as gifts from Spokane.

On January 16, 1959, the day after her arrival in Hawaii, Shirley was pleasantly surprised with a dignitary's welcome by Hawaii's official greeter, Mae Beimes. She called on Quinn, Blaisdell and Kaiser and delivered her greetings and apples amidst a bevy of reporters and photographers.

Following her term as the 1959 Miss Spokane, Shirley married Leon Robert Deranleau, also a credit department employee for Sears, Roebuck and Co., on July 9, 1960. Shirley and Leon have been active in the community since their marriage, and in 1966, they were chosen "Outstanding Washington State Jaycee Couple of the Year." They have three children: Marchelle Yvonne Deranleau, born in 1961; Loretta June Deranleau-Howard, born in 1963; and Yvette Marie (Deranleau) Millhorn, born in 1967. Shirley and Leon are also the grandparents of Katie and Trevor Millhorn.

Shirley has been employed as the office administrator for the Spokane Civic Theatre since 1976. Her special interest include theater, reading and aerobics.

The following is a short summary of the highlights of Shirley's tenure as Miss Spokane in her own words:

My Year as Miss Spokane, 1959

Written in 2000 by Shirley (Eagle) Deranleau.

The first wonderful and most surprising thing was being chosen Miss Spokane from such an outstanding group of young ladies. The whole year was very special and as someone said this will always be "your year" and it can never be taken from you.

Meeting people like Bing Crosby, Raymond Burr, Congressman Walt Horan of Washington's Fifth Congressional District, Ronald Reagan, Henry J. Kaiser (the industrialist) and General Curtis E. LeMay, was a very heady experience for a 19-year-old girl. But in retrospect, people whose names you wouldn't recognize (and most I don't remember) were the most fascinating. People who were president or convention chairman of their organization and shared with me many interesting stories about their group.

For a city girl like me, beating the Washington State Dairy Princess in a milking contest was quite an achievement. It was the closest I'd ever been to a cow and once I took the feather out of my headband the cow accepted me.

Attending other festivals and meeting young women representing their city or festival created many pleasant memories.

Being Miss Spokane was a definite growth experience. I learned a great deal about Spokane by doing research for my speeches. The opportunity to meet so many people was a character and maturity builder.

1959 was my year, filled with so many new and exciting things and I'm proud that I am able to be part of the group of Miss Spokanes.

Shirley Eagle as Miss Spokane meets Honolulu's official greeter, Mae Beimes.

The following article appeared in the *Honolulu Star-Bulletin* on January 16, 1959, following Shirley's arrival on the *Lurline* in Hawaii: "**Island Welcome** – Miss Spokane got a royal, flower-bedecked welcome as she arrived in Honolulu yesterday for a month's vacation. Nineteen-year-old Shirley Eagle was given a dozen floral leis, including one from Hawaii's official greeter, Mae Beimes. Miss Eagle was interviewed aboard ship by island reporters and featured on a radio broadcast. Among Miss Eagle's greeters were her grandmother, Mrs. T.J. Finnegan, longtime Honolulu resident, and aunt, Ethel Mary Finnegan, who is a year younger than Miss Spokane."

Shirley Eagle presenting Mayor Neal S. Blaisdell, of Honolulu, with a box of Washington State apples, courtesy of the Spokane Chamber of Commerce.

Returning from her trip to Hawaii in February 1959, Shirley stopped in Los Angeles, where she visited Bing Crosby in Hollywood during his filming of *Say One for Me*. He played the role of a priest in this Twentieth Century Fox film. Shirley's father, musician Don Eagle, had played in several movies, including Crosby's *A Connecticut Yankee in King Arthur's Court*.

A publicity shot in the office of Al Schilling, general manager of the Davenport Hotel, of Miss Spokane, Shirley Eagle, and actor Raymond Burr. Burr was in Spokane to attend a ground breaking for a new swimming pool at the Morning Star Boys' Ranch. This photo appeared in the Chamber bulletin under the heading "Take a Letter, Miss Spokane," alluding to his Perry Mason television character.

Left: Miss Spokane at Spokane's first Torchlight Parade, held in 1959. **Right:** Riding with Congressman Walt Horan in a 1959 Ford convertible during the Lilac Parade.

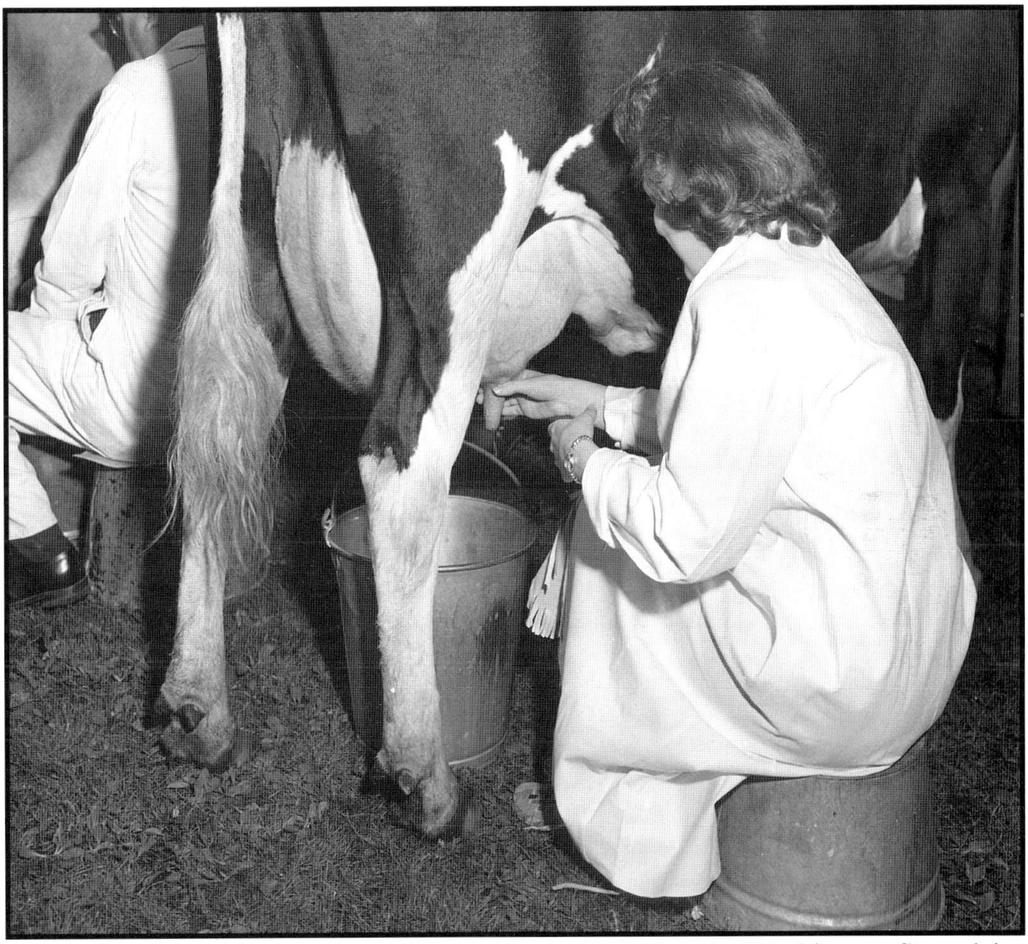

Miss Spokane at the controls during a program honoring the Washington State dairy industry. The Spokane Chamber of Commerce sponsored a milking contest on June 16, 1959, to be held in front of the Civic Building. The contest pitted Chamber president, J.W. Kipper, and Dr. Hampton H. Trayner, city health officer, against Shirley Eagle, Miss Spokane, and Marilyn Snydar, Washington State Dairy Princess. Shirley was easily the overall winner of the contest. Her prize? The contents of her bucket.

Shirley in Hawaii (left) and dressed in her official Miss Spokane Indian dress.

From left: Former Miss Spokane III, Margel (Peters) Ayars, and Miss Spokane XI, Patsy Kelly, with Shirley Eagle in 1959, holding the official Miss Spokane dress for a promotional advertisement announcing the 1960 Miss Spokane contest.

Shirley and Leon Robert Deranleau on their wedding day, July 9, 1960.

The Deranleau family, seated from left, Yvette (Deranleau) Millhorn holding Trevor Millhorn, Shirley (Eagle) and Leon Deranleau. Standing, from left, Marchelle Deranleau, Katie Millhorn and Loretta Deranleau-Howard.

(Green Gables Photography Studio photograph.)

Maureen Ann Brown

Miss Spokane 1960

Maureen Ann Brown, 1960

(All photos in this section are courtesy of Maureen Brown Pring.)

My Life As Miss Spokane and Beyond

Written in 2000 by Maureen (Brown) Pring

To be Miss Spokane was not really my dream – it was my mother's – and I had sort of looked on it as one of those "doting-mom" things, not too grounded in reality. However, when a member of the Spokane Ad Club asked if I would be willing to have them sponsor me as a candidate, I thought the contest would be fun – a great experience in itself – and it would make my mom happy. So what could it hurt? After all, it would only be for a few weeks. I certainly had no chance of winning. However, in a very short while, I was on my way to Pasadena, representing the city that had been my home since I was two years old.

Not only those first few months but the entire year, at this point in my life, exist in a sort of rosy mist of memory. A few memorable trips, meeting celebrities, attending social functions, all centered on the message: "Spokane is a friendly, welcoming city. You will be glad you visited us."

This was what made Miss Spokane unique. Visitors were intrigued by the fact that the person who greeted them was not a "beauty queen" with aspirations of bigger and better titles, or a representative of a particular industry or local events. This person was their hostess – the official city hostess – welcoming them to her home. (Or in a few cases inviting them to visit.) It was unique to Spokane, appreciated and admired by visitors and residents alike, and I was very sorry to see the tradition come to an end.

I met a number of celebrated people during the year: Darin McGavin – who insisted that it rained all the time in Spokane. Glen Ford and Maria Schell – once on the set of *Cimmeron* and again when they attended a banquet for the Spokane Horse Breeders Association; they were both delightful and charming people. Eddie Arcaro [one of the all-time greatest jockeys] – very courtly gentleman. Lyndon B. Johnson – gracious, interesting to talk with, and at that time in the campaign, appeared to be tired of traveling. Warren Magnuson – straight out of the movies – you know the "smoke-filled room," passing, gesturing with his cigar. Also, one very strange racehorse who was much more interested in nibbling on my corsage than getting his picture taken. Must not forget Betty Blue, who painted my portrait.

The people who made the biggest impression, though, were local. Perhaps because I got to know them – Jim Brennan, president of the Chamber; Tony Raiter, of the Chamber's Visitors and Convention Bureau and guardian angel of the Miss Spokanes; Luther Essick, who took the time to teach me Indian sign language. All of the doctors and nurses and especially the children, at the Shriners Hospital, one of my favorite places to visit. The many people in Spokane business and service organizations who worked so diligently to share with everyone their own perception of Spokane as a great place to be, whether it was for a brief visit or a lifetime.

There were also some significant events: the Rose Bowl, of course; the first international flight from the Spokane Airport to Calgary on West Coast Airlines; the ground breaking for Joe O'Leary's Payless Drug Store, the first store in Shadle Shopping

Center; opening of the air traffic control tower (when I overcame my fear of heights to climb the ladder – only to have it return with a vengeance when it was time to go down).

Then there was the day we were kept standing around at the airport waiting for a delayed flight when a bored Major Kenneth Lawsen decided to take a spin on a motorcycle, leaving a poor policeman wringing his hands and wondering what would happen to his career if the major injured himself – and worse yet – on the policeman's bike.

It was a great year, but all things come to an end. When it did end, I was already busy planning a wedding – to my high school sweetheart, John G. Pring. And here we are nearly 40 years later, with five children, five grandchildren and one cocker spaniel. Both of us grew up in Spokane, spent our lives working and raising our children here, and now in retirement we intend to stay here. Spokane is our home and we still think it is a great place to be.

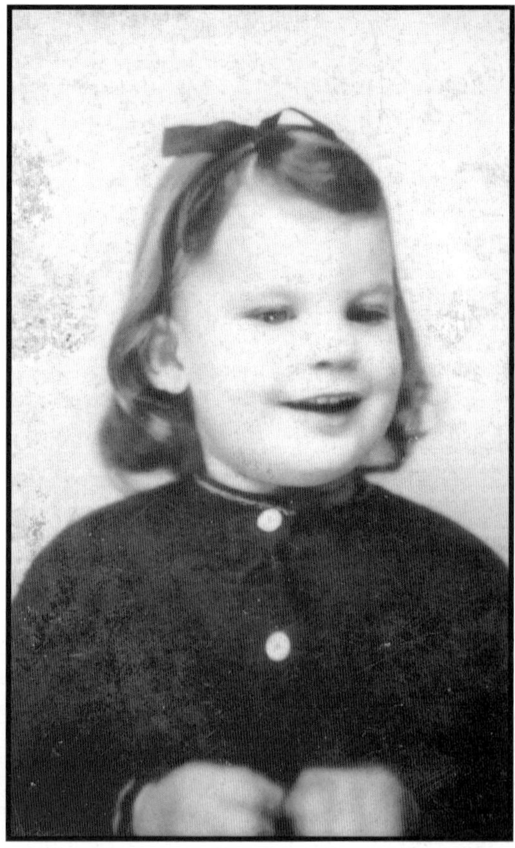

Maureen Brown was born in Deer Park, Washington, the daughter of Arthur H. and Sara Brown. She is shown here, as an infant, with her father (left) and at age three, sometime after the family had moved to Spokane. She attended Marycliff High School, where she was a member of the Cecilian Choir and the glee club, and lived at 5621 North Jefferson when she became Miss Spokane.

Maureen with her parakeets (left) and with the Calgary Stampede queen at a ribbon cutting ceremony for the first West Coast Airlines flight from Spokane to Calgary, Canada.

With Spokane Junior Police at a craft and hobby show (left) and at an auto show.

Maureen with a public relations delegate from Victoria, B.C. (left) and at a meeting of Northwest Indian tribes. Maureen was displaying the traditional Indian greeting of friendship. The arms crossed in this manner signify one is bearing no weapons.

Left: The delegation of young women from Washington State who went to the Rose Bowl in Pasadena. Maureen is fourth from left. While in California, Maria Schell and Glen Ford (center) gave them a movie studio tour. **Right:** Washington State's float in the Rose Bowl Parade. Maureen is sitting on the left side.

Left: The same group of women as above, pictured here with movie actor Darin McGavin. Maureen is second from left. **Right:** Kicking off the Toys For Tots drive.

Left: Maureen with her boss at the Caterpillar Company, where she worked when she became Miss Spokane XIII. **Right:** With Gordon Fowle from the Chamber of Commerce, who is holding the bracelet Maureen was given as a Miss Spokane candidate.

Maureen being introduced at an Eastern Star convention in the old coliseum.

John and Maureen with their daughter Kelly, her husband Matt Michels and Matt's mother, Levina Michels, on Kelly and Matt's wedding day, September 19, 1998.

Maureen and John's four daughters, from left, Kathy Hedgcock (second oldest), Kelly Michels (youngest), Kaycee Kaley (oldest) and Kristi Pring (second youngest). In 1987 Kristi became queen of the Deer Park Fair, the town where Maureen was born.

Left: Maureen and John Pring on their wedding day, January 21, 1961.
Right: Maureen with her parents, Arthur and Sara Brown, on her wedding day.

John and Maureen (Brown) Pring in August 2000.

Sally Ann Amick

Miss Spokane 1961

Sally Ann Amick, 1961

(All photos in this section are courtesy of Sally Amick Mauss.)

In the late fall of 1960, Sally Ann Amick was about to encounter a surprise that would greatly change her life-style and future. Without Sally's knowledge, her mother entered her in the Miss Spokane contest. Although this wasn't something Sally had intended to do, she went ahead with her mother's ambition. As a result, at the age of 18, she became the fourteenth Miss Spokane to serve in the role as the city's official hostess.

Sally, who was born in Salt Lake City, Utah, in 1942, is the daughter of Bruce and Betty (Boures) Amick. When Sally was young, the family, which also included Sally's two brothers and a sister, moved to 3904 East Eighth Avenue in Spokane.

Sally attended Sheridan Grade School, Libby Junior High School, Lewis and Clark High School, Whitworth College from 1960 to 1961 and the University of Washington in 1963. During her high school years, Sally was valedictorian of her junior class, president of the school girls' league and involved in high school speech and drama activities. She also modeled for many of the downtown stores. At the time of becoming Miss Spokane, Sally was a student at Whitworth College and working part-time at Phil's Café at 110 North Howard. Following her selection as Miss Spokane, she was hired by the Washington Water Power Company as a receptionist.

During Sally's Miss Spokane tenure she participated in over 64 official events, not including the numerous unscheduled courtesy events in which she assisted or the eight-day goodwill trip she and five other Washington State royalty made to the Los Angeles area to participate in the Tournament of Roses Parade and various Rose Bowl game activities. During her term, she officiated or participated in the usual types of activities required of the Miss Spokanes. For example, she welcomed delegates to conventions, greeted visiting dignitaries, was the guest speaker at various club meetings, assisted in benefits and dedications, such as the opening of the Shadle Shopping Center in September 1961, and, of course, participated in the Lilac Festival activities. The extensive list presented by the Chamber of Commerce at the beginning of Sally's term specified the type of attire she was to wear, which typically was the official Indian dress.

Following her term as Miss Spokane, Sally was chosen by the Spokane Junior Chamber of Commerce to represent Spokane in the Miss Washington contest held in Vancouver, Washington, July 13-15, 1962. The winner of this contest competed in the Miss America contest in Atlantic City, N.J. Sally became the second runner-up at the Miss Washington contest and won the evening gown competition. She was the only Miss Spokane to have won both contests, serving as the city's official hostess and representing the city as a contestant in the Miss Washington contest.

Sally married Bruce V. Mauss on June 7, 1968. They have one son, Cory Andrew Mauss, who at this writing is 26 years old. Sally and Bruce also have a two-and-a-half-year-old granddaughter, Chayla. Sally is currently the administrative assistant to the vice president of Mission and Community Relations at Holy Family Hospital in Spokane, a position she has held since 1991. Sally's current hobbies include collecting antique jewelry, reading, traveling and spoiling her granddaughter.

Bruce and Sally Mauss with son Cory in 1970.

Sally as a baby with her mother and father, Betty and Bruce Amick.

The eight finalists for the title of Miss Spokane for 1961, from left: Lynne Canwell, Ann Moeller, Linda Edburg, Donna Waters (in back), Sally Amick, Leona Doyle, Norma Johnson and Mary Kay Wallace.

Sally Ann Amick in 1961.

This was the first photo that appeared in the newspaper announcing the 1961 winner of the Miss Spokane contest. Following a judging session during the Spokane Chamber of Commerce's weekly membership session, 18-year-old Sally Ann Amick was chosen as Spokane's official hostess for 1961. At the time of her selection, she was attending Whitworth College and working at Phil's Restaurant in Spokane.

Sally riding in the lead convertible on May 20, 1961, during the Lilac Festival-Armed Forces Day Parade.

Left: Sally during a promotional campaign for her employer, the Washington Water Power Company.

Sally began working for Washington Water Power Company after becoming Miss Spokane. This proved to be a good match as they were exceptionally obliging in regards to her commitments for the city and allowed her whatever time she needed for her official functions.

Posing for a promotional ad in front of the Spokane Chamber of Commerce building at 1020 West Riverside Avenue.

A ceremony at Fort George Wright for the christening of an Atlas missile.

A truck carrying an Atlas Intercontinental Ballistic Missile crosses Fort George Wright Bridge over the Spokane River on March 29, 1961, on its way to the launch complex near Deer Park. Prior to this, ceremonies were held at the fort where Miss Spokane christened one of the missiles with a bottle of champagne. A press release described this missile as follows: "The Atlas missile is nearly 85 feet long and when fully fueled, weighs more than a four-unit freight diesel locomotive. It has a range of more than 9,000 miles and flies faster than 17,000 miles an hour. It is produced for the United States Air Force by Convair-Astronautics."

The photo to the left appeared in the *Spokesman-Review* on December 28, 1960, with the following caption: "Six beauties from as many cities in Washington arrived in Los Angeles yesterday en route to Pasadena and an appearance in the Tournament of Roses Parade on the Washington State float. The young women in front, from left, are: Peggy Kinney, Wenatchee; Sally Ann Amick, Spokane; Diane Harkness, Tacoma. Standing: Mary McManamy, Ellensburg; Constance Rae Hughes, Bellingham; Mary Jo Erickson, Seattle."

Left: Actor Tab Hunter and Sally sharing some Washington State apples at the MGM Studio in Hollywood, in 1961. **Right**: Sally delivering a box of Washington state apples to television personality Robert Cummings.

Upper left: Sally Amick, Robert Cummings and Diane Harkness, queen of the Puyallup Valley Daffodil Festival. **Lower left**: The six representatives from the state of Washington State during the Rose Bowl Parade. **Right**: From left, Miss Spokane XIV, Miss Seattle Seafair Queen and Miss Apple Blossom.

The Neal and Helen Fosseen Photo Album

The Miss Spokane Connection

In 1960 Spokane's political powers amended the Spokane City Charter to that of a mayor-council-city manager form of government. Neal R. Fosseen was elected mayor on June 7, 1960, and took office 16 days later. After a four-year term, he was reelected on March 10, 1964, and served two more years before resigning to devote more attention to his own affairs.

Prior to Fosseen's tenure as mayor, only one other mayor, Charles A. Fleming, had served more time in that position. From 1910 to 1960, Spokane mayors were appointed by the city commissioners. Fleming served a total of ten years. During that time, Marguerite Motie was the only official city hostess selected by the Spokane Ad Club or Chamber of Commerce.

By the time of Fosseen's tenure, the Chamber of Commerce had taken over the Miss Spokane contest and it was being held on an annual basis. Consequently, Fosseen served as mayor of Spokane during the reign of six official city hostesses. The following photos are from Neal and wife Helen's albums during this time:

Former Spokane mayor, Neal Fosseen, and his wife Helen.

(Photos this and facing page courtesy Neal and Helen Fosseen.)

Left: Spokane mayor, Neal Fosseen, prior to a 1,275-mile-per-hour flight with Air Force captain, Jackie Mootland, on May 31, 1962. **Right top**: Mayor Fosseen, Ed Sullivan and Art Selland in Berlin, on October 1, 1961. **Right bottom**: At ribbon cutting for the opening of Value-Mart in November 1965. At the center is Sharron Sweeny, Miss Spokane XVIII. To the left of her is Mayor Fosseen and to the right Al Janofsky and Walter Ludwig.

Left: Mayor Fosseen and John Parker presenting Terry Dawn Starr, Miss Spokane XX, with a cake in celebration of her 19th birthday in 1967. **Right**: The Hillyard Safeway Distributing Center opening on June 27, 1964. Mayor Fosseen and other dignitaries look on as the ribbon is cut by Rosemary Harness, Miss Spokane XVII.

Natalie Monte

Miss Spokane 1963

Natalie Monte, 1963

(All photos in this section are courtesy of Natalie Monte Rees.)

My Life As I've Known It

Written in 2000 by Natalie (Monte) Rees

It seems as though I was always destined to spend much of my life center stage. As the story goes, at the ripe old age of three, I would climb on top of the tables at my grandparents' restaurant and belt out songs at the top of my lungs for the unsuspecting diners. I really don't remember this dubious achievement, but I'm sure it must be true, given what's occurred the rest of my life.

All four of my grandparents emigrated here from Italy: Rosina and Joseph Migliuri, my mother's parents, and Guy and Marina Monte on my father's side. In the case of my Grandpa Monte, he actually came to America by himself first, leaving his wife and son in Italy until he could afford to send for them. I always considered him very brave. He had no funds, only a second-grade education, could speak no English, but knew he wanted to find a better way of life for his family in a promising new land. He made his way across the country to the Pacific Northwest and wound up as a camp cook in some logging camps. My grandma finally arrived on these shores, bringing my dad, who was around three years old by then. They eventually established an Italian Restaurant, Monte's Italian Dinners, at 410 West Sprague Avenue, which they operated until they were well into their eighties. My grandpa was one of

Natalie at age nine months (left) and at two years.

my life's heroes and one of the smartest people I've ever known. He was witty, self-educated, was a simply phenomenal cook (if I close my eyes and concentrate I can still taste his raspberry cream pie), and taught me how to do crossword puzzles at a very early age as a way to improve my vocabulary. And to this day, I still like to challenge myself with tough crosswords and always think of him.

I was born on June 1,1943, to Eleanor and Nat Monte at Sacred Heart Hospital in Spokane. My mom has always been called "Lee," so my name was a derivation of "Nat" and "Lee". My sister Deanna was born on my fifth birthday. And since my mother's birthday is May 31st, the occasions have always been a major family celebration. I attended St. Francis of Assisi Grade School and began my musical education at the same time. I was encouraged at a very early age to express myself and, boy, did I ever! Dad was always fond of the accordion, so it wasn't long before he'd set me up with lessons. And so it began. Of course, as most kids, I hated the lessons and especially having to practice, but I proceeded with diligence and took to it quickly. Before long, I was involved in music festivals and performing before small groups. That's when *Starlit Stairway* became part of my life.

As many Spokanites may remember, *Starlit Stairway* was an extremely popular KXLY television program that was broadcast every Saturday night for many years in the 1950s and early 1960s. It featured very talented and (sometimes not-so-talented) kids from ages one through eighteen competing in an amateur contest for monetary awards. Tap dancers (lots and lots of tap dancers), singers, musicians, all trying to make Mom and Dad and their friends watching at home very proud of them. And each year they would take all the winners and have a "finals" talent show for the top talent award. The Boyle Fuel Company sponsored the show

Playing the accordion in 1955.

I spent so many seasons performing on *Starlit Stairway* that everyone in the organization knew me personally, including Leon Boyle, who produced the show. Some years I won big, some years I didn't. But it led me straight to a performance on *The Lawrence Welk Show* on January 6, 1958. I was 14 at the time, and am not sure I comprehended the magnitude of appearing on a national television show. How did I get there? Mr. Boyle had chosen four or five of the *Starlit Stairway* regulars to perform at the Home Show in Spokane in 1957. As it happened, some members of the Lawrence Welk Orchestra were out on tour around the country and were appearing at this event also. Larry Hooper and Buddy Merrill watched me perform with the accordion and apparently went back to California and told Mr. Welk that he should put me on his *Top Tunes and New Talent Show*, which is exactly what he did. So off I flew with my parents and sister on a paid vacation to Hollywood, amidst much hoopla from the Spokane media. It was a wonderful experience for my whole family and I can sincerely say that Mr. Welk was a very nice man, and even took time to chat with a nervous little 14-year-old accordionist. My biggest thrill was meeting the Lennon Sisters. But then a strange thing happened. After listening to all those singers on the show, I just knew that I had found a new path for my life. I decided that I no longer wanted to play the accordion, now I wanted to SING – news that did not thrill my parents, I'm sure.

While at Marycliff High School, I was determined to embark on my fantasies of being a singer, so I joined all the musical singing groups, hoping one day to become a member of Marycliff's well-known Cecilians, twelve girls who performed all over the area singing in complex, tight-knit harmonies. I finally made it into this group as a Junior, acquired some great friends, and enjoyed every moment of our adventures in the spotlight. At about this same time, I discovered the theatre, and considering my dramatic tendencies anyway, determined that not only did I want to sing, but that I wanted to be an ACTRESS. Lofty goals for a 15 year old. So I joined the Drama Club and soon became president of the organization. Marycliff and Gonzaga Prep schools' production of the Rodgers & Hammerstein musical version of *Cinderella* in a joint production staged my first foray as a leading lady. I really have no idea if it was a truly good performance or not, but it didn't matter. I already had the theatre bug, and there is never a cure for that malady.

I entered Gonzaga University in 1961, majoring in English and education, with minors in music and drama. I was instantaneously drawn into everything that involved music or theatre, and in my freshman year played the lead in *South Pacific* as Nellie Forbush, a production that was directed by Spokane's grande dame of the theatre, Dorothy Darby Smith. This was by no means my last involvement with Mrs. Smith.

As the fall of 1962 rolled around, my mother began to read about the Miss Spokane contest for 1963. There was no question in her mind that I should become a contestant. Let me tell you, I was not at all sure about this prospect. When someone first tells you about this type of pageant, you immediately think of girls being judged on their beauty. At no time had I ever considered myself to be in this category. I had always achieved any previous successes through hard work, some innate musical ability, and a friendly, outgoing personality. But Mom explained to me that this position placed more emphasis on a young woman's ability to be the city's hostess and to be able to communicate with visitors and dignitaries in a poised, intelligent manner. So she convinced me to try, but I was never too certain that I could actually win.

It was customary to have a business group sponsor someone's candidacy for the position. And as fate would have it all those *Starlit Stairway* years as a child once again brought me to the attention of the Boyle Fuel Company, whose new president, Bob Ward, convinced the Fuel Dealers Association of the Inland Empire to sponsor me.

The contest itself consisted of a series of appearances in which we were to demonstrate our poise, speaking ability, personality and overall potential. Different judges were used for each segment of the contest, and eventually the field was narrowed to just three candidates. I well remember our final test. We were instructed to give a "Welcoming" speech, as if we were addressing one of the actual conventions scheduled for an upcoming event in 1963. I had been taking acting lessons from Dorothy Darby Smith while attending Gonzaga, so I pretended this was part of a play and that I needed to make my listeners believe what I was saying. She would always tell me that, "If YOU believe it, your audience will too." So that's what I did. I said things that I truly believed about my hometown of Spokane, its beautiful environment, and its friendly citizens.

On the evening of December 14, 1962, the history of my life truly changed forevermore, as they called out my name as the new Miss Spokane. At first it was really hard for me to believe that I'd heard them correctly. But after the applause, the hugs, the flowers, and when all the cameras finally stopped clicking and flashing, it dawned on me that this was really happening – and to me.

This photo was taken at the moment of the announcement of Natalie as Miss Spokane XVI. From left: Dale Stedman, chairman of the Chamber of Commerce Publicity and Promotion Committee; Susan Green, finalist; Shirley Hendricks, finalist; and Natalie, December 14, 1962.

The following year was an absolute whirlwind of events and appearances, wonderful moments to remember.

There were the conventions that came to town: the Pacific Northwest Farm Forum, National Association of Bank Women, Intermountain Logging Conference, Washington State Nurses, the Oregon-Washington Hotel Association, National IBM Convention, National Insurance Women Convention, the Canadian Mounted Police, the Inland Empire Industrial Exposition, the Association of Wheat Growers, and the list went on and on.

Natalie drawing the winning ticket for a Retail Trade Bureau promotional event on August 17, 1963. This was one of three events Natalie participated in that day.

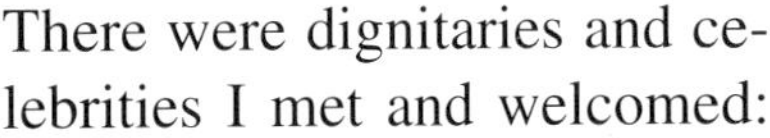

There were dignitaries and celebrities I met and welcomed: Ralph Edwards (of *This Is Your Life* fame), Rose Marie and Morey Amsterdam from *The Dick Van Dyke Show*, comedian George Jessel, actor Richard Crenna, various political figures, including then Governor Rosellini, and my favorites, members of The Blue Angels flying team. And there were so many more.

There were ribbon-cuttings and grand openings, like the Holiday Inn and the new Ridpath Hotel Motor Inn. We broke ground for the new Lincoln First Federal Building and for the Parade of Homes. I presented roses, trophies and awards, and sat in viewing stands for hydroplane races and parades. I kicked off telethons (and was often asked to perform as a singer, as well) and toy drives. I threw out the first baseball of the year for the Spokane Indians, threw the basketball onto the court for the State Class B Basketball Tournament, rolled the first bowling ball down the lane for the Professional Bowlers Association Pro-Am Tournament, dropped the first puck for a hockey game, and was "bat girl" one night for the Spokane Indians. I even christened an aircraft during Lilac Week, a B-52. She had been renamed the *City of Spokane*.

Natalie christening Fairchild AFB's B-52, the *City of Spokane*, on May 19, 1963.

So if you've ever wondered what it must have been like to be Miss Spokane, this gives you some idea. What was my favorite memory? It had to be the Lilac Parades (there were two of them in earlier years). I was asked to light the torch for the Torchlight Parade and then rode in a convertible in full Indian costume. I also rode in the Saturday morning Lilac Festival-Armed Forces Day Parade. It was great fun. Just about everyone I'd ever known went down to see the parade and to wave and yell at me as I went by. Some of my college chums would be yelling on one corner, and then would race down the street and would be hollering at me again three blocks farther along the route. They did that the whole length of the parade. I never knew how hard it was to smile and wave for three hours straight. And the costume was so *hot.*

Riding in a lilac-colored car with Lynn Cornish, president of the Chamber of Commerce, in the Lilac Festival Torchlight Parade, May 16, 1963.

I want to tell you about the Miss Spokane costume. It has its own story. During my reign, I would say I wore the costume for about half of my appearances. That decision was always left to the Chamber of Commerce. The costume was very authentic and, in fact, had its own history and symbolism. I used to go out and give speeches, in costume, on the meaning of the designs and beadwork. But what most of the public didn't know is that the costume was not new for each girl. It was passed on down the line. Consequently, it never fit any of us correctly. We were all different sizes and heights, and it had to be altered each year. Since the bottom of the dress was fringed, they couldn't just take up the hem. So they lifted it, or let it out, at the waistline. The costume was extremely heavy. I was shocked the first time I wore it. All that leather and beading added weight. It was bulky and very warm.

My funniest memory about the costume involved the long beautiful fringe adorning the sleeves. One evening I was sitting next to Mayor Neal Fosseen at the head table in the Marie Antoinette room at the Davenport Hotel. We often sat next to one another at head tables and had discussed the "fringe" problem when it came to maneuvering around a dinner table without dipping the fringe in my plate or in my neighbor's water glass. On this occasion the entree was some type of steak, and it was not particularly tender. As I was trying to encourage my steak knife to cooperate, the fringe, the steak, the knife and my frustration all came together when the steak went flying off my plate, up over my head and onto the floor behind me. I should have been mortified at this faux pas, but it was so silly and ridiculous, I just got the giggles – and so did the mayor. We never got our composure back the rest of the evening. And I told the waiter to "pass" on bringing me another entree, hoping that no one had noticed the cow jumping over the moon earlier.

Each girl was allowed to keep her moccasins. They were specially fitted and handmade for each Miss Spokane as soon as her selection was announced. I still have those moccasins and they're still in great shape.

All through my year of appearances, I was also a full-time student at Gonzaga University and worked part-time for Sears. In February of that year, I played a leading role in Gonzaga's production of *The Music Man*. My time was further occupied with our collegiate choir and the traveling performances we maintained, as well as my private voice lessons with the renowned Lyle Moore. I was also beginning to pursue my interest in singing jazz by performing on weekends with the Claude Myrhe Dance Band. As I look back on it all, I have no idea how I kept this kind of schedule. It must have been the exuberance of youth. There is no other explanation.

My tenure came to an end all too swiftly, and near the end of December, the Chamber of Commerce gave me a farewell luncheon. There were beautiful gifts and kind words of praise from so many city officials. I tearfully thanked them in return for my incredible year and all its memories, but also for the unique opportunity that had been given to me. As usual, when I get emotional, I tend to find a song lyric that can convey my feelings more eloquently. So I sang for them an old popular song of the day called "May You Always." And so it ended. I was probably the only Miss Spokane who sang her way out of office.

The kick off drive to find Miss Spokane XVII, November 1963. From left, Dale Stedman of the Chamber of Commerce; Natalie Monte, Miss Spokane XVI; Marguerite (Motie) Shiel, the first Miss Spokane; and Kathleen "Kaki" Smith, Miss Spokane XV.

Nothing this eventful in your life ever goes away, however. What I gained in knowledge, confidence and poise from this experience would stand me in good stead in future endeavors. Life would bring me twists, turns and surprises – with some great successes and a few heartbreaks along the way, but in general, years full of love and laughter.

In 1964 I married a young army lieutenant I'd met in college and we immediately headed to Europe on assignment. Our son Scott was born in Frankfurt, Germany. Unfortunately, the marriage had been unwise and was unsuccessful. We returned to Spokane and, by the time son Michael was born in early 1967, we had parted. My parents helped greatly during this unsettling period of my life and showered my children with much love and attention.

I once again turned to the staples of my life – music and the stage. I worked days and performed on weekends with some terrific jazz musicians in the area. And then one night in 1969 I had a date with destiny when I walked into an audition at Spokane Civic Theatre for a straight dramatic play called *Wait Until Dark*. Watching the audition that night was a man I hadn't met yet but who would change my life completely. His name was Lanny Rees.

I landed the part at the theatre, the start of a long and eventful association with that organization. Lanny was the resident set designer/lighting coordinator at that time. He'd been born in Spokane but had spent most of his childhood and teen years in California working in movies and television. He played "Junior" in *The Life of Riley*, both in the film and in the television series. As a child actor, he'd been featured in movies with the likes of James Cagney, starred in *My Dog Shep*, *Little Iodine*, *A Likely Story* and many more. His experiences in Hollywood would fill a book. When we met, he was a single parent with five children (four sons and a daughter). It was not love at first sight, but his sense of humor and great wit charmed me completely and we became great friends, working on many productions together, including *Funny Girl, Carnival*, and *Cabaret*. But in 1972,1 landed the lead in *The Sound of Music* and Lanny's youngest son, 12-year-old Mel, was chosen to play one of the children in the cast. That's when everything changed.

Friendship turned to romance during the rehearsals and performances of that show, with Lanny's son encouraging his dad all along the way. The show ran for almost two months, and at the closing night party, we announced our engagement to the cast. It was an emotional event that set off a joyful celebration for our theatrical troupe, but a much more important one for our two families.

We were married during Christmas week that same year and we're still together 28 years later. It was one of the smartest things I ever did. He is still my best friend, my biggest fan and my biggest critic (he always encourages me to reach my full potential), and has been a wonderful father to my sons, and to his own as well.

Lanny and Natalie Rees on their wedding day, December 29, 1972.

Combining two families was tough, but love and determination pulled us through. Four of the seven children lived with us – my two sons, along with Lanny's sons, Mel and Mitch. Our lives in the Spokane Valley were filled with our careers, school activities, dogs, cats, hamsters, gerbils, music lessons, baseball, marching bands, jazz band contests and what seemed like a house constantly full of teenagers. It was chaotic and wonderful. I continued to appear with jazz groups and musicians whenever possible and worked with the Civic Theatre on some wonderful shows, including two with my husband, *My Fair Lady* and *Funny Girl* (this time he played my love interest), and *The King and I,* one of my all-time favorites. Lanny and I also worked on two dinner theater productions of *I Do! I Do!* and he starred in *The Sunshine Boys*.

I lost my dad in 1983 and it was unquestionably the saddest experience of my life. He was the kindest person I'd ever known. He had never let me down – not once in my whole life – and was always there to offer his caring support and gentle guidance. Every time I step out onto a stage I know he is there beside me. He was always so proud of anything that I did. And he felt exactly the same way about my sister, Deanna. I miss him to this day.

In 1985 I appeared on the daytime version of *The Wheel of Fortune*. I had tried out for the program when they came to Spokane, was chosen as a contestant and went to California for the taping. It was such a unique experience – a real hoot! I appeared on three separate shows and came away with over $17,000 in prizes, including a diamond from Tiffany's and a fabulous vacation to the island of Barbados. That Caribbean adventure remains in our memories as the trip of a lifetime.

We moved to the Seattle area in the mid-1980s because of my husband's job opportunities and to explore a larger theatrical and musical market. Lanny has done some

Just before curtain time.

television advertising work and starred in *Guys & Dolls* with me, but has been content to be my cheerleader during the past ten years. We've met such talented musicians here and I've grown so much by working with them. I've been given opportunities to star in some terrific musicals: *Funny Girl* (third time), *42nd Street*, *Gypsy*, *Pal Joey* and *On Your Toes*. I also appeared in my all-time favorite role, the witch in Stephen Sondheim's *Into the Woods*, a musical staged in 1992 by Seattle's Civic Light Opera, which was critically acclaimed and voted the best Seattle production of the year – even triumphing over all the traveling Broadway shows. It was a very proud moment for me. Our lives have brought us the things that people cherish most – love and happiness. My mom still lives in Spokane and keeps me up to date on the news from there. Our children are doing well and have families of their own. Lanny has eight grandchildren, and my sons have each given me two beautiful little ones to spoil. I wish my dad had lived to meet them all.

My life seems to have come full circle. My first encounter with city government and the Chamber of Commerce occurred in my year as Miss Spokane. And here I am, all these years later, working for a city government – this time for Federal Way, Washington. I'm an administrative assistant in the office of the city manager, dealing with dignitaries, visiting politicians, diversity commissions and sister-city delegations. Looking back on that special year so long ago, I realize the great benefits given to me by the opportunity to serve as hostess for my hometown. It was a great honor that has not dimmed with the years. At the bottom of my career resume is a sentence on a line all its own: "Proudly served as Miss Spokane, Official City Hostess".

Olive Raymond, Chamber of Commerce staff, admiring one of two new outfits provided to Natalie as Miss Spokane as she began her year of service.

Left: The Monte family in 1953, from left: Natalie, her mother Eleanor, father Nat and sister Deanna. **Right:** Natalie's graduation day, May 31, 1961, with grandparents, Marina and Guy Monte, and her uncle, Gordon Monte (standing in back).

Left: Natalie with her sons in 1971: Michael Warner, age four (left), and Scott Warner, age six. **Right:** Natalie's sister, Deanna (Monte) Tiplin, with her husband, Rob Tiplin, and their children, daughter Tiffany (right) and son Derek about 1987.

Left: Ribbon cutting ceremony for the Holiday Inn grand opening on Sunset Hill, March 25, 1963. **Right:** A November 11, 1970, newspaper clipping of five former Miss Spokanes, from left: Gay LaRane (Mooney) Goerig (1966), Sharron (Sweeny) Grahlmann (1965), Vicki Miner (1969), Terry (Starr) Rifenbery (1967) and Natalie.

A photo montage of Natalie and Lanny's theatrical endeavors.

Top: From left, Lanny and Natalie in the Puget Sound Musical Theatre's *Guys and Dolls* (1987); as Professor Higgins and Eliza Doolittle in the Spokane Civic Theatre's *My Fair Lady* (1973) and *Funny Girl* (1970). **Center:** *Funny Girl*; Natalie backstage with her friend, the world-renowned musical director Mary Levine; Natalie as the evil, ugly witch who became the evil, beautiful witch in the Seattle Civic Light Opera *Into the Woods* (1992). **Bottom:** Natalie as the evil, ugly witch in *Into the Woods*; Seattle's Village Theatre's *Gyspy* (1988)*;* Natalie, as Maria, and Lanny's son Mel (standing behind Natalie) in the Civic Theatre's *The Sound of Music* (1972).

Natalie and Lanny on their 25th wedding anniversary, December 29, 1997.
"Still friends after all these years."

Leilani Ann Wickline

Miss Spokane 1970

Leilani Ann Wickline, 1970

(All photos in this section are courtesy of Lani Wickline Ellingsen.)

Leilani Ann "Lani" Wickline was born in Eugene, Oregon, the daughter of Mr. and Mrs. H.A. Wickline. She moved to Spokane with her family when she was a year old and lived at 3724 East Liberty. Lani went through the Spokane school system and graduated from Rogers High School. During her high school years, she became a cheerleader, a member of the Triple Trio (a girls' singing group), the National Honor Society and a Girls' State Representative.

In 1968 Lani represented Rogers High School as a Lilac princess. Following her graduation, she attended Spokane Community College and while there was chosen homecoming princess.

On December 10, 1969, while a student at Eastern Washington State College, Lani was chosen from a field of 21 contestants to be Spokane's 23rd official Miss Spokane. This contest was sponsored by the Spokane Chamber of Commerce, but during this time, each contestant was required to have an individual sponsor. Lani was sponsored by the Spokane Advertising and Sales Association, the organization that started this Miss Spokane contest in 1912.

In 1971 Lani married Dr. Donald A. Ellingsen, a local ophthalmologist. They raised four sons and a daughter and now have seven grandchildren.

Lani, as Miss Spokane, and Linda Wroe, Aqua Festival Queen from Austin, Texas, at the Armed Forces-Lilac Festival Parade in May of 1970.

Among other talents, Lani is an accomplished singer. She is shown here performing at one of the many functions she attended as Miss Spokane. One such event was for the Spokane Indians' opening-season pre-game festivities on April 24, 1970. That year the team's manager, Tommy Lasorda, was named the Minor League Manager of the Year by *The Sporting News.* During Lasorda's three seasons as manager of the Spokane Indians (1969-71), the club never finished lower than third in the minor leagues. In 1997 Lasorda was inducted into the National Baseball Hall of Fame.

The Ellingsen family in 1998

Lani and Don Ellingsen in 1999. Don is a retired ophthalmologist. Both Don and his father, Carl "Tuffy" Ellingsen, are included in Washington State University's Hall of Fame for their athletic accomplishments. The Rogers High School Field House was named in Carl's honor.

On March 11, 1976, the following article appeared in the *Spokane Daily Chronicle*:

Others to Run It?
Chamber Due to Drop Miss Spokane Contest

The Miss Spokane Contest is being dropped by the Spokane Chamber of Commerce, traditional sponsor of the city's official hostess program.

Chamber officials announced today that the organization will no longer sponsor the contest and that the program as it is now known will come to an end, but they expect another civic group to take up sponsorship and affiliate the program with state and national pageants.

Lack of such affiliation, which meant that Miss Spokane could not compete in either the Miss Washington or Miss America pageants, was increasingly regarded as a serious drawback in recent years. Indeed, the chamber had difficulty attracting candidates for the title and during the past few years the deadline for entry repeatedly had to be extended until a sufficient number of contestants could be persuaded to enter.

The image of the program also was somewhat marred by controversy in the most recent competition. A candidate eliminated in the first round of judging last fall for the title of Miss Spokane 1976 claimed she had been unfairly discriminated against by chamber staff members who raised questions about her character with judges. Toni Lynn Turner, a former masseuse, said judges were encouraged to downgrade her.

The first round of judging was nullified and candidates were "requalified." Chamber officials today said the controversy had no part in the decision to quit sponsoring the contest.

Chamber President M. J. Carter said in a prepared statement, "The chamber feels that it is unfair to limit the expectations and potential of local aspirants. Therefore, (with the chamber out of the picture) a local franchise can now be established to allow affiliation with state and national pageants."

Miss Spokane traditionally was chosen for speaking ability and general aptitude to welcome guests to the city and officiate at grand openings. Carter said today that, since the chamber would not go into the bathing beauty contest business, the competition didn't generate the level of enthusiasm and participation that might be expected if candidates could go on to higher competitions.

Other chamber officials said a number of groups have shown interest in establishing a local franchise to promote a Miss Spokane contest affiliated with the Miss America program.

They said they believe action will be taken by one of the interested parties in time for there to be a new kind of Miss Spokane next year, one that is more relevant to would-be contestants.

The chamber has sponsored the contest from the beginning – 1912. [Note: The contest was started and initially sponsored by the Spokane Advertising Club.] The first Miss Spokane, Marguerite Motie, served for a number of years until her marriage. The contest was discontinued during World War II. [Note: This is not entirely accurate. Catherine Bett's served in her official capacity until her marriage in August 1943, but was periodically called back to Spokane to officiate at various functions until 1947.] Selection of a new Miss Spokane on an annual basis began with the sixth official city hostess in 1953.

The reigning Miss Spokane, the 29th, is Susan Marie Laib. Chamber officials said the action announced today will be effective Jan. 1, 1977, and Miss Laib's reign during this year will not be affected.

The Spokane Chamber of Commerce was originally incorporated in 1891. Although the Chamber did not originate the Miss Spokane contest, they were active in its existence and continuance for a period of almost 65 years.

This photo, looking east on Riverside Avenue through the columns in front of the Chamber of Commerce Building, was taken in 1932, a year after the building was constructed. Notice the Indian head composites at the top of the columns. See page 215 for a front view of this structure.

(Photo courtesy Spokane Public Library.)

Chapter 4

Spokane's Miss Washington and Miss America Contestants

The original Miss Spokane contest was designed to select an official city hostess and representative. It was a service role, held with honor, to promote the city. There were few monetary enticements and the contest did not have the required components to qualify the winner to compete in the Miss Washington/ Miss America contests. Consequently, other contests sponsored by various organizations have provided that opportunity, but they have been transient in nature.

The first contest, only two years in duration (1926 and 1927), was unique among these contests in that cities could be represented in the Miss America Pageant. There was no required intermediate program, as there is today, in which the city titleholder must compete for the state title to be eligible for the national level. Because the position of the official city hostess was vacant (though Marguerite Motie still served in an unofficial capacity as the need arose), this contest was treated as the only Miss Spokane contest, although technically it was not. Its goal was to find a beautiful young woman to attend the Miss America Pageant. There were no required ongoing obligations on the part of the winner to the city.

By the late 1940s, when the next Miss Spokane contest was organized, Miss America contestants were required to hold a state, not city, title. The original Miss Spokane contest was going strong again, so sponsors of new contests had to use other names to identify their Miss Spokane. Although the goal of the various programs has been the same – to send a Spokane representative to the Miss Washington Pageant – the contest names have included: Miss Spokane County, Miss Greater Spokane, Miss America District Pageant and the Miss Spokane Scholarship Program. During the time the contests were running simultaneously, Sally (Amick) Mauss was the only one to win both contests (see pages 210-217). With the termination of the official city hostess program on January 1, 1977, the confusion over the name disappeared, but it was a mute point because the contest to compete for Miss Washington had ceased as well.

Over the years, the contest that began essentially as a beauty pageant has evolved into more of a scholarship program. The requirements have changed and pursuing a college education is a key component. Miss Spokane acts as a city hostess during her reign, but the main goal is to represent the city in the Miss Washington, and hopefully, the Miss America pageants. In most cases, when the Miss Washington contest is over, Miss Spokane makes few appearances in that capacity.

Glorian Smith, Miss Spokane 1926
and
Eva King, Miss Spokane 1927

A second Miss Spokane contest was initiated in 1926. The focus of this new contest was entirely different from the existing one originated by the Spokane Ad Club in 1912, which was somewhat inactive during these years. The sole purpose of the new program was to select a representative from Spokane to compete in the Miss America Pageant. The lucky woman chosen as Spokane's representative was rewarded with gifts, the support of local businesses and the publicity to be expected surrounding an event of this nature. However, she did not have a commitment to fulfill an ongoing role, such as the city hostess position in the other contest. For some undetermined reason, the contest was only held in 1926 and 1927.

At the time of this contest, the Miss America Pageant, which remains a popular event in the United States today, was still in its infancy. It began in 1921 as a promotional gimmick; Atlantic City, New Jersey, hotel owners decided to stage a flashy festival to entice summer tourists to stay in town beyond Labor Day. This festival included a "National Beauty Tournament" on the beach. Their goal was to select the most beautiful bathing beauty in America.

Atlantic City is located on the narrow island of Absecon on the Atlantic Ocean. The city was incorporated in 1854 and is nationally recognized as a resort and convention center. It is noted for its gambling casinos, clamming, shell fishing and candy manufacturing. Among many points of interest are a large convention center and a six-mile boardwalk with several amusement piers extending into the ocean. Since 1921 it has continued to gain recognition as the host city for the Miss America Pageant.

This pageant caught on immediately and was soon given its crowning touch when Atlantic City newsmen declared the winner of this new National Beauty Tournament would be called "Miss America." Press releases were sent to Eastern newspapers inviting them to run photo contests and pick winners to represent their communities at the new pageant. Eight contestants competed for the first title. The winner of the first Miss America contest was Margaret Gorman from Washington, D.C. At the time, she was 16 years old and a look-alike for the 1920s superstar Mary Pickford.

By 1923 over 70 contestants were competing for the title of Miss America and it was rapidly gaining recognition as a prominent event to attend. By the mid-1920s, it had become a national event, with contestants being sponsored by both the news media and local theaters from the East to West coasts.

From Miss Spokane to Miss America

On May 29, 1926, Spokane's Clemmer Theater and the *Spokane Press*, under the direction of the Clemmer Theater's manager, W.L. Doudlah, began a search for the prettiest girl in Spokane to send to the Miss America Pageant. Once this special girl was found, she would be called Miss Spokane and sent to Atlantic City to face national competition for the title of Miss America.

Few cities the size of Spokane (roughly 109,000 in population) were represented in the Miss America pageant and the local promoters felt this would be good publicity to attract attention to Spokane. Applications were made available throughout the city. The rules were simple. Actresses or models were not allowed to enter. Applicants had to be between the ages of 16 to 30 years of age and unmarried. (Interestingly, in 1923, when Helmar Leiderman won the Miss America crown from a field of 72 contestants, the pageant officials found that she was married. It was then they realized they had forgotten to include a "no marriage" rule.)

The winner of Clemmer/*Spokane Press* contest would be called Miss Spokane – a title necessary to qualify for the Miss America contest. She and her mother or chaperone would receive a first-class train fare to Atlantic City, where they would be put up in the best hotel with all expenses paid. The trip itself was valued at $500. In addition, the winner would receive a shopping spree worth about $1,000 to outfit her with clothing, jewelry and a visit to a beauty salon in preparation for the trip to Atlantic City. In addition, she was promised expense-paid trips to appear at theaters in other large cities, a chauffeured car at her disposal during these trips, and an opportunity for a movie screen test. What lovely young woman could resist such an offer?

The Winner

The Clemmer Theater was the setting for Spokane's young women to compete for the title of Miss America. A week of judging followed the close of the contest. Nearly a hundred bathing beauties paraded before the judges as they narrowed their choices. On the day before the winner was announced, the young women congregated at Manito Park for photographs to be exhibited at the Clemmer Theater and the best shots to be released through newsreels.

On the evening of July 30, 1926, in a ceremony at the Clemmer Theater, Mayor Charles A. Fleming announced the winner and crowned 17-year-old Glorian Smith as the city of Spokane's representative to Atlantic City. This striking blond North Central High School student, born May 11 1909, was the daughter of Mr. and Mrs. W.C. Smith.

Following her coronation as Miss Spokane, Glorian was treated to an all-expense-paid shopping trip in downtown Spokane and chauffeured from store to store in a

Top right: Clipping from the *Spokane Press* on July 31, 1926 announcing Glorian Smith as Miss Spokane.

MISS SPOKANE!

Glorian Smith, 17-year old student at North Central wins beauty title. Will represent Spokane at Atlantic City

Hail Miss Spokane!

Glorian Smith, 17-year-old student at North Central high school, has captured

Miss Margaret Mahoney was in charge of measuring of the girls. Photographs were taken by the Angvire studio in the Fernwell building.

—Portrait by Angvire Studio, Fernwell Bldg.

new Chrysler Imperial 80 sedan. On August 16, 1926, she boarded a Union Pacific train headed east for Atlantic City. Also on board were Miss Seattle and Miss Portland.

Little else is known about Glorian Smith and the outcome of her experience as Miss Spokane, but the following year, on August 5, 1927, nineteen-year-old Laura Eva King (who preferred to be called "Eve") was selected from about 110 contestants as the new Miss Spokane. Fortunately, because Eva has living descendants whom the authors were able to contact, much more is known about her. Two gracious daughters and a granddaughter generously shared photographs, memorabilia and stories of their mother and grandmother. They spoke lovingly about the kind of mother, grandmother and homemaker Eva was, remarking about her cooking abilities and her sense of humor. The photographs tell of her physical beauty.

Eva was born on December 23, 1907, in Craig, Montana, a town that took its name from her mother's family, but no longer exists. She was the daughter of Fred J. and Luella (Craig) King. Before the family moved to Spokane, they lived in Helena, Montana. Around age 16, Eva became Miss Coeur d'Alene. She was a North Central High School graduate, and at the time of the Miss Spokane contest, an employee of Culbertson's General Department Store.

Here's Miss Spokane.

Eva King, 19 Years Old, Wins Trip to Atlantic City

—Photo by Dorian.

It was a dramatic moment Friday night at the Clemmer theater when Miss Eva King, 19 years old, was crowned Miss Spokane.

By her victory Miss King won the chance to go back to Atlantic City and compete there against the country's best beauties for the national

"And we hope you come back as Miss America," concluded William Boate of Radio KGA as he set the crown of Miss Spokane upon Miss King's head.

After a week of preliminary tests the girls went into the finals Friday night at 9 p. m. while a record audience looked on.

finals, all beauties. The judges sat in the audience and kept incognito, in order to give utmost fairness to the contest.

After the first beauty parade, during which the girls were presented with boxes of candy, the judges retired to a private room for decision. They tangled on six of the entrants. A considerable lot of talk ensued.

(Continued on Page 2)

Lower right: Clipping from the *Spokane Press* on August 6, 1927 announcing Eva King as Miss Spokane.

Eva King Dixon, 1927 Miss Spokane

(All photos in this chapter are courtesy of Judy Dixon, Nancy Martin and Julie Bunch.)

The contest Eva participated in was sponsored by the Clemmer Theater and *Spokane Press* and was separate from the contest originated by the Spokane Ad Club. This photo of Eva was her husband's favorite and the one he kept on his desk for years.

Becoming Miss Spokane was the beginning of an exciting future for Eva. She was also treated to a shopping spree following her coronation. Although the scheduled event was similar for both Glorian Smith and Eva King, the article detailing Eva's shopping trip, which appeared in the August 6, 1927, issue of the *Spokane Press,* was more descriptive and provides a nostalgic glimpse of downtown Spokane. Excerpts follow:

Miss Spokane Has Fun at Shopping: Tours Downtown Merchandise Establishments; "Buys" Much Finery Without Cash.

Charming and poised, her dark beauty flashing through the crowds, Miss Eva King, crowned "Miss Spokane" Friday in the finals of The Press-Clemmer beauty contest, toured the smart shops of the city last Saturday, outfitting for her trip to Atlantic City. . . . as honors and gifts were showered on her. "It's simply wonderful. I'll never forget today. I'm just afraid I'll wake up." Miss Spokane was first driven to the Marcelle Shop in the Spokane Savings and Loan building in the Chrysler Brougham furnished for her tour by the Hatch Motor company.

Beautified in the Marcelle Shop

She was togged in a smart white flannel sports suit. Blond kid oxfords, with side cutouts, and peach stockings completed the ensemble. She wore a dainty pale pink "Lindy Lid" hat, which just now are so popular. . . . At the Marcell Shop Miss King had a manicure. The buffing completed her long slim fingers. She has splendid hands, according to artists who judged the contest. Miss Ella Smith, premier beauty culturist of Spokane, was closeted with the prize winner for an hour, giving her beauty hints.

Picked Finest Hat in Store

Next the entourage drew up at the Vogue millinery shop. There Henry Solomon, proprietor, aided her to select a smart black felt-and-satin riche hat. . . . "That girl has taste," remarked Solomon. "She picked the smartest hat in the store – a new Paris importation."

Lee H. Brooks of the Spokane Trunk and Grip shop presented Miss Spokane with a travelling bag. The lady's suitcase is alligator cowhide, silk lined and fitted with every convenience. . . . At the Aster Candy company, George Stark gave the beauty queen a huge five pound box of Dixon's Dixie chocolates. . . .

Poses With Burts Flowers

J.S. Ellis, at the Owl Drug Store, added a beautiful perfumerie [*sic*] set to the many presents . . . Miss Spokane posed in the window at A.J. Burt's House of Flowers. She also was given a beautiful corsage and a basket of cut flowers. At each stop the pretty brunette was photographed for the motion picture news reel by Art Stimson and Will Williams, local photographers. . . .

Gets Lunch at Dessert's

Next Spokane heard the lovely contralto of its chosen daughter over Radio Station KGA, in the Old National Bank building. "I'm so proud – thank you so much," the queen said, closing her talk. Then the crowd rolled into Vic Dessert's Oasis . . . After the luncheon, Miss King met several local notables . . . then journeyed to The Spokane Press, where she started the press that runs off the daily for Spokane. She was presented with an insurance policy by Henry Hansen, circulation manager of The Press.

Next Miss Spokane stopped at Lubin's big store, at Post and Main, . . . where she selected a smart frock which she will wear at Atlantic City. At M.M. Cohen's she received a smart underarm bag of black and tan, a jeweled comb and a novelty bracelet, . . . Crowds were attracted to Schuleins' shoe store at 509 Riverside, where Miss Spokane tried on some natty footwear in the window. She chose several pairs of smart footgear . . . Across the street, at the Hart, Schaffner & Marx shop, Miss Spokane picked her bathing suit. . . . a blue and tan two piece suit . . . .

Driving to the National Printing company at S 156 Browne, she ordered her cards for her trip east. She selected a plain engraved card, using remarkable taste. At the Dorian studio she again posed for her picture.

Cinderella Has a Great Day

. . . Finally Miss Spokane was driven to the Chrysler Community Dealer's at W606 Third, where the last stop was made. "Without the easy-riding Chrysler, I'd never have finished a hard day of shopping like this one. It's a wonderful car." So ended Cinderella's first day in her new role of queen of beauty in Spokane.

The Atlantic City Experience

On August 24, 1927, Eva departed Spokane on a Milwaukee train bound for Atlantic City. She traveled on the same train as Miss Seattle Peggy Maddieux, also en route to the Miss America Pageant.

The 1927 Atlantic City pageant lasted five days, from September 6th to the 10th. There were 72 contestants from major cities throughout the United States. During Eva's time in Atlantic City, she stayed in one of the city's finest hotels and was provided a chauffeured automobile. A personal escort was assigned to her and her chaperone.

Upon arrival at the Pennsylvania Station in Atlantic City on September 6th, the contestants were greeted by the mayor, president of the Chamber of Commerce, director general of the contest, pageant directors and all the Atlantic City commissioners. Each contestant was presented an official identification ribbon to be worn at all times during her stay and a program that outlined the upcoming four days of tense and grueling events.

After this greeting, photographs were taken and the girls were escorted to the mayor's office at City Hall, where they were officially welcomed to Atlantic City and presented with a key to the city by Mayor Anthony Ruffu Jr. From there they proceeded by car to Park Place and the Boardwalk where they participated in the opening of the pageant and the raising of the pageant colors. (Note the names in this narrative – the game Monopoly originated from Atlantic City.)

On Friday morning, September 9, 1927, the final judging of Miss America took place. Out of 72 contestants, Eva King placed second.

Miss Seattle Peggy Maddieux rode the train to the Atlantic City contest with Eva King in 1927. Peggy was the first wife of former Senator Warren Magnuson.

Each participant in the Miss America contest was presented a key to Atlantic City and a commemorative medal by Mayor Anthony Ruffu Jr. This copy shows Eva's key and her Miss Spokane commemorative medal. During the time Eva represented Spokane in this pageant, the requirement called for the participants to represent various cities in the nation. The contest later became limited to state titleholders.

After the Pageant

Following the Atlantic City beauty pageant, the contestants were besieged with contract offers. Representatives for everything from movies to promotional-advertising firms wanted their services. Eva, along with Miss El Paso, Miss Terre Haute, Miss New Orleans, Miss Minneapolis, Miss Brooklyn, Miss New Haven, Miss Bridgeport and the new 1927 Miss America (Lois Delander of Joliet, Illinois), signed a contract to appear in performances with a man named Mr. Lucille, who was proclaimed the world's fastest dressmaker. Eva said, "We appeared on the stage in bathing suits and then Mr. Lucille would use beautiful pieces of cloth to drape us in the latest styles of dress." They toured the East Coast with Mr. Lucille for seven months, putting on fashion shows in most of the major cities.

There were numerous highlights during these seven months. Eva and her group were the first women ever permitted to eat in the mess hall with the cadets at West Point. Eva met many movie actors, including John Gilbert, Douglas Fairbanks Jr. and Clara Bow. While on tour in Washington, D.C., she rode in the largest airplane in the United States and visited the White House.

Eva Returns to Spokane

Although Eva had many opportunities back East, including some tempting stage offers, and traveled thousands of miles visiting many cities, she always looked forward to returning to Spokane. Upon arriving home in April 1928, she publicly expressed her feelings for Spokane, "You find the old home town is some town, after all. I wouldn't trade Spokane for ten New Yorks."

Shortly after settling back in Spokane, Eva was employed in the beauty department of the Owl Drug Store at Wall and Riverside. On September 30, 1929, she married her childhood sweetheart, Hal Dixon, a graduate of North Central High School and Drake University in Des Moines, Iowa. He was born in Spokane on March 25, 1908, the son of Grant and Ruth (Parker) Dixon Sr. The Dixons were a self-made family of early lumbermen who had settled in Spokane about 1900. Among the Dixons' various enterprises, they were the owners of the Exchange Lumber & Manufacturing, Western Pine Manufacturing, and Lincoln Lumber companies. When the Dixon family sold their lumber holdings in the area, they purchased the Northtown Shopping Center in 1964 and built the Town and Country Shopping Center.

Hal and Eva became the parents of three daughters: Sally Jo (Taylor), Nancy Sue (Martin) and Judith Gay. They raised their family in Spokane and later move to Hayden Lake, Idaho, where they lived for 22 years. Hal passed away on April 25, 1985, at age 77, and Eva on January 19, 1993, at the age of 85.

A group of contestants in the Miss America Contest, who later worked for dressmaker Mr. Lucille in New York City. Eva is on the far right. This group toured the East Coast with Mr. Lucille for seven months, putting on fashion shows in most major cities. According to Eva, "We appeared on stage in bathing suits and then Mr. Lucille would use beautiful pieces of cloth to drape us in the latest styles of dress."

A photography session during the 1927 Miss America Beauty Pageant in Atlantic City. From left: Gladys Cookman, Miss Washington D.C.; Agnes Hill, Earl Carrol's Vanities; and Eva King, Miss Spokane.

Hal and Eva (King) Dixon in the early 1930s.

The Clemmer Theater, located at 910 West Sprague Avenue, was built in 1915 by Dr. Howard S. Clemmer, and at the time was considered the finest theater in Spokane. It was Spokane's first air-conditioned theater. Large fans circulated warm air from a steam-heated basement chamber through ducts vented over the heads of the audience. In the summer this system was turned into an air conditioner by filling the basement area near the furnace with an average of six truckloads of ice a day and running the fans.

The Clemmer Theater, 1916.

(Photo courtesy Spokane Public Library)

Dr. Clemmer, a local dentist, was an active participant in his theater and often became involved in unique promotional projects. One of these was a free weekly show for all redheaded boys in Spokane. (Dr. Clemmer was a redhead). He was not only involved in the 1926 and 1927 Miss Spokane contests, but was also the president of the Spokane Ad Club when they started the first Miss Spokane contest and the advertising campaign featuring Marguerite Motie.

In 1929, at the onset of the Depression, the Clemmer fell on hard times and closed for a year. It reopened in 1930 as the Audian Theater. Two years later, it was renamed the State Theater. In more recent years, it was acquired by the Sandifer family, who completed a major restoration, and named it the Metropolitan Performing Arts or commonly known as just "The Met." It is no longer a movie theater and now used mainly for concerts.

(Photo courtesy Ernie Wales.)

When Dr. Clemmer's wife died in the mid-1920s, his son John went to live with relatives in Washtucna. On April 1, 1928, three of John's Spokane friends made a trip to Washtucna to visit him (left). From left: Fred Bartleson, Lewis and Clark High School; Jack Hangauer, Gonzaga High School and the owner of the 1916 Model-T Ford; Ernie Wales, Lewis and Clark.

A newspaper clipping of Eva King as "Miss Pontiac" during an auto show in Spokane.

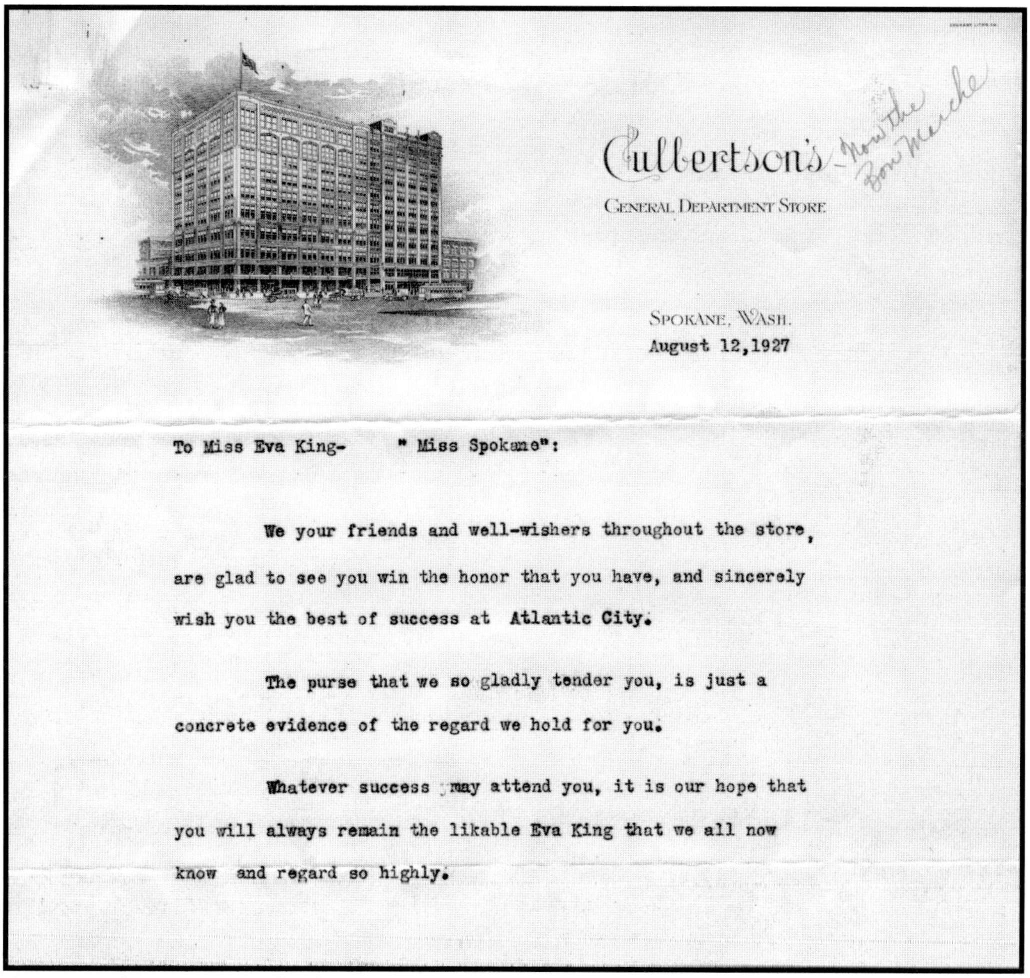

Culbertson's — now the Bon Marche

General Department Store

Spokane, Wash.
August 12,1927

To Miss Eva King- " Miss Spokane":

We your friends and well-wishers throughout the store, are glad to see you win the honor that you have, and sincerely wish you the best of success at Atlantic City.

The purse that we so gladly tender you, is just a concrete evidence of the regard we hold for you.

Whatever success may attend you, it is our hope that you will always remain the likable Eva King that we all now know and regard so highly.

A copy of page one of a four-page letter of encouragement from F.R. Culbertson and 212 well-wishers from Culbertson's Store (located in the building of the present Bon Marche). Eva worked for Culbertson's prior to becoming Miss Spokane.

Dixon Lumber Company, circa 1900. In 1929 Eva King married her childhood sweetheart, Hal Dixon. The Dixon family were early pioneers in the lumber industry and, at the time, owners of the Western Pine Lumber and Exchange Lumber companies.

Eva and Hal Dixon attending the Tenth Annual Loggers Banquet in the Marie Antoinette Room at the Davenport Hotel. Hal was the toastmaster for this occasion.

Eva Dixon with her daughters Sally (left) and Nancy.

Left: Eva and Hal Dixon with their daughters Nancy (left) and Sally.
Right: Eva and Hal in front of their home at Hayden Lake, Idaho.

Eva (King) Dixon and her daughters, from left, Sally Jo, Judy and Nancy.

Donnagene Herr

Miss Spokane County 1949

In 1949, at the age of 18 and while still attending Rogers High School, Donagene Herr (now O'Dell) won the title of Miss Spokane County. This new contest, sponsored by the Spokane Junior Chamber of Commerce, contained the necessary elements for the winner to participate in the Miss Washington Pageant, which ultimately could lead to the Miss America Pageant. Twenty finalists competed for this new title, which rewarded the winner with a new wardrobe and a trip to the Miss Washington contest in Seattle. Donnagene placed fourth at the Miss Washington contest. Along with her duties as Miss Spokane County, she was also crowned queen of the Lilac Festival. Following the end of her term, Donnagen crowned her successor, Barbara Crosby, Miss Spokane County of 1950.

Donnagene Herr, crowned Miss Spokane County on May 13, 1949.

Donagene was born and raised in Spokane. She married at the age of 20 and has two sons, Daniel and Jay, and a daughter, Pamela Jo, four grandchildren and one great grandchild.

She worked as a secretary for the personnel department at Lincoln Savings and Loan in Spokane until 1960, when she moved to San Francisco. She has lived the majority of her life in California, where she has had numerous careers, including her own business, Model Home Enterprise. From 1985 to 1987, she managed a Christian shelter for abused mothers. During Donnagene's career, she has been able to travel extensively, both within and outside the United States. She is now retired.

In 1998 she moved to Palm Springs, California, where she now lives. All three of her children live nearby.

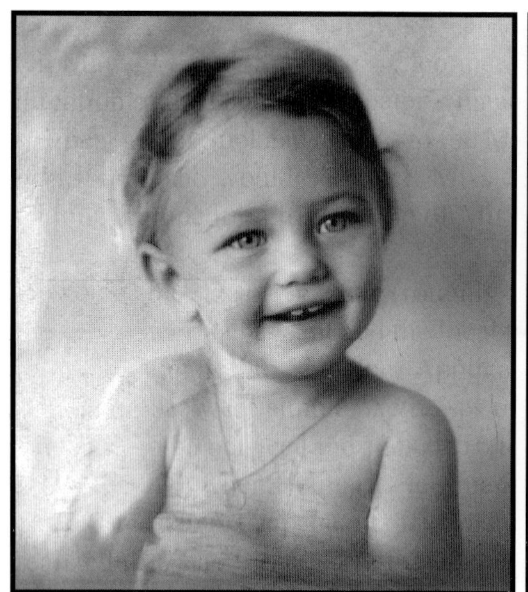

Donnagene at 18 months (left) and with her brother Richard.

Donnagene's eighth grade class at Franklin School, 1945. **Front row**, from left: Barry Dunlop, Roy Ulrich, Herbie Brown, Gary Kerr, Bill Reese, Don Farley, Maynard Stone. **Second row**: Dwyla Seehorn, Louise Henager, Laura Lee Foster, Mollie McGovern, Eileen Todd, Donnagene Herr, Berneice Tarbert, Lucille Todd. **Third row**: Donna Lea Bedinger, Marie Witter, Myrna Abbott, Joy Ann Wynia, Margery Mendenhall, Barbara Anderson, Sue Emery, Patricia Kirkpatrick, Donna Rae Hern. **Fourth row**: Darrell Allen, Weldon Ferry, Dan Rafferty, Dale Pointer, Earl Witter, Randall Stone, Bill Hoisington and Lanunce Macumber.

Donnagene's 1949 graduation photo from Rogers High School (left) and a promotional photo of her picking fruit as Miss Spokane County during "Valley Day."

Left: Donnagene with (from left) Spokane mayor, Arthur A. Meeham; Otto Warren, Chamber of Commerce president; and Jerry Camp. Mayor Meeham had just proclaimed September 17th "Spokane Day." **Right**: Donnagene Herr and other contestants at the Miss Spokane contest.

Left: Donnagene, at the age of 20, in her wedding gown at the Whitworth Presbyterian Church. Donnagene designed her own wedding gown. **Right**: Feeding a parrot.

From left, Donna O'Dell with her stepfather and mother, Ken and Mary Lou Shields, in 1989

Donnagene (right) with her daughter, Pamela Jo, and her mother, Mary Lou.

Donnagene (center) and family members, from left, grandson Michael Schmidt, grandson Able Leher, son Daniel Schmidt, son Jay Wilson, daughter Pamela Schmidt and granddaughter Kelly Schmidt.

The Miss Spokane Contest for the Miss America District Pageant

Sponsored by the Spokane Jaycees

In 1958 the Spokane Jaycees initiated what was called the Miss America District Pageant. The existing Miss Spokane contest, sponsored by the Spokane Chamber of Commerce, was not designed to send its city hostess representative to the Miss Washington Pageant. However, for young women who wanted that opportunity, the district pageant provided the necessary components, namely talent, swimsuit and evening gown competitions. The year this contest was initiated, Anne Sylvia Henderson was selected to represent Spokane in the Miss Washington Pageant. Much to the delight of Anne and the city, she became the first, and to this date, the only representative from Spokane to attain the title of Miss Washington. The following press release, kicking off the search for Anne's successor, provides some of the pertinent details regarding this contest:

PRESS RELEASE – January 5, 1959

It was announced today by Ed Roe, Project Publicity Chairman, at the "Spokane Jaycees Pepsi-Cola, Miss America District Pageant" kickoff at the Desert Hotel, that a "Spokane Jaycees Miss America" will represent the Northeast corner of the state at the Miss Washington Pageant in Seattle, March 27 - 28.

The Spokane Jaycees are planning an intensive search for the "Miss America" contestant from our area not only to aid this outstanding national program and to give a local girl the chance of a lifetime...but also, to promote local business through the favorable attention and publicity that will come from the selection of 'Miss Washington" and "Miss America" from the Spokane area.

We hope that every girl who can qualify will enter this local contest. Any one of the entrants might very well be the next "Miss America." You may see her everyday and never suspect that a year from now she will be pictured on magazine covers, touring foreign capitals, and representing the young women of America. Miss America, 1960, will receive $10,000 in scholarships plus an estimated $75,000 in modeling and personal appearance contracts. There will be another $21,000 in scholarships to be divided among the other finalists.

Last year we had the good fortune of our local winner, Miss Anne Henderson, capturing the Miss Washington crown. She was awarded an expense-free trip to Atlantic City for the Miss America Pageant. Miss Henderson placed fourteenth in the judging and won a total of $1,200 in scholarships.

This contest is sponsored by the Spokane Junior Chamber of Commerce aided by the Pepsi -Cola Bottling Company. The project is being conducted by the Jaycee Trade Promotion Committee under the direction of Robert H. Clausen. The chairman of the project is Herbert H. Cardle.

Any girl may nominate herself personally, or any business, organization, or individual may nominate a girl with her consent. The deadline for entries will be February 10, 1959.

Anne Henderson

Miss Spokane 1958 and Miss Washington 1959

Anne Henderson, Miss Washington, 1958.
Anne is the only Miss Spokane to date to have won that title.
(All photographs in this section are courtesy of Anne Henderson Anderson.)

Anne (Henderson) Anderson, a Brief Autobiography

Written in 2000 by Anne Anderson

I was born to Virginia and Bob Henderson at midnight on August 2, 1939, in Sacramento, California. My brother, Jim, was born in San Mateo four years later. Our father was in the oil business and we moved a lot during my early years, ending up in Spokane when I was six.

I attended Finch and Jefferson Elementary, Lewis and Clark High School and Eastern Washington University. We moved briefly to Billings, Montana, when I was in the seventh grade, but returned to Spokane. I had a great time in high school. It was wonderful growing up in the 50s with rock-and-roll and carefree times. Life was good to me; I had many friends and dated constantly. I didn't get straight A's, but was an average student with many things to do and places to go. I kept busy entertaining groups with pantomime of popular female artists. Being one of the first in the area to offer this type of entertainment, I became in much demand. As my social life flourished, I was chosen the jolliest sophomore girl, along with Gary Cogdill (jolliest sophomore boy), and in my senior year, chosen Lilac Princess. Back then, it was sponsored by the American Federation of Garden Clubs and the Lilac court consisted of five girls.

One of the most important aspects of my high school years was being introduced to Young Life, an international Christian group that reaches high school students and offers a life-style devoted to Christianity. I was active in this group and attended meetings every week as well as attending Malibu Camp in Canada every summer as a member of the work crew and Colorado Springs during the winter. This life-style has kept me on track all my life.

After high school graduation, my intentions were to work and put myself through college. I enrolled at Eastern Washington State College (now EWU) and commuted daily during the first few months, until I read an article about tryouts for the Jaycees-sponsored Miss Spokane contest for the Miss America District Pageant. It involved college scholarship money and I decided to "go for it." I was astounded when I won the local contest and was so excited to continue on to the Miss Washington Pageant in Seattle. Needless to say, my college aspirations went on hold for a while. After I won Miss Washington (the first and, to this day, the only one from Spokane to win the title), my life became very busy preparing for the Miss America Pageant in Atlantic City. There were luncheons, boat and auto shows, banquets, fashion shows, speaking engagements, various groups to entertain, Seafair in Seattle, and modeling daily at the Bon Marche in Seattle. There were luncheons with Senator Henry "Scoop" Jackson and Governor Albert Rosellini. I lived with my Aunt Milly in Bellevue until the time I went to Atlantic City on September 12, 1958.

My mom, grandmother, chaperone and I flew to Atlantic City, which was a very long trip in those days. From Spokane, we were escorted to the airport by 20 cars and four police motorcycle escorts. It was the first airplane trip we had ever taken and was quite an experience. It was also the first time I had traveled back East. Following registration, we were whisked to our hotels in limousines and it was nonstop until the end: rehearsals; parades; photo, radio and television sessions; more rehearsals; walking the boardwalk; swimming in the ocean; interviews with the judges (among whom were Kitty Carlisle, Moss Hart, Bennett Cerf and wife Phyllis, Mitch Miller and Heidi Krall); autograph signing, etc., with only a few hours of sleep each night. At the Dennis Hotel where we were staying, they had items on the menu named after each of us and mine was the Miss Washington Sundae, which was topped with bing cherry sauce. One interesting side note was an article that appeared in the Atlantic City newspaper; twenty-six press writers, who were predicting the outcome, placed me in a tie for fifth place with Miss New Jersey. It was a whirlwind experience and an honor to be chosen to represent the state of Washington. As it turned out, I placed 14th and was only eight points away from being among the top ten.

After arriving home, I continued to make appearances and decided to move to California to continue my college education and to work in San Francisco, where I began a modeling career. Within a year, I was a top model and had to put my education on hold again. It was such an exciting career. I met many people and traveled throughout the area. Being spiritually and emotionally stable helped me through all of this. The Lord blessed me and continues to bless my family and me. In 1961 I was chosen National Wine Queen and promoted California wines, attended numerous wine tastings, state fairs and luncheons. That same year, I met my husband-to-be, Ted Anderson. He was a junior executive with Shell Oil. We were married the following year in San Mateo. I continued to model and even after we were transferred to Sacramento, I commuted to San Francisco until I became pregnant with my first child, Kristen. We were transferred to New York and my second child, Jeff, was born. After we moved to New Orleans, Steve was born.

I loved being a "stay-at-home mom." Houston was the final move for us. We were there five years before our divorce in 1976. The children and I then moved back to Spokane and I started work at the Crescent as their store model. Soon after that, I began working full time at Ferris High School and remained there for almost 10 years. In 1989 I started work at the Spokane Symphony as receptionist and secretary to the music director, where I am presently employed.

After moving back to Spokane, I became active in the "Ham On Regal" productions at Ferris High School for a number of years, helped judge various contests, and became involved with the Spokane Symphony Associates. In 1989 I was an original committee member for the Miss Spokane Scholarship Program when it was started up again after a 25-year absence. I have been responsible for booking appearances for Miss Spokane and, as you can tell by this book, the program is still going strong!

My children have all graduated from college. Jeff and Steve reside in Western Washington. Kristen lives in Spokane with her husband, Gregg Powell, and their beautiful two-and-a-half-year-old daughter, Annie Elizabeth. My father passed away in 1985 and my mother, who is still very active and healthy, lives a few blocks from me. My brother Jim and his family live in Mission Viejo, California. We are a close-knit family and love doing things together.

Left: Anne's grandmother, Ada Mutch, with her daughters, Dorothy and Milly, in front of their home at 4526 North Walnut Street in Spokane in 1915. **Right**: The Mutch sisters, Virginia (Anne's mother), Milly and Dorothy in 1933.

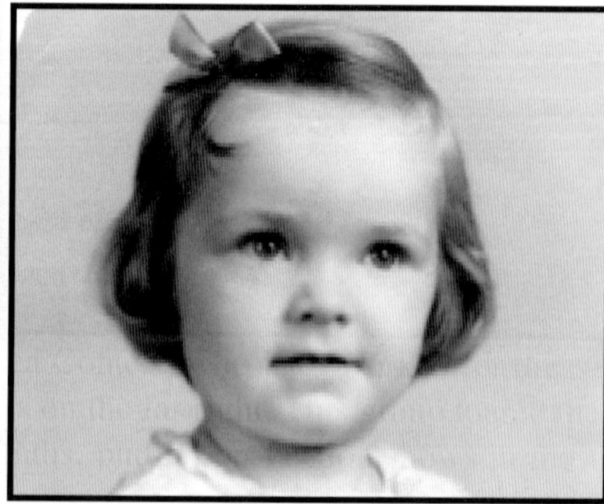

Left: The Henderson brothers, Fred, Bob (Anne's father) and Sam. **Right**: Anne, age 2.

Anne Henderson, at the age of three.
She became Miss Spokane and Miss Washington in 1958.
To date, she is the only Miss Spokane to have become Miss Washington.

Anne at about four years of age (left) and with her brother Jim and father Bob.

Left: Anne practicing golf in 1953. **Right**: Bob and Virginia Henderson in Hawaii.

Anne as a teenager in 1952 (left) and her graduation picture in 1957.

Above: The 1957 Spokane Lilac Festival Court. From left: Ann Bradford, Anne Henderson, Lilac Queen Kay Levesque, Judy Mead and Sally Schaefer. **Left**: Gail Cogdill and Anne at the Lewis and Clark's Sadie Hawkins Dance in 1956. After high school, Codgill played football at WSU and then professionally, becoming a star for the Detroit Lions. In 1960 he was named NFL Rookie of the Year and in 1962 Detroit's most valuable player.

Anne Henderson
Miss Spokane, 1958

Spokane's Winner

Anne S. Henderson, 18-year-old Eastern Washington col lege blonde, last night was named to represent Spokane i the Miss America contest. Her record pantomime of th popular rock and roll tune "Same Old Jazz, Mama" captivate five judges and an audience of about 250 at the Davenpor hotel. With the title, she wins a $100 scholarship, a $30 wardrobe and an all-expense trip to Seattle for the Mis Washington eliminations.

The 1958 news clipping that announced Anne as the winner of the Spokane Jaycees' first Miss Spokane contest. The purpose of the original Miss Spokane contest, which began in 1912, was an official representative position for the city, not a preliminary to the Miss Washington and Miss America contests. The Miss Spokane contest Anne won and the one that is active today sends the winning contestant to the Miss Washington Pageant. The winning contestant competes for Miss America.

One of the highlights of Anne's Atlantic City experience was the final evening after the coronation of Miss America. She went backstage to leave when she heard someone call her name. Looking toward the backstage door, she saw her friend, Pete Riley, and a friend of his waving at her. They had driven up from the University of Pennsylvania on a motorcycle to see her. She was elated! A couple months later, when Pete was returning home to Spokane for the Christmas holidays, he and three of his fellow students from ministerial school were killed in an auto accident. Anne said, "I'll never forget him and the influence he had on my life. He was truly my life's soul mate."

Anne on the Miss Washington float during the Miss America Pageant in Atlantic City.

Anne in her official Miss Washington car, a new Oldsmobile convertible, in front of her home. The car was provided for her use during her year as Miss Washington.

Anne being crowned the 1961 National Wine Queen by California Governor and Mrs. Edmund Brown at a ceremony held in San Francisco. As National Wine Queen, Anne was provided a wardrobe by Koret and acted as hostess for the California wine growers during National Wine Week in October. The annual National Wine Week, which was started in 1939, included civic events, luncheons, banquets and wine tasting.

Anne Henderson as the 1961 National Wine Queen with her official car.

The actor Jack Kelly, from the famed television show *Maverick,* is being served champagne in a silver wine tasting cup by Anne Henderson, National Wine Queen.

Anne touring the vineyards (left) and doing a cooking demonstration with wine.

A large billboard pose for an Italian restaurant in San Francisco.

National Wine Queen Anne Henderson in various poses in 1961.

Anne's Modeling Career

Informal Modeling:
San Francisco Fashion Industry, Lorie Deb, Magnins, Macy's, Emporium, Roos Atkins, J.C. Penney, Wards, Sears, City of Paris, Livingston Brothers. Also, various stores in Sacramento, Seattle, Spokane, Houston, New York, New Jersey and New Orleans.

Fashion and Commercial Photography:
Corvette, Sweet 10, Macy's, Ernie's Restaurant, Alfreds Restaurant, Viking Sauna, *Life Magazine*, Matson Lines, Emporium, U.S. Steel, U.S. Gypsum, Bogward Auto, Falstaff Beer, Lucky Lager Beer, Lane Furniture, Del Monte, Quantas, Friden, J.C. Penney. Pacific Northwest Bell, East Bay Utilities and Arrow Shirts.

Movies:
Half-hour comedy with Paul Speegle for the San Francisco Ad Club, half-hour film in San Antonio, Texas, for Wine Industry, half-hour film in Sacramento for California State Fair.

Television:
Numerous fashion show for local stations in San Francisco, Seattle, Spokane, Los Angeles, Houston. Various talk shows.

Miscellaneous:
Buyers fashion market weeks, boat, auto, sport shows. Hundreds of conventions, including U.S. Air Force, American Medical Association, American Dental Association, American Seating. Worked with various stars (including Jock Mahoney, Esther Williams, Jack Kclly) and politicians (including Gov. Edmund Brown, Gov. Rosellini, Sen. Henry Jackson and various mayors). Performances included musical comedy for Macys in Sacramento and Phono Mimic for various conventions. Lorie Deb Bridal designed their gowns on her for five years.

Anne modeling a wedding dress in 1962 (left) and on her own wedding day when she married Ted Anderson in Redwood City, California, in 1961.

Modeling in Houston, Texas, in 1976.

Anne modeling for The Emporium in San Francisco during the early 1960s. At the time, The Emporium was one of the larger store chains in that area. It had stores in downtown San Francisco and at Stonestown, Stanford and the Stevens Creek area.

Anne in Houston, in 1976 (left) and, as National Wine Queen (right), presenting movie actor Joe E. Browne a bottle of champagne, a key to the wine cellars of California and a kiss. This event took place in San Francisco.

Anne in Houston in 1976 (left) and San Francisco in 1979

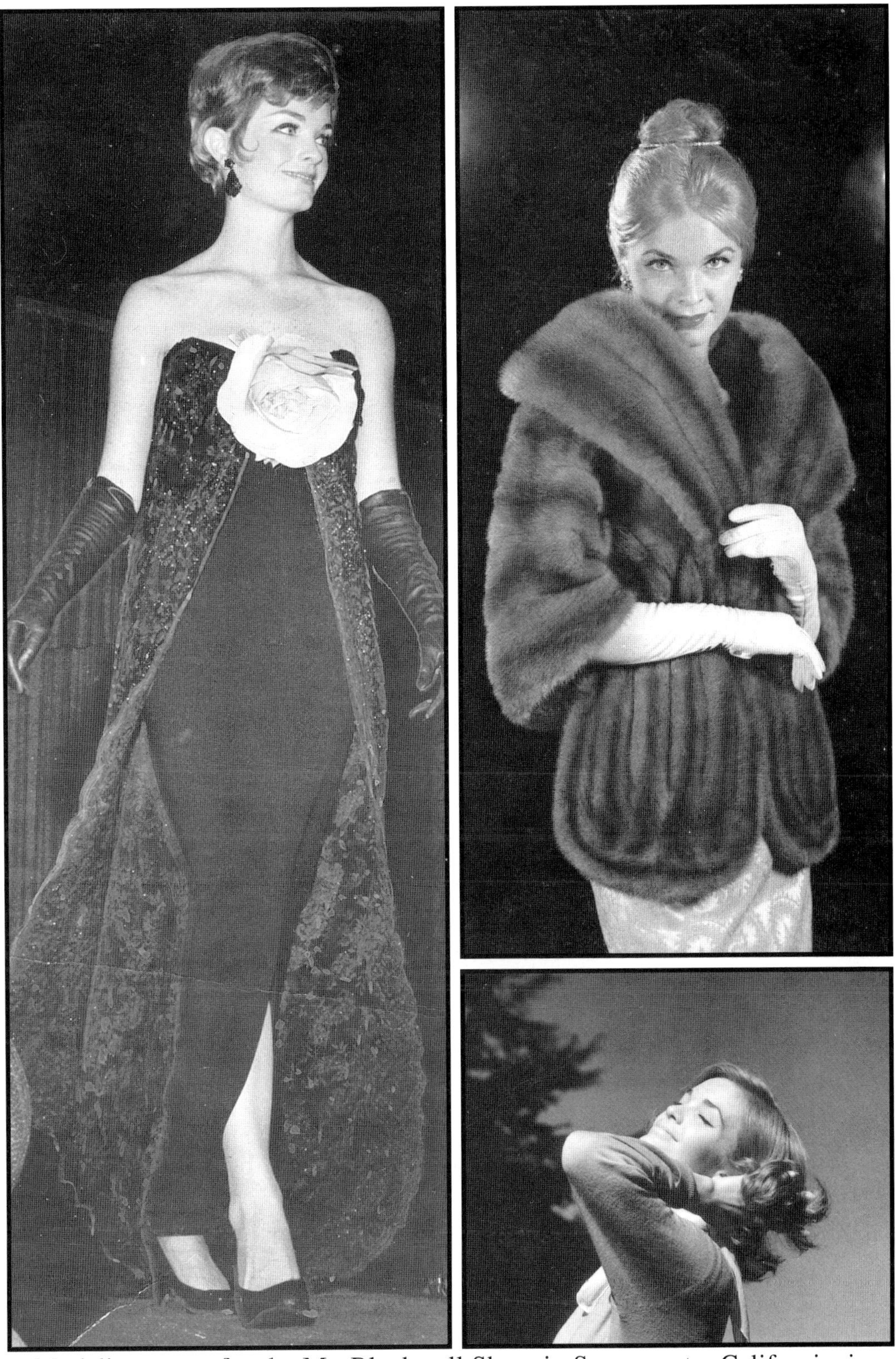

Modeling poses for the Mr. Blackwell Show in Sacramento, California, in 1963 (left) and the Stefani Brothers in 1961 (upper right).

Left: Anne's mother, Virginia Henderson, in 1999. **Right**: Anne and son Steve, 1999.

Left: Anne's daughter Kristen, granddaughter Annie, and son-in-law Gregg Powell. **Right**: Anne's brother, Jim Henderson, in 1999.

From left: Jeff Anderson, Virginia Henderson, Anne Anderson and Steve Anderson in front of Applebees Neighborhood Grill & Bar at 2007 East 29th Avenue, July 2000.

Left: Anne and her granddaughter, Annie, opening presents on Christmas 1999.
Right: Anne's daughter and granddaughter, Kristen and Annie Powell, on Easter 2000.

The Miss Spokane Scholarship Program

In 1989, after a lapse of over 25 years, a contest to select a Miss Spokane to compete in the Miss Washington Pageant was organized, called the Miss Spokane Scholarship Program, which is active today. When it began, the Miss Spokane selection process took place in the fall to prepare the young woman for the Miss Washington Pageant held the following summer. For that reason, the winner's title included the year of the Miss Washington Pageant, not the year she was chosen as Miss Spokane. In the year 2000, a change was initiated to hold the Miss Spokane contest in the same year (in January) as the Miss Washington contest. For more information on the pageant, also see the letter from the executive director on page 343. The following is a list of contestants since the inception of this program.

1990	Jennifer Williams
1991	**Amy Sturtz**
1992	**Brenda Grizzle Janke**
1993	**Jennifer Soo Fryhling**
1994	Ann Marie Kuhn
1995	**Victoria Nicacio Van Inwegen**
1996	Sarah Etzler
1997	No Miss Spokane
1998	**Sarahlynn Aanderud**
1999	**Abigail Palmer**
2000	**Fianna Dickson**

The **bolded names** indicate the young women in the Miss Spokane Scholarship Program who contributed photographs, and in most cases, their own personal reflections on their experiences as Miss Spokane and as a contestant in the Miss Washington Pageant. These accounts are contained in the following pages. They not only are a representative cross-section of the Miss Spokanes, but also of the Miss Washingtons, and are examples of some of the area's finest young women.

Amy Sturtz

Miss Spokane 1991

Amy Sturtz, 1990

(All photos in this section are courtesy of Amy Sturtz.)

My Life Before, During and After Miss Spokane

Written in 2000 by Amy Sturtz

I was born in Chelan, Washington, on May 7, 1967 to Steve and Kathy Sturtz. My father was the choir and band director of Chelan Junior and Senior High School. My enjoyment of music and thoughts of a teaching career began at an early age. We attended the Little Stone Church, and although I was a shy youngster, I began performing at a young age, singing and acting in church programs. When I was three years old, my sister, Stefani, joined our family on July 26, 1970.

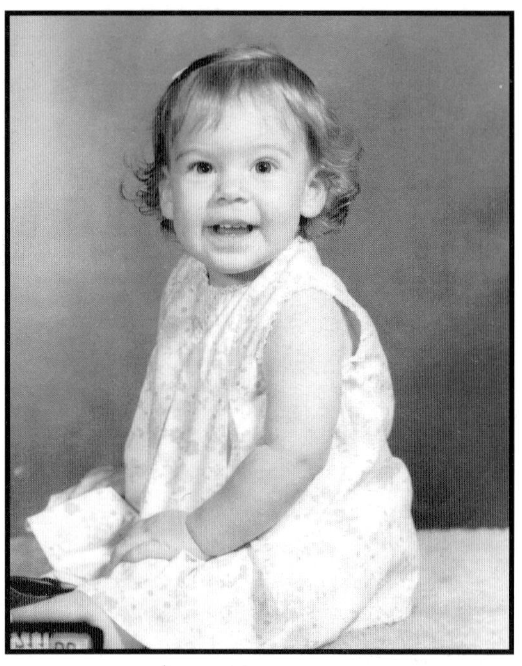

Amy at age one.

During my childhood years, I was very much a tomboy. I loved to go to my grandparents' house in Tonasket to play on the farm, hike, camp, fish, ride motorbikes and play basketball with my uncle and his friends. Time spent with my uncle inspired me to get involved in sports. I began playing "hoops" with the boys in fifth grade and began winning awards in "Run, Dribble and Shoot," "Spot Shooting," and "Hoop Shoot" contests.

Although I was very active in elementary school and was not much into "girly" activities, I remember watching the Miss America Pageant year after year and dreaming of being on the stage in Atlantic City. I always thought what an incredible feeling it must be and of all the opportunities bestowed upon the young lady crowned. Although most years I dressed up as a famous sports figure for the annual "Fiction Fantasy Day" at school, in fourth grade I dressed up as Miss America. Also during this time, I was performing at piano recitals, church functions, school concerts and talent shows.

In junior high and high school, I was actively involved in competitive sports, playing volleyball, soccer, basketball and running track. In high school, I also became a varsity football cheerleader, lettered three out of the four years in basketball and all four years in track, and broke numerous school track records. I also pursued my love of music, was in the school band and continued singing and playing the piano within my community and my church. Though not an outgoing person, I had a heart for competition and loved performing. When put in competition or on a stage, I was a different person – I came to life and I felt no insecurities.

I began working at the age of 13 during the summer months, school breaks and on weekends, and learned early to be a responsible student, balancing work and school. I was a quiet, self-conscious, conscientious individual. In high school, I became involved in student government as a student council representative, both vice president and president of our pep club, and student body vice president.

Amy (left) and her sister, Stefani, on Fiction Fantasy Day in April 1977. Amy dressed up as Miss America and Stefani as Daisy May.

Whatever I took on as a commitment, I always devoted myself to doing my very best. I received many honors throughout my high school years in sports, music and scholastic achievement, including "Most Inspirational" awards for both basketball and track, making the honor roll and being named in *Who's Who in Music*. I was also selected for various high school royalty positions and vied for the title of Miss Lake Chelan.

Amy going for a lay-in during her senior year of basketball at Chelan High School. This was during a game with the Omak Pioneers. Chelan won.

In 1985 I graduated from Chelan High School and began to pursue a Bachelor's Degree in Education. I attended Wenatchee Valley College for two years and then transferred to Eastern Washington University, where I made the national dean's list. Becoming an educator was the perfect choice for me; my ultimate dream is to have a large family and be in a vocation in which I can spend as much time with my children as possible.

In college I played basketball for the Wenatchee Valley College Lady Knights; sang in the Wenatchee Valley College Collegiate Singers, a select choral jazz group; and was on the WVC dean's list. During one of our Collegiate Singers' performances, as entertainment for the Miss Greater Wenatchee Pageant, I became interested in the Miss America Scholarship Program. After the pageant, Deloma Sherwood, one of the Miss Greater Wenatchee board members, approached me about becoming a contestant for the following year. Her encouragement was the boost of confidence I needed to push me towards a long-awaited dream.

In 1987 I began my pursuit of the Miss America crown. My first year I was not granted a single award, but I felt as if I was on top of the world. I learned so much about myself and gained a confidence I had never felt before. I knew immediately after the crowning had taken place I would be back on stage the following year; I wanted to be crowned Miss Greater Wenatchee.

The following year, although a junior at Eastern Washington University, I was still eligible to run for Miss Greater Wenatchee; my permanent address was in Chelan, which was part of the pageant's territory. I chose my vocal performance early, *Don't*

Rain On My Parade, began working on choreography and studying for the interview portion of the contest. Practicing my talent was the easy part. I loved to sing! My roommates were so supportive. No matter how tired I was, they never let me go to bed without performing for them at least once. They were extremely helpful in choreographing my song, critiquing my performance and boosting my confidence. Studying for the interview was difficult. For the talent competition, I knew what I had to do – get on stage and perform. But the interview was the unknown; I didn't know what they would ask me. Being such an active person, I never enjoyed sitting still to read the newspaper or listen to the news. Plus, to add to my discomfort, I was going to be in a room with five strangers.

In 1988 all my hard work paid off – I was crowned Miss Greater Wenatchee 1989. I was ecstatic! God had graciously granted me the gift. It was a year full of excitement and hard work. I had to learn to balance school in Cheney with my responsibilities of appearances and practices for Miss Washington back in Wenatchee, which meant many long hours on the road. The greatest highlights of my reign were entertaining at many of the Washington Centennial Games ceremonies, along with competing in the Miss Washington Pageant. And another, which I would not realize until later, was meeting Lynne Schuster and Gail Gallik.

Lynne Schuster, Amy Sturtz and Gail Gallik.

After a lapse in the Miss Spokane contest of over 25 years, Lynne and Gail were in the beginning stages of preparing to once again have representation from Spokane at the Miss Washington Pageant and each served terms as executive director. Gail, who had been a former Miss Walla Walla, had a belief in the Miss America scholarship system and three years earlier had begun working towards bringing the pageant back to Spokane. It was a task few would have taken on, let alone succeeded in. In October of 1989, Gail's aspirations became a reality. The Miss Spokane committee, comprised of Anne Anderson, Lynn Forbes, Michelle Vanderline, Sandi Bentz and Roberta Greene, did a magnificent job. The quality of the pageant in all aspects – contestant preparation and activity, committee outreach, directing and production of the show – were superior.

After I won Miss Greater Wenatchee, Lynne and Gail heard I was attending Eastern Washington University and were eager to meet with me. Lynne was excited when she discovered I grew up in Chelan because she was also a native of Chelan and her mother still resided there. I began attending mock interviews at Lynne's home. They, along with the Miss Spokane committee, helped me to prepare for the interview portion of the competition.

The Miss Washington Pageant 1989 experience was similar to my first Miss Greater Wenatchee Pageant – it was an education. I was overwhelmed by the pageant flair and hoopla. I really had no idea what to expect and was I ever amazed by the caliber of talent, confidence, poise, intelligence and professionalism of the contestants. I soon learned that the pursuit of the Miss America crown was not an easy one and many young ladies would not have been crowned at the local, state or national levels if not for perseverance. Some ran as many as five times at the state level to make their way on to the Miss America stage and some have even been to Miss America with different state titles. I walked away with the mere satisfaction I had made it to the Miss Washington Pageant, I had learned more about myself and the dedication and commitment it would take to become Miss Washington, I had an enormous support group of family and friends, and there was now a Miss Spokane committee enthusiastic to greet me as a contestant for the resurrected Miss Spokane Pageant.

I am a perfectionist and put a lot of pressure on myself. And I had a fear of not being crowned Miss Spokane. During dress rehearsal the night before the pageant, I came down with a miserable 24-hour flu. Surviving on little sleep, I was able to compete. I felt I was strong and did well in all phases of the competition, and was chosen as second runner-up. Jennifer Williams, a beautiful young lady and talented pianist, was crowned Miss Spokane. There were highlights to just being a contestant, however. I made some friendships I still treasure dearly and was able to stand with the other contestants in the VIP section to see and hear President George Bush during his visit to Spokane for the Washington Centennial Celebration.

I was not ready to give up on my dream. I was determined to become Miss Spokane and to have another opportunity at Miss Washington. Back home in north central Washington for the summer, I drove to Seattle weekly to take voice lessons from Jeff Francis. In the fall of 1990, I was doing my student teaching at Chester Elementary in the Central Valley School District in Mr. Hussey's fifth grade class. The pageant and my teaching complemented each other very well. Preparation for both kept my mind occupied and focused in a variety of arenas. Being center stage in front of my students, facing their unknown questions and actions on a daily basis helped to prepare me for the pageant, and having performed in front of strangers, keeping abreast of current events for contest interviews helped me to be a better informed and confident teacher. For as long as I can remember, I have had a love for children and the desire to be a teacher. My goal is not only academic education, but to also help children realize their potential and their responsibilities, and to accomplish this with love, support, discipline and encouragement.

I competed for Miss Spokane 1991 with the most confidence I had ever had, knowing I was well prepared. I came out of my interview feeling certain, my voice was strong as I sang *The Glory of Love*, and I was relaxed and poised in swimsuit and in evening gown. My short speech was *Miss Sturtz Can You Help Me*? "I sure can Mikey. What can I do for you?" I was self-assured of my overall performance. It was now in God's hands.

On October 20,1990, my dream came true and I was crowned Miss Spokane 1991. Although I had not been privileged to be crowned the first Miss Spokane in this newly-revived pageant, I was the recipient of the first "Touch of Class" award, named after Gail Gallik. Gail had moved out of the area during 1991 and the committee chose to name an award in her honor. Secondly, Sheri S. Barnard, mayor of Spokane, proclaimed Miss Spokane would serve in an official capacity as hostess of the city. Being Miss Spokane and official hostess of the city, many opportunities were presented and I enjoyed an exciting year of events.

It all started the following Monday, October 22, when I greeted my fifth grade students with crown and banner on. They were overwhelmed with excitement! Most of them already knew their teacher had won. One of the students, Shane Douglas, had attended the pageant and received a lot of attention because he had taken a picture of Miss Sturtz in her swimsuit! Those students, along with the entire Chester staff, will never know how much they helped me in my endeavor, how much I still think of them, and how they truly made me feel like a queen!

The Sturtz family following an evening of competition at the Miss Washington Pageant, from left, Kathy, Amy, Steve and Stefani.

Amy greeting Spokane mayor, Sheri Barnard, at the Friends of the Davenport "Christmas Elegance."

The following is a sampling of Amy's appearances and involvement during her reign, which provides a glimpse of what the role of Miss Spokane entails: **Fund-raising events** for WAMPUM, Children's Miracle Network, Cheney Cowles Museum, Miss Spokane Scholarship Program, Police Guild. **Grand openings** for Ernst Hardware at Northpoint and J.C. Penney at Northtown shopping centers. **Fashion show participation** to benefit the Spokane Symphony Associates and Goodwill Industries. **Trade shows:** Ag Trade; Boat; Home and Yard; and Big Horn Sports. Amy also was a judge for the North Central Lilac princess, selecting Amy Cartledge, who later became the Lilac queen.

I kept a very busy schedule throughout my reign, but managed to work all but five days of the remaining school year as a substitute teacher. I had received my teaching degree with a K-8 elementary education endorsement with a major in math, and a K-12 endorsement in both choral and instrumental music in December of 1990. I juggled many appearances in the evenings and weekends.

I was elated when requested to sing at my appearances and especially enjoyed singing our national anthem. I sang for the Manito Lions, the Gem and Mineral show, the Christmas Tree Elegance at Inn at the Park, at Sacred Heart's "Baby's First Christmas," and several schools in the Central Valley School District. The three greatest highlight appearances and performances for me were at the Spokane Chiefs opening hockey game, the opening of Playfair, and above all, the welcome-home party for the troops returning from the Persian Gulf War at Riverfront Park after the mayor gave her speech.

In June of 1991, I did compete in the Miss Washington Pageant and was extremely pleased at my efforts toward achieving my goal. Sometimes we want something desperately, but it doesn't happen to be in God's Master Plan. Obviously, I was disappointed at not becoming Miss Washington, but I had a wonderful journey. I gained an enormous amount of maturity, opportunity, experience, confidence, friendship, faith and memories from my year as Miss Spokane. It was time to move on, to take what I had gained from the ride of my dream, and begin my other dream to motivate young people to their highest potential.

In July I was hired as a sixth grade teacher at Cashmere Middle School and assistant basketball coach at Cashmere High School. I was disappointed I would be leaving Spokane, but if I had to leave, Cashmere was my first choice to begin my teaching career. It is a small community located in north central Washington, well known as a top district in the state. It also happens to be my hometown's (Chelan's) rival.

On October 19, 1991, I gave up my reign, crowning Brenda Grizzle as the next Miss Spokane. I performed *Someone Up There Loves Me.* My father and I sang a duet *What A Difference You've Made in My Life,* which I dedicated to the Miss Spokane committee, and then had a tape of my farewell speech played.

As I look back over the year as Miss Spokane, I can hardly believe how quickly it passed. It seems like just yesterday that I was a student teacher standing in front of my fifth graders at Chester Elementary receiving good luck hugs, cards and gifts, and then greeting them on Monday morning as Miss Spokane with my crown and banner on. They were thrilled, excited and proud. I was not only their teacher, but in their eyes, a real queen. I had a busy year and loved every minute of it, not to mention the wonderful people I came in contact with and the enduring friendships because of that incredible year! I enjoyed entertaining at exciting places and competing in the Miss Washington Pageant. All have been quite overwhelming and I will treasure the memories and friendships for a lifetime.

Amy signing autographs for her Chester Elementary students.

Reflecting back, not only on the year as Miss Spokane, but on the four-and-a-half years of active involvement in the Miss America Scholarship Program, I know I would not be the self-assured woman I am today if it weren't for this program. Along with the personal growth, I have had the opportunity to achieve some of my goals and live some of my dreams, such as being a positive role model, an entertainer and somewhat of a celebrity. On top of all that, I was awarded a total of $3,200 in scholarship monies to further my education and earn my Master's Degree in Curriculum and Instruction from Lesley College in Cambridge, Massachusetts, which I completed in 1995. I found my one moment in time when I was more than I thought I could be. However, I did not leave with sadness, but with sincere gratitude.

I am still teaching sixth grade at Cashmere Middle School, where I have been for eight years, and coaching Cashmere High School girl's junior varsity basketball. I have also enjoyed being the assistant director for the annual sixth grade musical for six years, and supervising middle and high school students on trips to Washington D.C., Boston and New York, and Walt Disney World and Kennedy Space Center. In 1998, after seven years at Cashmere, I took a leave of absence for a year to teach sixth grade and coach freshmen girls' basketball in Lake Havasu City, Arizona. It was a great experience, but I missed my family dearly. I was able to return to Cashmere and regain my positions. In 1996 I was honored in *Who's Who Among America's Teachers*.

I am still very physically active. I enjoy playing basketball, lifting weights, snow skiing, hiking and running. Although I've always enjoyed running, my dear friend, Nyana Sims, whom I met while living in Lake Havasu, inspired me to taking running to new heights. I have now run two marathons: the Rock-n-roll Marathon in San Diego (3:37:41) and the Portland Marathon (3:37:42). I look forward to running another this fall.

Another love of mine is to drive my convertible with the top down. Nothing makes me feel freer. My first car when I got my teaching job was a red convertible Mazda Rx7. I now drive a Mitsubishi Spyder Eclipse. There's nothing like your hair blowing in the wind as you drive over a mountain pass. My dad, nephew and 90-year-old grandfather enjoy it as well!

I am still single and searching for the love of my life to begin my family with. I have faith God has a special man chosen for me. I pray I will be the wife and mother to which I have always aspired. In the meantime, I enjoy being Aunt Amy to my niece and nephew, McKenna and Gunnar Rice.

Amy's recent school photo.

Amy running in the Rock-n-roll Marathon in San Diego (left) and just after being crowned Miss Greater Wenatchee in 1989.

Amy on a hike to Mt. Cashmere.

Amy Sturtz being crowned Miss Spokane on October 20, 1990 by Jennifer Williams, Miss Spokane 1990.

In front of the Met Theatre, where the Miss Spokane Pageant took place, preparing for the limousine ride to the Awards Ball at the Holiday Inn.

Amy, as Miss Spokane 1991, performing *Someone Up There Loves Me* at the Miss Spokane Scholarship Pageant on October 19, 1991, when Brenda Grizzle was crowned Miss Spokane 1992.

Brenda Grizzle

Miss Spokane 1992

Brenda Grizzle, official Miss Spokane portrait, 1992

(All photos in this section are courtesy of Brenda Grizzle Janke. Above photo taken by Rob Behm.)

Brenda Kay Grizzle was born in Burbank, California, on July 10, 1970. In 1979 she moved to Spokane with her parents, Charles R. and Janet M. (Ramsey) Grizzle and her older sister, Victoria Lynn (Vicki). She attended and graduated from the following schools: Hamblen Elementary, Sacajawea Junior High, Ferris High School, Eastern Washington University and Whitworth College. Her sister, now Vicki Grizzle-Clancy, is also a graduate of EWU.

Brenda's father is a retired publicist and advertising executive and her mother a library clerk. Brenda is an elementary school teacher and her husband, David Martin Janke, is a radiologic technologist for the Heart Institute of Spokane. Brenda and

David are the proud parents of one-year-old-daughter Madison Malia Janke.

During her tenure as Miss Spokane and throughout her life, Brenda has projected an image of sincerity and thoughtfulness towards others. Her involvement with hundreds of children throughout the Spokane area as a counselor, tutor, teacher and volunteer has affected many lives. The 1992 Miss Washington Pageant named Brenda as the recipient of the first "Washington Cares for Children Award." This award is presented to a contestant who demonstrates creativity, a long-term impact upon the community, and the likelihood of continued involvement with children.

Brenda's hobbies include reading, aerobics, hiking, camping and surfing the internet. In addition to being selected as Miss Spokane, she was also a Spokane Lilac Festival princess and the Ferris High School 1987 homecoming queen.

In 1997 Dan Brown of the Miss Spokane Pageant Committee asked Brenda to write a brief resume of her thoughts and experiences during her tenure as Miss Spokane. Brenda's following response best sums up her personal history of that event:

Letter to the Miss Spokane Pageant Committee

Written on March 11, 1997 by Brenda Kay (Grizzle) Janke

Thank you for contacting me. I am glad to hear there are people pulling together to keep our pageant alive. What you are doing will make a difference in the lives of many young women. I have condensed my story as much as possible. I hope this fits your request.

My interest in the Miss Spokane Pageant began when I watched my friend Jennifer Williams crown her successor. Amazed at the beautifully composed woman she had become, I watched her in awe never dreaming I would one day be in her place. Working hard to pay my way through college, I was always on the lookout for scholarship possibilities. I asked a lot of questions, watched contestants, and with Lynne Schuster's encouragement, auditioned to be a contestant in the 1992 Miss Spokane Pageant. Participating in the Miss Spokane Pageant has influenced me so much. It is difficult to imagine how my life would be different if I had not taken this road.

The most helpful skills I developed involve confidence in public speaking and interview situations. Committee volunteers spent hours of their time training, encouraging, and guiding all of the contestants. We learned how to sit, walk, make eye contact, and answer difficult questions. I began a habit of reading the newspaper thoroughly, hungry for information on current events. I strengthened my own opinions and learned how to express them clearly and confidently.

Along with these skills, the committee helped us to improve physically. We spent time learning about makeup, hair, and clothing styles. We were challenged to set personal goals for fitness and talent. As a dancer, I had never performed alone on stage. I had never choreographed my own routine, and I was not even close to being professionally trained. Yet, with the incredible support systems of the pageant committee, the other contestants, and my family, I worked very hard and performed to the best of my ability. And I won!

Brenda Grizzle being crowned Miss Spokane 1992 by the 1991 Miss Spokane, Amy Sturtz, with assistance from Shannon Edwards.
(Rob Behm photograph.)

My year as Miss Spokane was a wonderful whirlwind year of appearances, performances, and preparation. As the official greeter for the city of Spokane, I was able to experience many aspects of our community. I met interesting people, attended elegant parties, and spent time as a role model for children. When I could catch my breath, preparations were made for the Miss Washington Pageant in June. All this and I was still enrolled in school full time also. What a way to learn how to organize yourself and your time!

With help from the Miss Spokane pageant, I graduated from Eastern Washington University in 1993 debt free! Later that year, I interviewed for my first teaching job wearing my professional suit (from the Miss Washington Pageant) and applying my renewed confidence and interview skills. My dream came true: a third grade classroom of my own!

I am convinced that the pageant experience has contributed to my successes today. At this writing, I have completed five years of teaching elementary school and am earning a masters degree from Whitworth College in Elementary Education. Being involved in the Miss Spokane Pageant will always be a highlight in my life. I am grateful for the opportunity to share this with you.

Brenda with runners-up for the 1992 Miss Spokane contest. From left: Heather Carlson, fourth runner-up; Carla Larson, second runner up; Brenda Grizzle, Miss Spokane; Sabrina Jones, first runner-up and Joyce Hester, third runner-up.

(Rob Behm photograph.)

Brenda and pageant committee members at the Lilac Festival Royalty luncheon. From left: Evelyn Conant, Gail Scanlan, Nikki Niederhauser, Cathy Tunstall, Roberta Greene and Anne Anderson, former Miss Spokane and Miss Washington.

Brenda riding high with her father Charles, mother Janet and sister Victoria in the San Gabriel Mountains of southern California.

The Grizzle girls, Brenda and Victoria (seated), posed in old-fashioned dresses with their mother, Janet, in 1972.

Brenda and her first boyfriend, Greg Fisher, in 1973. She and her family lived for ten years in the foothill community of La Canada/Flintridge north of the Pasadena Rose Bowl. Her craftsman father, a television and motion picture publicist and audiovisual product development manager at Walt Disney Productions, built this play house.

After years of serious consideration, the family decided to move from the megalopolis of Los Angeles to the small city life-style of Spokane.

Right: Brenda posing as a farm girl with straw hat.

During her senior year at Ferris High School, 1987-1988, Brenda (center) became a cheerleader for all major sports. Here she struts through a routine at Albi Stadium with classmates Kim Pearson (left) and Ann Hagen.

Using props and costumes created by her parents, Brenda captured the attention of her audiences in unique and humorous dance routines.

Brenda's older sister, Vicki, Eastern Washington University 1986 homecoming queen, has always been an inspiration to Brenda, five years her junior, and an avid supporter.

Left: As a 1988 Spokane Lilac princess, Brenda flew with the Air Force in a KC-135 tanker out of Fairchild Air Force Base. **Right**: The talent competition of the Miss Spokane Pageant was Brenda's first solo dance performance.

Brenda's (second from right) confidence in dance and performance grew through her experiences with the Eastern Washington University Jazz III Unlimited Dance Team.

Moments after being crowned Miss Spokane, Brenda is whisked to the reception at the Sheraton Hotel in a private, personally-assigned limousine, courtesy of Embassy Limousines, on October 19, 1991.

Brenda dressed as an elf with Santa Claus and Vakhtang Jordania, conductor of the Spokane Symphony Orchestra.

Singing up a storm at a Christmas party for the Spokane Child Abuse and Neglect Prevention Center (SCAN).

Sharing a ride on the Looff Carousel at Riverfront Park during Washington Trust Bank's family night.

Brenda's role as Miss Spokane royalty gave her a wonderful opportunity to meet people and make new friends in a variety of public appearances. Here she visits with aspiring young girls while signing autographs prior to the 1992 Miss Washington Pageant in Vancouver, Washington.

Relaxing at home with the Grizzle family, from left, Charles (father), Janet (mother), Brenda, Victoria (sister) and Buffy, circa 1990.

On December 18, 1993, Brenda Grizzle married David Janke, her college sweetheart of five years.

Brenda, husband David and daughter Madison celebrate Christmas 1999 together.

Jennifer Soo Fryhling

Miss Spokane 1993

The official Miss Spokane portrait of Jennifer Soo Fryhling in 1993.

(Richard Behm photo, courtesy of Jennifer Soo Fryhling.)

Jennifer Soo Fryhling graduated from Eastern Washington University in 1993, while serving as Miss Spokane. At Eastern she received her Bachelor of Arts Degree in International Affairs and Economics, graduating Magna Cum Laude. At EWU she was in the Phi Kappa Phi honor society, on the national dean's list, received the Trustees' Scholarship and numerous awards. She was also recognized in *Who's Who*. Following her graduation from EWU, she attended and graduated Cum Laude from the Seattle University School of Law, with a J.D., in 1997. While there, she also received the Year End Achievement and the Asian-American Bar Association of Washington scholarships.

Jennifer worked in Seattle at the Court of Appeals before moving to San Francisco. She currently practices law in the area of intellectual property, which includes trademarks, copyrights, unfair competition and patents. In June 2000 she married her law-school sweetheart on the *Queen Mary,* docked in Long Beach, California.

Recent photo of Jennifer Fryhling.

Victoria Nicacio

Miss Spokane 1995

Victoria Nicacio being crowned Miss Spokane at the Met Theatre on October 28, 1994.

(All photos in this section are courtesy of Victoria Nicacio Van Inwegen.)

My Year As Miss Spokane
Written on March 29, 2000 by Victoria Nicacio Van Inwegen

My name is Victoria Van Inwegen, formerly Victoria Nicacio, and I was Miss Spokane 1995. I am currently residing in Chicago, where I live with my husband, Patrick. I work in the Information Technology Department at Unext.com, a company that develops business courses for delivery via the Internet. Patrick is pursuing his Ph.D. in Political Science at Loyola University.

I was crowned Miss Spokane in October 1994, while I was junior at Gonzaga University. I had moved to Spokane from my hometown of Pasco, Washington. Spokane had always held a special place in my heart because my maternal grandparents lived in Spokane while I was growing up. I have many pleasant memories of my family's visits to see Grandma and Grandpa. Many of my relatives had been pioneers in Washington, settling in Spokane Falls before Washington gained statehood. These relatives included my great great grandparents, E.E. Alexander and Bertie Louis Alexander. Bertie was in the first graduating class at Lewis and Clark High School.

My reign got off to a wonderful start because the other ladies who competed were so friendly. We had so much fun during rehearsals and constantly got in trouble for talking too much. I have enclosed one of my favorite pictures from my year as Miss Spokane, which shows the contestants grouped together after the show was over and I had been selected as Miss Spokane 1995. We were hugging and laughing about how good we felt now that the pressure was off and the show was over. No more production numbers to remember! I also recall standing in the foyer waiting to go to the reception and a little girl asked me for an autograph. Me? An autograph! That was just the beginning.

The highlights of my year include singing with the Jim Baker Band during one of the Saturday dances at the Davenport Hotel. It had always been a dream of mine to sing with a big band and this was my chance. I had rehearsed the song, Nat King Cole's *Orange Colored Sky* only once with Jim Baker, but about a million times in my head. When I sang it with the band, Mr. Baker was so surprised that he yelled, "One more time!" and I got to sing it again. I was floating for days. I also remember the time I addressed the mayor as "Mayor Geraghty" and he said, "Just call me Jack." I was thinking, "Of course, I should just call him Jack."

Christmas was a busy time of year. I can now say I've "played" with the Spokane Symphony. For their Holiday Pops concert I played a wayward elf that caused all kinds of ruckus while Santa was looking for me. The audience was on my side when Santa finally got a hold of me so he had to forgive me.

I got to do so many fun things. I was in parades and realized the importance of the "parade wave." If you don't wave from the elbow, your wrist will hurt. I actually got to say, "Let the games begin," while I was the Chieftess of the Highland Games. I was on the radio and had a lot of fun playing practical jokes on the listeners and responding to the callers.

My year as Miss Spokane also afforded me the opportunity to be of service to the community. I participated in events that raised over $500,000 while I was Miss Spokane. I did everything from playing "Vanna" [White] at charity auctions to visiting children and their families at the Shiners Hospital. I spoke numerous times to various civic organizations on my platform "Parental Involvement in Education." I had the wonderful opportunity to give a message that I thought was important for people to hear. The fact that I was Miss Spokane encouraged people to really listen to what I had to say. I always loved the question-and-answer sessions after a speech I had given. Those sessions made me believe I had an effect on people and maybe they would be more involved in their child's education because of me. I was so excited when I was interviewed for a local television show because it opened up the doors to a much wider audience.

I learned so much while I was Miss Spokane. I used to joke that I could be a "professional mingler." But I realize how important it is to be comfortable around people and to make people comfortable around you. I am still convinced that all the intensive interview practice sessions we had while preparing for the Miss Spokane and Miss Washington programs enabled me to secure a job offer from Andersen Consulting five months before I graduated from Gonzaga. My vocal skills improved tremendously since I performed so many times. I got to sing at a Chiefs' game. I was so proud of myself for choosing a vocally challenging aria to perform at Miss Washington. That song required so much energy I had to get my LEGS into it. When I first started practicing, I could barely get through the song once, and even then, I felt like I needed a nap. My vocal range was at its peak that year.

I also learned time management and organization skills. I was a full-time student at Gonzaga, majoring in mathematics and getting certified to teach high school. I worked part-time at Washington Water Power. I was dating my future husband, who got to serve as my escort to many events. In my spare time I slept.

All of these fun, wonderful opportunities and I got scholarship money, too! How lucky can a girl get?

My year as Miss Spokane ended in October 1995. I graduated from Gonzaga with my B.S. in Mathematics and my secondary education certificate in May of 1996. I moved to Seattle, but returned to Spokane in August to be married in St. Aloysius

Church to Patrick, whom I met on our first day of school at GU. We lived in Seattle for two years before moving to Chicago. While we enjoy Chicago, we both know we'll end up back in the Pacific Northwest again. Once you've experienced the best, it's hard to settle for anything less.

I realized that above I speak of myself as Miss Spokane in the past tense. I think I will always be Miss Spokane. Are there still 76 lakes in a 50-mile radius? Or was it 76 lakes in a 25-mile radius? I am still a compulsive newspaper reader, all those current event questions. You need someone to sing the national anthem? I'm your "man." How about the Canadian anthem? I can do that too. Do you need someone to make a prospective customer/employee comfortable and sell them on your company at the same time? Count on me. Not only do I have a very solid year of experience, I have the crown to prove it.

Victoria's official Miss Spokane portrait (left) and playing Santa's elf at the Spokane Symphony's Holiday Pops Concert. Mike Cantlon as Santa

Victoria with other contestants immediately after winning the Miss Spokane contest. This is one of Victoria's favorite photos because of the reactions of the other contestants, who were so happy and excited about her success.

A Christmas party at the Davenport Hotel. The other three young women on the left were also Miss Spokane contestants. Lynne Schuster, who was executive director of the Miss Spokane Scholarship Program, is on the far right.

Victoria at her good-luck reception on June 10, 1995, before leaving for the Miss Washington Pageant. The reception was held at the top of the Shilo Inn. Gonzaga University is visible in the background.

A group of supporters and committee members on the day Victoria left for the Miss Washington contest. She is wearing her white "I Love Spokane" shirt. Many of her well-wishers are holding photos of Victoria, one is wearing a shirt with her image on it, but the cat at the right had to be restrained to be photographed for the occasion.

Victoria with Jean Silver, state representative, during a visit to the Washington State Legislature in Olympia.

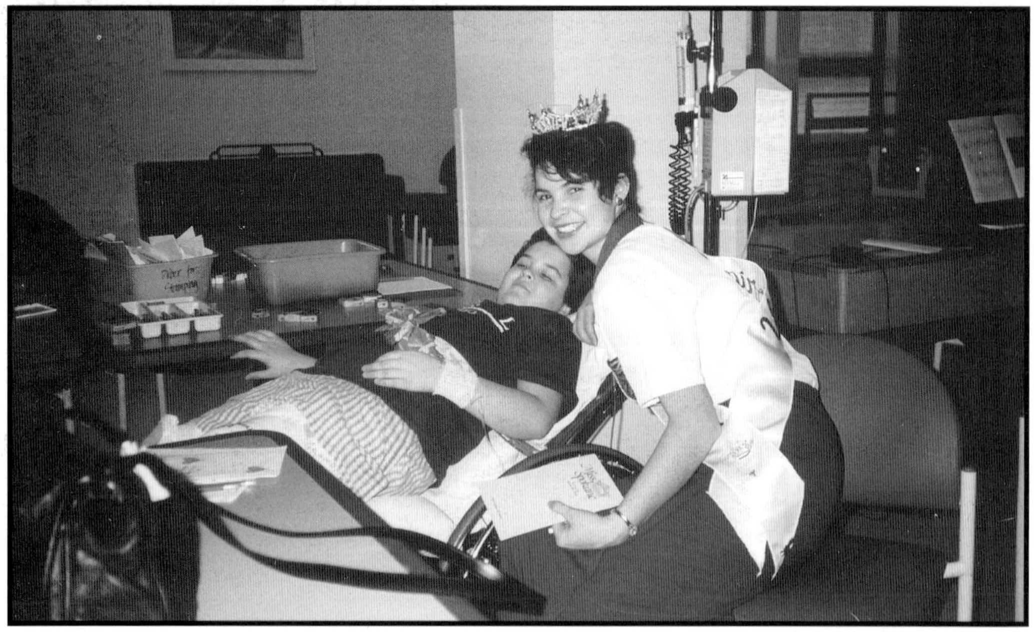

During a visit to the Shriners Hospital. While at the hospital, Victoria sang for the children and their families and signed autographs.

Victoria Nicacio and Patrick Van Inwegen walking down the isle of St. Aloysius Church on their wedding day, August 31, 1996.

Sarahlynn Aanderud

Miss Spokane 1998

Sarahlynn Aanderud's official Miss Spokane photo, 1997.

(All photos in this section are courtesy of Sarahlynn Aanderud.)

Sarahlynn Aanderud was born on December 20,1974 in Thermopolis, Wyoming. She grew up in the town of Blackfoot in southern Idaho. She later moved to Puyallup, Washington, where she graduated from Governor John R. Rogers High School in 1993. Following her high school graduation, she attended Gonzaga University in Spokane from 1993 through 1998, majoring in pre-med biology and music. During this time, she also studied in Florence, Italy, for a year. While overseas, she traveled in Italy, France, Germany, Austria, Ireland, England, Spain, Hungary, the Czech Republic, Egypt, Israel and Jordan.

While a student at Gonzaga, Sarahlynn noticed a small sign advertising scholarship money for women. At the time, she had no idea what an impact that little sign would have on her life. As a result of pursuing the information on the sign, she was crowned Miss Spokane in October 1997 and competed in the Miss Washington Pageant held in the Tri-Cities, June 18-20, 1998. She placed eighth and was the recipient of the National Miss America Community Service Award. She also received a scholarship for her work on her platform, "Ending the American Tragedy of Drinking and Driving," and efforts to eliminate underage drinking through her Alcohol Free Kids program. Following her reign as Miss Spokane, she went on to become Miss Puget Sound 1999.

At the present time, Sarahlynn is attending the University of Washington in Seattle, where she is finishing a degree in philosophy with a concentration in medical ethics, and is interning at KIRO 7 News in pursuit of a career as a health reporter. As a classically trained clarinetist of 13 years, she enjoys playing in the pit orchestras for local musicals in Seattle. She hopes to venture into jazz and swing music soon.

Highlights of My Reign
Written in 2000 by Sarahlynn Aanderud

The biggest highlight of my reign as Miss Spokane was the wonderful people I got to meet. The opportunities that opened up for me were innumerable: feeling like a princess while leading the Lilac Parade in Spokane, speaking at the local schools to implement my program and educate our community, leading a city council meeting, visiting the local hospitals to brighten the days of sick children. Being in medicine, this was incredibly special to me, particularly one young cancer patient that I met named Danielle.

Danielle and I became close, and I visited with her several times. On one occasion, she was supposed to ride in the car with the mayor of Spokane, John Talbott, during the Lilac Parade. Unfortunately, she became very ill and was not allowed to leave the hospital. She was devastated. I got a call from the mayor about two hours before the parade was to start saying that maybe we could bring the parade to her since she could not go to the parade. So, I got all dressed up in my huge dress and raced to the hospital to meet the mayor and visit Danielle. She was thrilled.

Danielle passed away just shortly before I gave up my crown. She was only ten. I will never forget her spunk and energy, even at the worst of times. I remember one visit when I asked how she was feeling, she gave me a big toothy grin and said, "Great. I didn't even throw up after my 'chemo' today." She always made me so grateful for what I have, a lesson I think all could benefit from.

Left: Sarahlynn, in 1995, with her best friends: Karissa Warner, Julie Smith and Cami Blanchard. **Right:** Just after being crowned Miss Spokane in 1997.

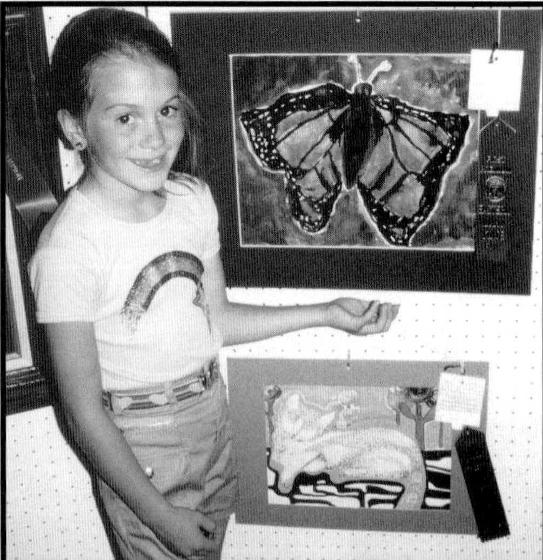

Left: Sarahlynn at age two. **Right**: Sarah at the Eastern Idaho State Fair, age seven.

Left: Sarahlynn attending the Locals dinner at the Miss Washington Pageant. **Right**: With her "wonderful chaperone," Pat Ulrich, at the Miss Washington Pageant.

Left: Sarahlynn and Miss Seattle, Wendy Burke, at the Miss Washington Pageant. **Right**: Competing in the talent portion of the Miss Washington Pageant.

Sarahlynn competing in the swimsuit competition at the Miss Washington Pageant.

Sarahlynn with her best friend, Kim Brockbank.

Sarahlynn with a young cancer patient named Crystal at Sacred Heart.

Sarahlynn with her parents, Rich and Suzanne Aanderud.

Left: Sarahlynn at the St. Patrick's Day parade in downtown Spokane. **Upper right**: Sarahlynn with Spokane mayor, John Talbott. **Middle right**: With Mr. and Mrs. Stockton, the grand marshal of the St. Patrick's Day parade.

Sarah with her dear friend, Cabot Guidry.

Abigail Palmer

Miss Spokane 1999

Abigail Palmer, 1998

(All photos in this section are courtesy of Abigail Palmer.)

Born in Peekskill, New York, on November 15, 1977, Abigail Palmer moved to Spokane with her mother, Linda Palmer, when she was less than a year old. In 1995 she graduated from West Valley High School, where she was on the honor roll. Other high school activities included being president and national qualifier for Distribution Education Clubs of America (DECA), senior yearbook editor, varsity cheerleader and a participant in Running Start, a program that offers college classes to high school juniors and seniors. She was also the Lilac Festival queen in 1996.

Following high school, she enrolled in Spokane Community College, graduating in 1998 with an Associate of Arts Degree. She is currently in her last quarter at Eastern Washington University as a pre-law student, while working at Global Credit Union.

Following her graduation from EWU, she plans to obtain a law degree from Gonzaga University, work as a prosecuting attorney for Spokane County and eventually become a judge. She is active as a Court Appointed Special Advocate (CASA)/ Guardian Ad Litem. In addition to this, she still finds time enjoy snowmobiling, snow skiing, fishing, hiking and music.

Abigail was chosen on October 24, 1998, to reign as Miss Spokane for the following year. Her platform on the prevention of child abuse and her vocal talent contributed to her success at receiving the honor of being selected. She chose the Judy Garland song *Come Rain or Come Shine* for the talent competition.

During Abigail's term, she maintained a busy schedule. She immediately became involved in various holiday activities: preparing and serving Thanksgiving dinner to women and children at St. Paul's; appearing at the Spokane Valley Mall Santa Celebration, Patsy Clark's Mansion's lighting ceremony and the Friends of the Davenport Christmas party fund-raiser; performing at the Spokane Symphony's Christmas Tree Elegance fund-raisers and Support Care and Networking for Families' Christmas party; and participated in the Toys for Tots drive. Typical of the Miss Spokanes' obligations throughout their yearlong reign, Abigail also gave speeches (generally on her platform of child abuse prevention), television and radio interviews, helped judge or appeared at other pageants, rode in parades, made guest appearances at conferences and sporting events, participated in fund-raisers, and of course, prepared to compete in the Miss Washington Pageant, which began on June 26, 1999, in the Tri-Cities. Always eager to advocate against child abuse, Abigail had frequent interactions with agencies, such as the Vanessa Behan Crisis Nursery, involved with the care and protection of children.

Abigail's appearance schedule for the month of March 1999, which follows, gives a more detailed account of her what her obligations were and what might be expected of a Miss Spokane during her reign:

Mar 1	Assisted in delivering items collected at area Global Credit Union Branches for the Vanessa Behan Crisis Nursery.
Mar 3	Miss Spokane preparation-for-state meeting and official photo shoot.
Mar 6	Judged the Block Kids Competition for the National Women in Construction.
Mar 10	St. Patrick's Day luncheon at C.I. Shenanigans.
Mar 13	St. Patrick's Day parade with television coverage and program article.
Mar 15	Judged the Mt. Spokane Lilac Princess Coronation for Spokane's Lilac Festival.
Mar 16	Read to children and parents for Holmes Elementary Family Reading Night.

Mar 22	Miss Spokane preparation-for-state meeting.
Mar 23	Official Miss Spokane photo shoot.
Mar 26	Miss Spokane preparation-for-state meeting.
Mar 27	Sang two songs for the Mrs. Washington International coronation.
Mar 30	Guest at the Chase Youth Awards at the Spokane Opera House - Channel 4 News at 11:00 p.m.

Abigail's official Miss Washington photo (the result of one of the photo shoots listed in her above appearance schedule) submitted to the judges of the Miss Washington Pageant, a requirement to participate. *(Photo by Green Gables Photography Studio.)*

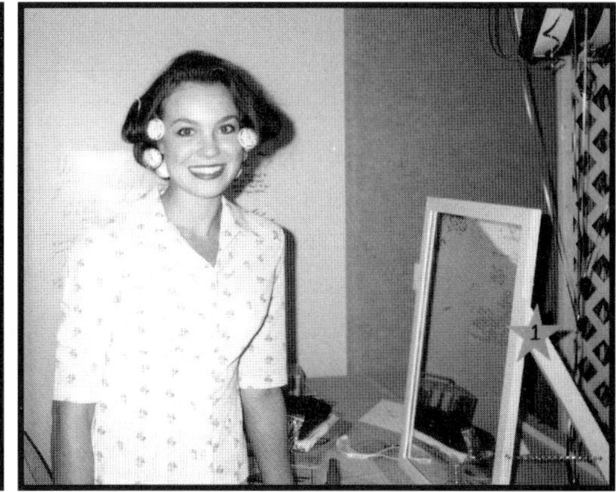

Left: Abigail Palmer with Spokane mayor, John Talbot, at a Friends of the Davenport meeting at the Davenport Hotel. **Right**: Abigail preparing for her appearance in the Miss Washington Pageant in June 1999.

Left: Abigail's brother, Jed Palmer, congratulating her on becoming Miss Spokane. **Right**: St. Patrick's Day celebration. Former mayor, Jack Geraghty, is at the right.

From left: Abigail Palmer, Miss Spokane 1999; Abbi Reynvaan, Miss Gig Harbor; and Sarah Aanderud, Miss Puget Sound 1999 and Miss Spokane 1998.

Fianna Dickson

Miss Spokane 2000

Fianna Dickson, 2000

(All photos in this section are courtesy of Fianna Dickson.)

On May 19,1979, as the Lilac Parade made its way through the streets of Spokane, Fianna Marie Dickson burst into the world with her award-winning smile. This was one year and a day before the eruption of Mt. St. Helens and the inches of ash it deposited in the Spokane area. A true Spokane native, she has lived all 21 years in her South Hill home, just a few blocks from Ferris High School, with her parents, David and Patti Dickson. Her father worked in the

Spokane area as a welder and steelworker. For the past 10 years, her mother has been an assistant in Traffic Safety Education (TSE) for Spokane Public School District #81. Fianna is an only child and was raised with her constant companions, three Pembroke Welsh Corgie dogs: Bilbo Baggins, Hobbs and Tasha.

Fianna's grandparents are Cecil and Josephine Nuxoll of Spokane and Warren and Anita Dickson of Okanogan. Fianna's family history has its roots in one of the first "mom and pop" grocery stores on East Sprague. Fianna's great grandparents, on her mother's side emigrated from Italy. In 1926 Michele and Carolina Mossuto opened their store in a new building at 2423 East Sprague. This building is located across from Northwest Seed and Pet. Mossuto's store was in competition with what is now Rosauers, a successful supermarket chain.

Fianna attended Adams Elementary and quickly became a focused student. Homework was always easy for her. For fun, she began taking baton lessons at the age of seven and twirled her baton for events around Spokane. Coached by Donna Ryan, at age nine she became a Ryanette majorette and was always a regular in the Junior Lilac Parade. This was the beginning of Fianna's parade career. Since then she has marched in parades from coast to coast, Washington, D.C. to Pasadena, California.

She entered Libby Junior High with a full set of new braces to enhance her smile. She was always active in school. She contributed to her school yearbook as a representative for her journalism class, became involved in student government as Associated Student Body Secretary and, as captain of the High Stepper Drill Team, got her start doing choreography.

At fourteen, Fianna purchased a 1963 Nova SS and over the next couple of years, she and her dad created a beautiful, bright-red beauty. Her love of cars came from her dad, as did her interest in classic cars and their restoration.

Even in high school, Fianna was serious about her education, was on the National Honor Society and in advanced placement classes at Ferris. Education is a serious pursuit for Fianna. She was awarded drill team captain in her senior year, the year the team and band were featured in the Pasadena Rose Bowl Parade. In 1997 she was honored by being chosen Lilac princess for Ferris High School. She traveled across Washington State promoting the Lilac Festival during her yearlong reign.

In the spring of 1999, Fianna graduated with honors from Spokane Falls Community College, receiving her Associate of Arts Degree. While there, she became involved with the poetry club as an associate editor and writer. She was also inducted into the Phi Theta Kappa Honor Society, on the National Dean's List, was an academic scholarship recipient and made the President's Honor Roll.

One-year-old Fianna performing on her Grandmother Nuxoll's organ in 1980. This was one of her first significant performances. Many others would soon follow. Inset is Fianna's grandparents on her mother's side, Josephine and Cecil Nuxoll.

Fianna in 1987 as a majorette (left) and as a princess in 1985 performing for her Grandma Dickson. Inset is her grandparents on her father's side, Anita and Pete Dickson.

During this time, Fianna began teaching and creating choreography for halftime football shows. Her skills with the baton were applicable for the flag work that is popular with drill teams and Winterguard. (Winterguard is a color guard and dance unit that uses a theme and props to present a ten-minute show for competition on a basketball court during intervals of a game. These teams compete locally, statewide and nationally and are the ultimate drill dance team activity.) Fianna became known throughout the Northwest as a coach, choreographer and judicature for band and drill competitions. She has worked as coach or assistant coach for Wenatchee, University and Ferris high schools. This a love and a passion for Fianna. As a result, she has been negotiating her own contracts with these schools for the past four years.

In the fall of 1999, Fianna transferred to Gonzaga University. She plans to graduate in 2001 with degrees in public relations and speech communication and a minor in political science. As a junior, she was one of twenty selected from 500 applicants to become a Gonzaga Ambassador, giving tours, traveling and promoting the school throughout the Northwest. She enjoys supporting Gonzaga basketball as a ZAG dance team member and choreographer.

The year 2000 has brought many opportunities, one of which was the offer to try for the title of Miss Spokane 2000. Unlike the early Miss Spokanes, today's applicants are no longer affiliated with the Spokane Chamber of Commerce, although the chamber continues to promote the program. Today, Miss Spokane is chosen by state and national judges from the Miss America Scholarship Organization. In essence, the winner has specific responsibilities and is awarded college scholarships. A young woman can only reign one year and must meet certain criteria. She must be between the ages of 17 and 24, never married, never had children, live in the region she would represent, have a platform issue, compete in the Miss Washington Pageant and commit for one year. The contest involves an intense interview process, community service platform work, evening gown, swimsuit and talent competitions. Just like the Miss America program seen on television by millions, the Miss Spokane Scholarship Program promotes a well-rounded young woman who is involved in her community and is willing to speak on a platform of her choosing. She must also demonstrate physical fitness and attend college.

This challenge and opportunity interested Fianna. Her decision to enter the competition had a lot to do with the chance to be heard on issues. On January 8, 2000, Fianna Dickson was chosen as Miss Spokane. She won a $2,000 scholarship, the chance to compete for the title of Miss Washington, and was given many speaking and promotional opportunities. To date, she has won nearly $9,000 in scholarships, including the Miss America Community Service Award for the state of Washington and the chance to continue on for a $5,000 scholarship. This is in addition to numerous television and radio appearances and guest speaker invitations.

Posing in the family's parklike backyard for the first day of the eighth grade at Libby Junior High in 1992 (left) and her Ferris High School graduation photo in 1997.

Left: Fianna as the Ferris Lilac Princess, 1997. **Right**: SFCC graduation with an AA degree and honors in the spring of 1999. She then went on to Gonzaga University.

Fianna has chosen "Lighting the Way to Lifelong Safe Driving" as her platform during her reign as Miss Spokane. She has spoken to area high school students and to driving school students and their parents about the need for more time behind the wheel, with an emphasis on forming better driving habits and more parental involvement with their novice driver. Fianna developed a brochure, "Lighting the Way to Lifelong Safe Driving," and a web page to provide links and resources for her platform.

In the spring of 2000, Fianna was the motivational speaker for the Street Law Youth Summit in Olympia. This Washington D.C.-based organization, directed by Erin Hull, promotes youth involvement in their community through the National Highway Safety Association. During her visit to Olympia, Fianna met and spoke with Lt. Governor Brad Owen, several senators and Rep. Jeff Gombosky concerning House Bill #6264 on a graduated driver's license. This bill passed and will be in effect June 2001. It requires 50 hours behind the wheel with a parent (only four hours are presently required) and other restrictions for novice drivers, which hopefully will result in fewer tragic accidents.

In March 2000, Fianna was asked to be a presenter and guest speaker to the 350-member Traffic Safety Educators Conference in Tacoma. In her speech "Sharing the Vision," Fianna talked about the effect safer driving would have on our communities and the lives that could be saved with more parental involvement. She received a standing ovation and the Commitment to Excellence plaque for her efforts.

Another opportunity, since 1998, has been an internship with Mayor John Talbott. After working three months as the temporary receptionist for the city council at City Hall, Fianna was given a plaque and high praise from both the mayor and Joan Poirier, city manager assistant.

At the Miss Washington Pageant, Fianna took first runner-up and a scholarship of $4,000. She also won the community service award (a scholarship of $1,000) and the swimsuit award (a scholarship of $300). Another of the many prizes awarded the first runner-up is a chance to compete in the National Sweetheart Pageant, the only pageant outside the Miss America Organization that is sanctioned by them. It took place in Hoopestan, Illinois, Labor Day Weekend 2000.

Among Fianna's many accomplishments, with a fourth of her term left to complete, are over 500 hours she has dedicated to community service. This time does not include the countless hours preparing for her numerous appearances. She supports various public concern and safety issues, especially promoting her safe-driving platform. She makes numerous appearances to promote the Miss Spokane contest and the Lilac Festival and inspire other young women to participate in these programs, and is a motivational speaker for various youth programs.

In the future, Fianna plans to continue her public-service projects in the Spokane area and complete a Masters Degree in Communications, marry "Mr. Right" and be a role model for young women in the community. As she said during an interview for the January 20, 2000, *Gonzaga University Bulletin* just after her crowning, "The important thing is that I make a difference and that I'm not just walking around with a crown on my head."

Mossuto's store.

Fianna's roots in Spokane go back to 1926. Shown above is the interior of her grandparents' grocery store located at 2423 East Sprague Avenue. From left: Michele, Dominic and Carolina Mossuto in 1926. In the photo on the left, Michele in standing in front of the store.

Fianna in the Senate Chambers at Olympia with Lt. Governor Brad Owen promoting the graduated driver's licensing bill (left) and in Washington, D.C. with Erin Hull and John Harvey, ESD 101, promoting youth involvement in Traffic Safety Education.

In Tacoma at the fall conference for the Washington State Traffic Safety Education with Dr. Terry Bergeson, Superintendent of Public Instruction for Washington State and Dave Kuennen of OSPI Traffic Safety (left) and AAA for a speech promoting safe driving habits and good decision making.

At Spokane Community College with TSE instructor, Gordon Elmes, learning to use the teaching tool – Fred Mottola's "Skid Monster" (left) and at the Spokane Market Place with Tullia Barbonte. According to Fianna, Tullia makes the best sauce in town.

With Spokane mayor, John Talbott, and his wife Claudia (left) and with her parents, David and Patti Dickson, at the Hotel Lusso. This was during a reception banquet for Miss Spokane prior to leaving for the Miss Washington Pageant.

Fianna at the Lilac Parade with Mrs. Washington International, Heidi Stephens, (left) and during the swimsuit contest in the Miss Washington Pageant. Fianna won this contest and $5,000 in college scholarships for her platform on safe driving.

Left: Fianna being interviewed by Tina Willis, Miss Washington 1999. Fianna was chosen first runner-up to Miss Washington 2000. **Right:** Photo taken by Henry Schultz in August 2000 for the National Sweetheart Pageant held in Hoopestan, Illinois.

The Miss Spokane Scholarship Program

A letter from Carol Grover, Executive Director since 1997, written in October 2000

Carol Grover (second from right) with her husband Lewis; Miss Spokane 1998, Sarahlynn Aanderud (center); and Miss Spokane 1999, Abigail Palmer.
(Photo courtesy Sarahlynn Aanderud.)

In 1989 I began a wonderful adventure as one of many volunteers to work with the Miss Spokane Scholarship Program, being brought back to Spokane after a 25-year absence, through the efforts of Lynne Schuster and Gail Gallik. What a tremendous honor it has been for the past 12 years to be the production co-coordinator responsible for putting together the final-night production to crown the new Miss Spokane each year.

Over the next 12 years, I became not only a volunteer but also an advocate and supporter of the largest scholarship program for women in the country. I have witnessed the growth of countless young women who have given their time, energy and enthusiasm to compete with each other. Young women who, through the program, grew to greater heights of self-esteem, more polished public speakers and quality assets to the community.

The winners each year are all the contestants, not just the one chosen to wear the crown and receive the title of Miss Spokane. Prior to the contest training, some individuals had been unable to speak fluently to a panel of judges, but learned to do so with ease and professionalism. Many have obtained employment as a result of the "job interview" rehearsal they received from a volunteer committee, which guided them through the process. The scholarship dollars have assisted many of the young women to further their education. Since 1989, the Miss Spokane Scholarship Program has awarded close to $35,000 in scholarship assistance.

My sincere desire is to increase community awareness of the program, not just of the production seen on the final night after training for eight weeks, but also the "behind the scenes" program, efforts by contestants and volunteers alike. The hard work, growth, development and achievements, which make this the best educational program for women in the world, is often not recognized by the general public.

The Miss Spokane Scholarship Program is proud to be the preliminary program to the Miss America Scholarship Program. All women ages 17-24 are welcome to participate on this opportunity. We sincerely appreciate the community's financial and emotional support, and the opportunity to serve the people of the great city of Spokane.

Index

Aanderud, Rich 328
Aanderud, Sarahlynn 284, 322-329, 333, 343
Aanderud, Suzanne 328
Abbott, Myrna 258
Abraham Lincoln speech contest 179
Abrams, Shirley 141
Acacia Cemetery 129
Adams Elementary School 335
Adams, Daniel 180, 181, 185
Adams, Elizabeth (see Armstrong, Elizabeth)
Adams, Gordon E. 180, 185
Adams, Harry G. 14
Adams, Jean (Tang) 181, 185
Adams, Peter 180, 181, 185
Adams, Madeleine 181, 185
Adams, Suzanne (see Thompson, Suzanne)
Adams, Teresa (Timons) 185
Aeroflight Executive Flight Services 188
Albert, G.S. 96
Alexander, Bertie 315
Alexander, E.E. 315
Allan, Mrs. Bruce 140
Allen, Darrell 258
Alumnae News 182
American Federation of Garden Clubs 264
Amick, Betty 210, 212
Amick, Bruce 210, 212
Amick (Mauss), Sally Ann 33, 210-217, 240
Amsterdam, Morey 225
Anaconda, Mont. 187
Anderson, Anne (see Henderson, Anne)
Anderson, Barbara 258
Anderson, Jeff 265, 266, 283
Anderson, South Carolina 160
Anderson, Steve 265, 266, 282, 283
Anderson, Ted 265, 278
Anderson's Print Shop 112
Andersonian, The 112
Ankeny, Levi (senator) 102
Ankeny's Restaurant 102
Anthony, H.T. 96
Anthony, Janet 141
Apple Blossom Festival 145, 157
Applebee's Neighborhood Grill & Bar 283
Apple Valley, Calif. 149
Aqua Festival Queen 235
Arcaro, Eddie 203
Armed Forces-Lilac Parade (see Lilac Festival)
Armstrong, Brian 181, 185
Armstrong, Dan 180, 185
Armstong, Elizabeth (Adams) 180, 181, 182, 185
Arneson, Arthur 110
Arthur D. Jones & Co. 70
Aster Candy Company 245
Atlantic City, N.J. 211, 241, 243, 245, 246, 248, 249, 251, 262, 264, 265, 270
Atlas Intercontinental Ballistic Missile 215, 216
Audian Theater 252
Auditorium Building 17, 72, 76, 102
Austin, Texas 235
Avant Junior Toastmistress Club 194

Baker, Jim 315
Bamonte, Tony 29
Banff Winter Carnival 132, 134-137
Barbonte, Tullia 341
Barnard, Sheri 291, 292
Barnes, John 37
Barnes, Mary Ruth 131
Barnes, Motie & Ready Real Estate Firm 66
Barrymore, Ethel 87
Bartleson, Fred 252
Bartlett, Patricia 135, 140
Bayne, Emily (see Motie, Emily)
Bayne, Marilyn 50
Bayne, Roland 35, 37, 38, 50, 54
Bayne, William 50, 119
Bearden, Mrs. H.B. 156
Beardsmore, William 96
Beaverhead, Pete 170
Beaverton, Oregon 180
Bedinger, Donna Lee 258
Beimes, Mae 94, 96
Bellingham, Wash. 216
Bentz, Sandi 289
Berg, F.O, 15, 26
Bergen, Edgar 157
Bergen, Eva 147, 151, 158
Bergen, George 147, 151, 158
Bergen (Thompson), Glenda 33, 145, 147-162
Bergeson, Terry 341
Berle, Milton 165
Bernhardt, Sarah 87
Berry, Beverly 153
Betts (Williams), Catherine "Cay" 33, 74, 83, 115, 121, 130-146
Bett's Oil Company 131, 135, 138
Betts, Chauncey 131,
Betts, Clark 131
Betts, Marcieta 131, 142, 144
Betts, Ray Sr. 131, 142,
Betts, Ray Jr. 131, 138, 142
Bidds (major) 96
Bigelow, Marcia (see Gusman, Marcia)
Bigelow, Mark 164 177
Bigelow, R.E. 70, 78, 113
Bigelow, Rick 164, 177
Bigelow, Robert 164, 177
Bigelow, Scott 164, 177
Bigelow, Tracey 164, 177
Billings, Mont. 264
Bird, Carol 175
Birke, Marion 139
Blackfoot, Idaho 323
Blackfoot Indian Tribe 86, 95
Blaisdell, Neal S. (mayor) 194, 197
Blakely, H.M. 96
Bleecker, H.L. 78
Blue Angels Flying Team 225
Blue Book Directory 98
Blue Mountains 133
Blue, Betty 203
Bodeneck & Jacobs 72
Boise, Idaho 37
Bon Marche 253
Bow, Clara 249
Boyd, Lucille 159
Boyd, Mattie 146, 156
Boyd, Sam (chief) 146, 156
Boyd, William (Hopalong Cassidy) 172
Boyle Fuel Company 222, 224
Boyle, Leon 222
Branson, Missouri 183
Brashears, Howard 37, 62, 63
Braun, Carol 175
Brennan, Jim 203
Bridgeport, Wash. 164
Briley, Bob 22
Britten, L.T 88
Brockbank, Kim 327
Brooklyn Dodgers 186
Brooks, Lee 245
Brown, Annie 170
Brown, Arthur H. 204, 209
Brown, Dan 299
Brown, Herbie 258
Brown, Les 133
Brown, Margaret 159, 170
Brown (Pring), Maureen Ann 33, 202-209 209
Brown, Edmund (Calif. governor) & Mrs. 272
Brown, Sara 204, 209
Browne, Joe E. 280
Browne's Addition 53, 166
Browning, Mont. 86
Brunswick, Maine 180
Bulkley, Mrs. George 140
Burbank, Calif. 298
Burch, Toni 33
Burke, Wendy 325

Burr, Raymond 195, 198
Burt, A.J. 245
Buscho, Ruth 141
Bush, George (president) 290
Butler, Frank 38
Butte, Mont. 102

C & C Spokane Flour Mill 20
Cable Addition streetcar line 53
Cagney, James 228
Cahill, Miles 96
Cahokia, Ill. 36
Caldwell, Chad 116
Caldwell, Christine (Neu) 116
Caldwell, Jeff 116
Caldwell, Jim 116
Calgary Herald 132
Calgary, Albert 203, 205
Calgary Stampede 205
California Hotel 102
California House 10
Camp, Jerry 259
Campbell, Janet 134, 135, 140
Cannon Hill 65
Canwell, Lynn 212
Cape Girardeau, Missouri 37
Capeloto, Alexandra 116
Capeloto, Ben 116
Capeloto, Bob 84, 116, 127, 128
Capeloto, Claire 116
Capeloto, Dorothy "Dodie" (Shiel) 35, 65, 84, 114-116, 121, 122, 127, 128
Capeloto, Jay 116, 128
Capeloto, Maribeth 116, 128
Capeloto, Mark 116, 128
Capeloto, Paul 116, 128
Capeloto, Shelly 116, 128
Capeloto, Tony 116
Cardle, Herbert 262
Carlisle, Kitty 265
Carlson, Heather 301
Carmichael, Calif. 149
Carrol's Vanities 251
Carter, M.J 238
Cartledge, Amy 292
Cashmere High School 293-4
Cashmere Middle School 293-4
Cashmere, Wash. 295
Cathedral of St. John the Evangelist 184
Caudill, Pamela 33
Cecilian Choir 204, 223
Central Pre-Mix 50
Central Valley School District 292
Cerf, Bennett 265
Cerf, Phylis 265
Chapin, E.P. 96
Chelan High School 286, 288
Chelan Jr. High School 286
Chelan, Wash. 286
Cheney, Wash. 159, 289
Cheney Cowles Museum (see also Northwest Museum of Arts and Culture) 74, 146
Chester Elementary School 290, 293
Chicago, Ill. 115, 188
Children's Hospital & Medical Center 115
Chronicle, The 78
City of Spokane (airplane) 225
Cincinnati, Ohio 101
City of Spokane (B-52 airplane) 160, 182
Clark, Buddy 133
Clark, F. Lewis 20
Claude Myrhe Dance Band 227
Clausen, Robert 262
Clemmer Theater 242, 244, 252
Clemmer Theatre /*Spokane Press* Miss Spokane contest 241-246
Cleveland, Ohio 28
Clifton, Nora 135
Clinton, Iowa 37, 38
Coeur d'Alene, Ida. 108-109
Coeur d'Alene Indian Reservation 146
Coeur d'Alene Indian Tribe 135
Coeur d'Alene Mining District 11, 24
Cogdill, Gail 264, 269
Columbia Basin Water Festival 174
Columbia Cavalcade 132
Columbia River 133
Comanche, Iowa 38
Conant, Evelyn 301
Cone, Marilyn 153
Connolly, M.B. 96
Continental Airlines 188
Convair-Astronautics 216
Cook Francis 78, 79
Cook, Harl 78
Cook, Silas 78
Cookman, Gladys 251
Corbaley, Gordon 70
Corbin, D.C. 24
Cornish, Lynn 226
Cottrell, Jimmy 139
Cottey College 180, 182
Cowles, William H. 85
Cox, Chuck 170
Cox, Etta Adams 170
Coyle, W.J. (Lt. gov.) 96
Craig, Mont. 243
Crenna, Richard 225
Crescent Block 13
Crescent Store 70, 72, 265
Crime in Spokane 11, 12
Crommelin, Connie 135, 137, 140
Crosby, Barbara 257
Crosby, Bing 66, 69, 139, 153, 172, 195, 198
Crosby, H.L. Sr. 139
Crosby's Hayden Hellcats 153
Culbertson's Store 243, 253
Culbertson, F.R. 253
Culhane, Patricia 33
Cummings, Robert 217
Cunningham, C.D. 96
Curtis, Frank 20
Cutter, Kirtland 29, 85, 142

Dasidrian talent club 179, 194
Davenport Hotel 84, 85, 86, 88, 89, 92, 93, 94, 95, 96, 99, 101, 134-5, 167, 198, 315, 318, 333; Coffee shop 86; Hall of Doges 70, 90, 94 Italian Gardens, 86, 93; Marie Antoinette Room 86, 87, 90, 92, 99, 226, 254
Davenport, Iowa 37
Davenport, Louis 30, 70, 84-88, 95, 97, 135, Obituary 86
Davenport Restaurant 71, 90, 91
Davenport, Verus 84, 88
Davenport's Waffle Foundry 84
Davenport, Wash. 51
Davison, Andy (mayor Calgary, Alberta) 136
Day, Claude D. 160
Day, Doris 133
Dayo Elementary School 149
de Merry, Major 96
Deer Park Fair 208
Deer Park, Wash. 204
Delander, Lois 249
Deranleau, Leon 194, 201
Deranleau, Marchelle Y. 194, 201
Deranleau, Shirley (see Eagle, Shirley)
Deranleau (Millhorn), Yvette 194, 201
Deranleau-Howard, Loretta J. 194, 201
Desert Hotel 262
Desticker , General 96
Detroit Lions 269
Detroit, Mich. 35
Dewey, Thomas (New York governor) 132, 155
DeWolf, Frances 55
DeWolf, Gerald 37, 55
DeWolf, Helen 55
DeWolf, Vivian (see Motie, Vivian)
Dickson, Anita 335-6
Dickson, David 334, 342
Dickson, Fianna 284, 334-342
Dickson, Patti 334, 342
Dickson, Pete 336
Dickson, Warren 335
Dimond, Joyce 193
Disney, Walt 59

Dixon Lumber Company 254
Dixon, Eve (see King, Eva)
Dixon, Grant Sr. 249
Dixon, Hal 249, 251, 254-6
Dixon, Judith G. 249, 256
Dixon (Martin), Nancy S. 249, 255, 256
Dixon, Ruth (Parker) 249
Dixon (Taylor), Sally Jo 249, 255, 256
Dobish, Bill 29
Dorian Studio 246
Doudlah, W.L, 242
Douglas, Shane 291
Doyle, Leona 212
Drain, James 96
Drake, Francis E. 96
Drake University 249
Drumheller, Joseph 153
DuBois, Elizabeth 141
Duffy, Leo 96
Dunlop, Barry 258
Dunning, Chappie (Mrs. J.W.) 135, 146, 165
Dupper, Charlene 33
Dyer, Doris 141

Eagle, Don 193, 198
Eagle, June 193
Eagle (Deranleau), Shirley 33, 193-201
Earhart, Amelia 87, 88
Eastern Star 207
Eastern Washington State Historical Society 144
Eastern Washington University (also State College) 235, 264, 288, 289, 298, 300, 306, 313
Ecker, Roland K. 152
Economic panic of 1893, 10
Edburg, Linda 212
Edris, William 88
Edwards, Ralph 225
Edwards, Shannon 300
Egan, George E. 160
Eggers, Matthew 192
Eggers, Patricia "Patsy" (see Kelly, Patricia)
Eggers, Arthur 188, 191, 192
Eggers, David 192
Eggers, Mathew 188, 191
Eggers (Stevens), Sarah 188, 192
Elks Club 88
Ellensburg, Wash. 216
Ellingsen, Carl "Tuffy" 237
Ellingsen, Donald 235, 237
Ellingsen family 237
Ellingsen, Lani (see Wickline, Lani)
Ellis, G.H. 96
Ellis, Genie Lynn 33
Ellis, J.S. 245
Ellsworth Air force Base, South Dakota 149
Emery, Sue 258
Empire Furniture Legion Team 153
Emporium (store) 279
Englewood, Colorado 193
Erickson, Mary Jo 216
Erwin, E.K. 96
Essick, Luther 179, 203
Etzler, Sara 284
Eugene, Oregon 129, 234
Eureka, Calif. 38
Evanco, Michael 160
Ewing, B. Gard 96
Exchange Lumber & Manufacturing Company 249
Exchange Lumber Company 254
Explorer I 187
Fair and Warmer (play) 103

Fairbanks, Douglas Jr. 87, 249
Fairchild Air Force Base 87, 133, 130,149, 160, 164, 179, 182, 190, 225
Falls City Block and Opera House 14, 102
Farley, Don 258
Farmers' Market 27
Fayle, Louise (Motier) 36
Fayle, William 36
Felts Field 88
Ferris High School 266, 298, 299, 334
Ferry, Weldon 258
Filio, Charles 96
Fillingham, William R. 189
Finch Elementary School 264
Finnegan, Ethel M. 196
Finnegan, Mrs. T.J. 196
Finney, Frank 106
Fisher, Greg 304
Fleming, Charles A. (mayor) 96, 218, 242
Flowerfield 88
Flowers, Shirley 174
Flying Squadron 133, 141
Foch, Ferdinand (French general) 87, 96
Foley, Tom (U.S. Rep.)182
Forbes, Lynn 289
Forbush, Nellie 223
Ford, Glen 203, 206
Ford, Lizzie 146
Fort George Wright 72, 215-16
Fosseen, A.B. 96
Fosseen, Helen 218
Fosseen, Neal (mayor) 218, 219, 226-227
Foster, Laura Lee 258
Fowle, Gordon 206
Francis, Jeff 290
Frankfurt, Germany 228
Fry, Sue 141
Fryhling, Jennifer Soo 248, 312-313
Fulbright, J.W. 179

Gaddis, Eleanor 71, 72
Galena Army Air Corps Base 88,
Gallik, Gail 289, 291, 343
Gandy, Lloyd 110
Garrison, Donald E. 160
Geiger Air Force Base 189
Gellert, Nathan H. 184
Geraghty, Jack (mayor) 315, 333
Gilbert, John 249
Gill, Roy 96
Gillooley, Joseph 36
Gillooley, Mary (Motier) 36
Glacier National Park 85, 95
Global Credit Union 330, 331
Godlewski, Helen 54
Goerig, Gay LaRane (Mooney) 231
Gombosky, Jeff 339
Gonzaga Prep School 223
Gonzaga University 66, 139, 159, 223, 224, 227, 315-317, 323, 331, 337, 338, 352
Good Roads Assoc. 78
Gordon, Mrs. B.L. 70
Gorman, Margaret 241
Graham, John W. 138
Grahlmann, Sharon (Sweeny) 231
Grand Coulee Dam 100, 132, 159, 189
Grandma's Kitchen 78
Granite Building 72
Granite Creek 148
Grant School 50, 55, 56
Graves Music 78
"Great Big Baked Potato" 97
Great Lakes 109
Great Northern Railroad 86, 95, 99, 105, 133
Green, Alex 70, 72
Green, Susan 224
Greene, Roberta 289, 301
Grizzle (Janke), Brenda 284, 293, 297-311
Grizzle, Charles 298, 302, 310
Grizzle, Janet 298, 302, 303, 305, 310
Grizzle-Clancy, Victoria 298, 302, 303, 306, 310
Grove, C.E. (Dr.) 96
Grover, Carol 343
Grover, Lewis 343
Grub Stake, The 101
Guidry, Cabot 329
Guilbert, Frank 78
Guilbert, W.S. 96
Gunn, George 125
Gusman, Alexander "Joe" 163, 166

Gusman, Bertha 163, 166, 167, 176
Gusman, Celeste 176
Gusman (Bigelow), Marcia 33, 163-177
Gwyer, Jack 178

Haas, Carol 175
Hagen, Ann 305
Haley, Francis 54
Hall, Halliene 70
Hamblin Elementary School 298
Hangauer, Jack 252
Hansen, Henry 245
Harkness, Diane 216, 217
Harness, Rosemary 33, 219
Harrison, Ida. 108-109
Hart, Louis F. (governor) 96
Hart, Moss 265
Hart, Schaffner & Marx Shop 246
Hartman, Mary 38
Harvey, John 341
Hatch Motor Company 245
Havermale Junior High School 193
Hay, Marion (governor Washington State) 78, 79
Hayden Lake, Idaho 139, 159, 249, 255
Hayward Larkin Advertising Co. 72
Hayward, Harry 102
Hedgcock, Kathy (Pring) 208
Heink, Schumann 87
Helena, Mont. 243
Hello Miss Spokane, (song) 74, 106
Henager, Louise 258
Henderson (Anderson), Anne 262-283, 289, 301; Resume of modeling career 277
Henderson, Bob 264, 266, 268
Henderson, Fred 266
Henderson, Jim 264, 266, 268, 282
Henderson, Sam 266
Henderson, Virginia (Mutch) 264, 266, 268, 282, 283
Hendricks, Shirley 224
Henrichs, Emma 148
Henrichs, Ralph 148
Henrietta, Sister Mary 36
Hercules Mine 24
Hern, Donna Rae 258
Herr (O'Dell), Donnagene 257-261
Hester, Joyce 301
Heylman, Harry 96
Hickman, C.E. 72
Hill, Agnes 251
Hill, James J. 85, 95
Hill, Louis 85
Hilton, James 138
Hindley, William (mayor) 70, 78, 79
Hogan, Walter 96
Hopalong Cassidy (see Boyd, William)
Hoisington, Bill 258
Holiday Inn 225, 231
Hollywood, Calif. 101, 134, 139, 198, 217, 223, 228
Holmes Elementary School 193
Holy Family Hospital 211
Holy Names College 145
Home Telephone Company 78
Honolulu, Hawaii 124, 197
Honolulu Star-Bulletin 196
Hooper, Larry 223
Hoopestan, Ill. 342
Hoover, Herbert (president) 86
Hope, Bob 139
Hope, Idaho 152
Hopkins, W.P. 96
Horan, Walt (congressman) 195, 199
Hotel Lusso 342
Houston, Texas 188, 278, 280, 287
Hudson's Bay Co. 133, 146
Hughes, Constance Rae 216
Hull, Erin 341
Hunter, Tab 217
Hutchinson, Rachael 74
Hutton, Levi 24
Hutton, May 24
Hutton Settlement 24

Illeana (Princess) 87
Indian costume (see Miss Spokane Indian costume
Inland Automobile Association (also Club) 78, 97
Inland Empire Industrial Exposition 225
Inland Truck and Diesel Co. 163, 166
Insinger, Robert 78, 96
Intel Corporation 181
Intermountain Logging Conference 183, 225
Interstate Fair, 1910, 22
Interurban Terminal 25
Ione, Wash. 101
Isadora, Sister Mary 36

Jackson, Henry "Scoop" 179, 265
Janke, Brenda (see Grizzle, Brenda)
Janke, David 298, 299, 311
Janke, Madison M.. 299, 311
Janosky, Al 219
Jefferson Elementary School 264
Jensen, Margaret 74
Jessle, George 225
Jim's Place 23
Joel Ferris Perennial Gardens 140
John Rogers High School 147
John the Baptist 100
John W. Graham & Company 107
Johnson, E.L. 160
Johnson, Lyndon B. (president) 203
Johnson, Norma 212
Jones, Arless O. 160
Jones, Arthur D. 78, 96
Jones, Sabrina 301
Jordania, Vaktang 308
Joseph, Oregon 148
Joseph, Sister Miriam (see also Motie, Frances A.) 37, 39, 58
Joy's Opera House 102

Kaiser Aluminum 132
Kaiser, Henry J. 132, 194, 195
Kaley, Kaycee (Pring) 208
Kaskaskia, Ill. 36
Kaye, Danny 133
Keating, Edward 36
Keating, Eleanore (Motier) 36
Keene, Thomas 96
Keith, George 96
Kelly Clarke Inc 115
Kelly Gardens 187
Kelly, Albert A. Sr. 187
Kelly, Albert Jr. 187
Kelly, Emmaleta (Sims) 187
Kelly, Jack 274
Kelly, Larry 187, 189
Kelly (Eggers), Patricia "Patsy" 33, 186-192, 194, 200
Kelly, Raymond 135
Kemp, Blanche 74
Kerr, Gary 258
Ketterer, John 38
Ketterer, Joseph 38
King and I, The (play) 229
King Edward Hotel 136
King, C.L. 96
King (Dixon), Eva 241-256
King, Fred 243
King, Luella (Craig) 243
Kinman Business University 180, 184
Kinney, Peggy 216
Kippen, Herbert 72
Kipper, Joseph W. 194, 199
Kirkpatrick, Grace 132
Kirkpatrick, Patricia 258
KIRO 7 News 323
Klondike Gold Rush 24
Knights of Columbus 66, 40, 51
Knights of Pythias 179
Knott, Louise 36
Korean War 160
Krall, Heidi 265
Kuennen, Dave 341
Kuhn, Ann Marie 284
KXLY Television 222

Lafayette, Edward Motier 35
Lafayette, Marquis de 35
Lafayette, Michel Louis 35
Lafferty, Perry 133
Laib, Susan 33, 239
Lakes, Coeur d'Alene 74, 109; Pend Oreille 105, 148; Priest 101; Thomas 101; Twin Lakes 42, 46, 47; Washington 116, 122, 127
Lamberton, Harold (Dr.) 144
Lane, Thaddeus 78, 97
Larson, Carla 301
Lasorda, Tommy 236
Lawrence Welk Orchestra 223
Lawsen, Kenneth 204
Leiderman, Helmar 242
LeMay, Curtis 195
Lenhart, Margaret 139
Lennon Sisters 179, 183, 223
Letsch, Lee 131
Leuthold, Caroline 135
Levesque, Kay 269
Levine, Mary 232
Levitch, Sally Butterworth 176
Lewis and Clark High School 59, 65, 66, 68, 69, 114, 119, 131, 142, 168, 179, 180, 211, 252, 264, 269, 315
Lewiston, Idaho 163, 164
Lewiston Roundup 175
Libby Junior High School 211, 335
Libby, Charles Sr. 72
Life of Riley, The (film and TV) 228
Life Magazine 164
Liftchild, Charles & Mrs. 131, 142
Likarish, Judith 33
Lilac Festival (also Armed Forces Day-Lilac Festival, Lilac parade) 134, 158, 175, 176, 182, 188, 190, 211, 214, 226, 235, 257, 292, 301, 323-324, 331, 338, 342; First Torchlight Parade 199
Limacher, P.J. 149
Lincoln First Federal Building 225
Lincoln Lumber Co. 249
Lincoln Savings and Loan 257
Lindberg, Charles 87
Lindsley, Marjorie 74
Liner, C.O. (Dr.) 96
Lionhead Lodge 101
Little Miss Portland 81
Little Spokane River 88, 100
Livengood, Lester 96
Lloyd, F.H. 72
Looff Carousel 309
Los Angeles, Calif. 37, 56, 98, 99, 165, 198, 216, 304
Lott, Agnes 159
Lowe, Kristin Kay 33
Loyola University 315
Lubins (store) 246
Lucille, Mr. 246, 250
Ludwig, Walter 219
Lurline (ocean liner) 115, 196
Lynch, Marguerite (Motier) 36
Lynch, Michael 36
Lyons, Iowa 38

Mack, Ted 179
Macumber, Lanunce 258
Maddieux, Peggy 246, 247
Magnuson, Warren (senator) 203, 247
Maguire, John 102
Maguire, Mary 37
Malmgren & Cutter (architects) 85
Malmgren, Charles 142
Mamer Transport Company 88
Manito Lions 292
Manito Park 140, 142, 174, 242
Mann, Samuel A. Mrs. 72
Mann, Vera 72
Marcelle Shop 245
Marchi, Dorothy 50
Marchi, John 50
Marie, Rose 225
Markey, John 96
Marshall, General 87
Martha, Princess of Norway 87
Martin, Janet 135, 137, 140
Martin, Nancy (see Dixon, Nancy)
Marycliff High School 204, 223
Marycliff Prep School 223
Masons, The 88
Mattes, Abel 38
Mattes, Anna 36, 37
Mattes, Brigetta 38
Mattes, Eleanore 36
Mattes, Ella 36
Mattes, Emily 38
Mattes, family genealogy 38
Mattes, George 36
Mattes, Henry 36
Mattes, John 37, 38
Mattes, Joseph 38
Mattes, Mary 36, 38
Mattes, Prisca 38
Mattes, Roman 38
Mattes, Rose 38
Mattes, Wentzel 38
Mattes, William 38
Mauss, Bruce 211
Mauss, Cory 211
Mauss, Sally (see Amick, Sally)
Maverick (TV show) 274
McCabe, Mary 141
McCarthy, Charlie (puppet) 157
McCarty, Colleen 33
McCarty, Ella 146, 179
McCarty, Mary Edith 152
McCollough, Frank 96
McConville, Jim 164
McDonald, Jackie 175
McGavin, Darin 203, 206
McGoldrick, James 110
McGovern, Mollie 258
McKinley, William (president) 86
McManamy, Mary 216
McNider, Hanford 96
Mead, Judy 269
Medicine Hat, Alberta 54
Meehan, Arthur (mayor) 145, 259
Mendenhall, Margery 258
Merrill, Buddy 223
Merriman, Charles 110
Metropolitan Investment Securities 180
Metropolitan Mortgage and Securities, Inc. 180
Metaline Falls, Wash. 145
Met Theatre 296, 314
MGM Studio 217
Michalski, James 160
Michael, Susan (also Michele, Susan) 146
Michels, Kelly (Pring) 208
Michels, Levina 208
Michels, Matt 208
Migliuri, Joseph 221
Migliuri, Rosina 221
Miller, Mitch 265
Millhorn, Katie 194, 201
Millhorn, Trevor 194, 201
Millhorn, Yvette M. (Deranleau) 194, 201
Milton, Fla. 181
Milwaukee Railroad 109
Miner, E. Vicki 33
Minnehaha Park 99, 101
Minnehaha Studio 101
Miss America Pageant 9, 240-242, 246, 248-251, 262, 264, 265, 270, 271, 286-288, 337
Miss America District Pageant 262, 264
Miss Chicago 115
Miss Coeur d'Alene 243
Miss Columbia 70
Miss Greater Spokane 240
Miss Greater Wenatchee 288, 289, 295
Miss Lake Chelan 288
Miss Pasco 175
Miss Pontiac 253
Miss Spokane (airplane) 74, 110
Miss Spokane (steamer) 74, 108, 109
Miss Spokane contest,

Miss America District Pageant 240, 262, 264-5
Miss Spokane contest, official city hostess, origination 9, 33, 70-72; termination by Chamber of Commerce 238-239
Miss Spokane County 240, 257, 259
Miss Spokane Indian costume (information about) 32, 72, 135, 146, 156, 164, 169, 226
Miss Spokane memorabilia 111
Miss Spokane Scholarship Program 240, 266, 284-343
Miss Sunshine 171
Miss Walla Walla 289
Miss Washington 9, 240, 262-267, 270, 271, 284, 289, 290, 291, 293, 299, 300, 301, 310, 319, 323, 325, 326, 331, 331, 333, 337, 339, 342, 343
Mission Street Bridge 26
Mission Viejo, Calif. 266
Mississippi River 35, 36, 38
Mississippi Valley 36
Missoula, Mont, 24
Moeller, Ann 212
Monaghan, James 31
Monroe Street Bridge 19, 28, 29; longest concrete span in the world 29
Monte (Tiplin), Deanna 222, 229, 231
Monte, Eleanor 222, 231
Monte, Gordon 231
Monte, Guy 221, 231
Monte, Marina 221, 231
Monte, Nat 222, 231
Monte (Rees), Natalie 220-233
Monte's Italian Dinners 221
Moomaw, Donna 159
Mooney, Gaye LaRane 33, 231
Moore, Herbert 96
Moore, Lyle 227
Moorehouse, H.L. (Dr.) 96
Mootland, Jackie 219
Morning Star Boy's Ranch 198
Morris, William 70
Moser, Marie 38
Mossuto, Carolina 335, 340
Mossuto, Dominic 340
Mossuto, Michele 335, 340
Motie, Anna (Mattes) 37-39, 49-55, 62, 66, 72, 119
Motie (Strebe), Dorothy C. 37, 40, 49, 50, 55 56, 59, 62, 64
Motie (Bayne), Emily 35, 39, 42, 50, 51, 54, 56, 64, 98,
Motie (Brashears), Esther L. 37, 39, 40, 62-64, 98, 119
Motie family 10, 25, 31; genealogy 35-64
Motie, Frances A. (see also Sister Miriam Joseph) 37, 39, 57-58, 98
Motie, Francis Patrick "Frank" 36-39, 50-53, 54, 55, 62, 66, 96, 119
Motie (Shiel), E. Marguerite 9-11, 32- 35, 37, 38, 39, 42-50, 59-62, 65-129, 131, 132, 146, 218, 227, 239, 240, 252
Motie (Reeder), Miriam J. 37, 39, 42, 58-59
Motie (Regan), Ruth 37, 39, 42, 44, 49, 58
Motie (DeWolf) Vivian M. 37, 3 9, 55-56
Motier, Alice (Ryan) 36
Motier, Emily (also Sister Mary Henrietta, B.V.M) 36
Motier, Felicite (Constant) 36
Motier, Felicite (Rollet) 36
Motier, Francois 36
Motier, George 36
Motier, Henry 36
Motier, Joseph 36
Motier, Josephine (also Sister Mary Isadora, B.V.M.) 36
Motier, Louise (Knott) 36
Motier, Mary (Keating) 36
Motier, Mary (Maguire) 36
Mottola, Fred 341
Mt. Spokane 140, 189
Mutch, Ada 266
Mutch, Dorothy 266
Mutch, Milly 266
Mutch, Virginia 266 (see Henderson, Virginia

NASA 187
Natatorium Park 173
National Wine Queen 265, 272, 273, 274, 276, 280
Nervig, Helen 153
Neu, Carl 115, 116, 126
Neu, Carl Jr. 115, 126
Neu, Christie (Caldwell) 116, 126
Neu, Kelly 116
Neu, Mary Ann (Shiel) 115-116 121, 122, 126
Neu, Max 116
Neu, Peter 116
Neu, Sally 116
Neu, Sam 116
Neu, Tom 116, 126
New Orleans, Louisiana 36, 188
New York City 109
Nicacio (Van Inwegen), Victoria 284, 314-321
Niederhauser, Nikki 301
North Central High School 66, 69, 103, 104, 164, 193, 194, 243, 249
Northern Pacific Railroad 16, 23, 24, 97
Northtown Shopping Center 249
Northwest Museum of Arts and Culture (see also Cheney Cowles Museum) 146
NorthwesternUniversity 61, 115, 181
Nuxoll, Cecil 335, 336
Nuxoll, Josephine 335, 336

Odebolt, Iowa 37, 50 56, 66, 129
O'Dell, Donnagene (see Herr, Donnagene)
Ofstad, Arnt 140
Olaf, Crown Prince of Norway) 87
Old National Bank 70, 88
Old National Bank Building 245
Oldershot, Connie 33
O'Leary, Joe 203
Olive, Harry 96
Olmsted, E.D.(mayor) 11
Oppenheimer, Ruth 74
Oppenheimer, Simon 20
Overhauser Candy Company 71, 111
Overhauser, J.H. 71
Owen, Brad (Lt. gov.) 339, 341
Owl Drug Store 245, 249

Pacific Coast League 186
Paine, Waldo 96
Pal Joey (play) 230
Palmer, Abigail 284, 330-333, 343
Palmer, Jed 333
Palm Springs, Calif. 257
Panama Pacific Universal Exposition 80, 113
Pangborn, Clyde 110
Parker, Frank 96, 179
Parker, John 219
Parkwater 110
Parrish, Randall 36
Pasedena, Calif. 203, 206, 211, 216, 217
Pasco, Wash. 88, 174, 315

Pathfinder Promotion Trips 97
Payless Drug Store 203
Peaceful Valley 12
Pearson, Kim 305
Peekskill, N.Y. 330
Peouse, Christine 159
Perry, Edward A. 190
Pershing, John J. (general) 87
Persian Gulf War 293
Peters, Frank 145
Peters, Lloyd 101
Peters, Margel 33, 145, 146, 200
Peters, Paul 101
Peters, Ray 101
Petty (Skok), Mary Lou 139
Peyton Building 15
Pfeffer, Marian (Leavett) 152
Phil's Café 211, 213
Phillips, George A. 96, 110
Pickford, Mary 87, 241
Pike's Peak 78
Platt, Elizabeth 38
Playfair Race Track 77
Pocahontas 72
Pocatello, Idaho 160
Porter, Del 139
Pointer, Dale 258
Police Benefit Ball 173
Police Guild 292
Pope, Suzanne 153
Porter, Richard 30, 88
Portland Flowering Mill 20
Portland, Ore. 81, 102, 175, 181
Portland Oregonian 135
Portland Rose Festival 175
Post, Frederick 20
Potlatch, Idaho 159
Potvin, E.D. 96
Powell, Annie 266, 282, 283
Powell, Gregg 266, 282
Powell, Kirsten 266, 282, 283
Power, Frederick Tyrone II 98-101
Power, Harold 99
Power, Tyrone (the elder) 99
Power, Tyrone III 99
Priest River, Idaho 145
Princess Spokane 79
Pring, John G. 204, 208, 209
Pring, Kathy 208
Pring, Kaycee 208
Pring, Kelly 208
Pring, Krista 208
Pring, Maureen (see Brown, Maureen)
Pryde, James A. 173
Puget Sound, Wash. 120
Putnam, Amelia Earhart 88

Queen Marie of Romania 87
Quinn, William (governor) 194

Rafferty, Dan 258
Raiter, Tony 203
Raymond, Alice 159
Raymond, Olive 230
Ready, Austin 37
Reagan, Ronald (president) 195
Reardan, Wash. 51
Red Collar Line 108-9
Red Front Grocery 37
Reeder, George 37, 53, 59
Reeder, Miriam (see Motie, Miriam)
Rees, Lanny 228-9, 232, 233
Rees, Mel 228-9, 232
Rees, Mitch 229
Rees, Natalie (see Monte, Natalie)
Reese, Bill 258
Regan, Ruth (see Motie, Ruth)
Regan, Stephen A. 37, 58
Review Building 78
Reynvaan, Abbi 333
Rice, Curtis L. 160
Rice, Gunnar 294
Rice, McKenna 294
Rice, Ren (Chief of Police) 11
Richardson, Mrs. W.W. 140
Richfield Oil Company 55, 59, 62
Ridpath Hotel 175
Ridpath Motor Inn 225
Rifenbery, Terry Dawn (Starr) 231
Riley, Pete 271
Riverfront Park 309
Robert, R.W. 78
Roche, Gus W. 72
Rocky River Bridge 28, 29
Rodgers & Hammerstein 223
Roe, Ed 262
Rogers High School 148, 223, 234, 235, 237, 257, 259
Rogers, A.F. 78
Rogers, Virginia 141
Rogers, Will 87
Rollet (Motier), Felicite 36
Roosevelt Grade School 142
Roosevelt, Eleanor 141, 179
Roosevelt, Theodore (president) 76
Rose Bowl 203, 206, 211, 217
Rosellini, Albert (governor) 186, 194, 225, 265
Rounds, Doreen 137
Royal Canadian Mounted Police 137
Ruffu, Anthony Jr. (mayor)) 246, 248
Rumberg, Diane 33
Rutter, Carol 74
Rutter, Lewis 70
Ryan, Alice 36
Ryan, Donna 335
Ryan & Newton Company 88

Sacajawea Junior High School 298
Sacred Heart Hospital 30, 222, 328
Sacramento, Calif. 112, 264, 281
Salt Lake City, Utah 58, 165, 210
San Diego, Calif. 120
Sandifer Family 252
San Francisco, Calif. 80, 85, 100, 113, 115, 164, 188, 275, 279, 280, 313
San Gabriel Mountains 302
San Mateo, Calif. 264, 265
Santa Fe, N.M. 135
Scanlan, Gail 301
Schaefer, Sally 269
Schell, Maria 203, 206
Schmidt, Burton 183
Schmidt, Daniel 257, 261
Schmidt, Kelly 261
Schmidt, Michael 261
Schmidt, Pamela 257, 261
Schultz, Henry 342
Schuster, Lynne 289, 318, 343
Seattle University School of Law 313
Seattle, Wash. 9, 115, 129, 132, 141
Seehorn, Dwyla 258
Selland, Art 219
Shadle Shopping Center 203, 211
Shaffer, Robert L. 160
Shelly, Kate 38
Sheraton Hotel 307
Sheridan Grade School 211
Sherwood, Deloma 288
Sherwood, Winifred 170
Shiel, Dorothy "Dodie" (see Capeloto, Dorothy
Shiel, Howard 119
Shiel, Marguerite (see Motie, Marguerite)
Shiel, Mary Ann (see Neu, Mary Ann)
Shiel, Patty (Harrison)
Shiel, Walter 37, 47, 74, 114, 115, 117-120, 122-5, 127, 129
Shiel, Walter Jr. 115, 121-124
Shields, Ken 260
Shields, Mary Lou 260
Shilling, Al 198
Shilo Inn 318
Shipman, Nell 101
Shore, Dinah 133
Shriners Hospital 203, 316, 320
Silent movies in Spokane 57, 98
Silver, Jean (state rep.) 320
Sims, Gertrude 187
Sims, Nyana 294
Sims, Richard 187
Skok, Mary Lou Petty 139
Smith, Dorothy Darby 224
Smith, Ella 245

Smith, Glorian 241-3, 245
Smith, Kathleen "Kaki" 33, 227
Snake River 133
Snyder, Marilyn 199
Solomon, Henry 245
Sondheim, Stephen 230
South Central High School 65-69, 114
Spokane Advertising Club 32, 59, 71-74, 81-83, 98-9, 101, 103-4, 106-7, 110, 113, 130-1, 145, 202, 218, 239, 241, 244, 252
Spokane Airport 203
Spokane Amateur Athletic Club 88
Spokane and Eastern Trust Company 70, 88
Spokane Aviation Story, The (James McGoldrick) 110
Spokane Chamber of Commerce 33, 70, 78, 87, 103, 130-2, 135, 145, 148, 153, 156, 178-9, 186, 194, 197, 199, 203, 206, 211, 213, 215, 218, 224, 226, 227, 230, 235, 238, 259, 262
Spokane Child Abuse and Neglect Prevention Center 308
Spokane Chronicle 59, 78, 103, 110, 135, 148
Spokane City Hall 10, 339
Spokane City Jail 10
Spokane Civic Theatre 195, 228, 229, 232
Spokane Club 88
Spokane Community College 235, 330, 341
Spokane County Club 88
Spokane County Courthouse 12
Spokane Daily Chronicle 71, 72, 76, 145, 189, 238
Spokane Fairgrounds 132
Spokane Falls Community College 335
Spokane fire of 1889, "Great Fire" 10, 13, 84
Spokane flag (official city) 75
Spokane High School 69
Spokane House Hotel 164
Spokane Indian Reservation 158-9, 169
Spokane Indian Tribe 135, 145-6, 168, 180
Spokane Indians' Baseball Team 72, 186, 225, 236,
Spokane Interstate Fair, 1915, 30
Spokane Natural Gas Company 178, 184
Spokane Park Board 78, 88, 99
Spokane Press 87, 99, 100, 102, 243, 245
Spokane Savings and Loan 245
Spokane Ski Club 140
Spokane Symphony 265-6, 317, 308
Spokane Trunk and Grip 245
Spokane Women's Club 133
Spokane's Crime Check Program 50
Spokane's Greatest Advertising Campaign 104
Spokane's official flag 79
Spokesman-Review 181, 216, 70, 132, 138, 148, 151, 168, 78
St. Aloysius Church 25, 51, 66, 316, 321
St. Francis of Assisi Grade School 222
St. George's School 88
St. Louis, Missouri 35
St. Luke's Hospital 131
St. Maries, Idaho 108
Standard Fuel and Ice 31
Stanton, Frances 135
Stark, George 245
Starlit Stairway (TV program) 222, 223, 224
Starr (Rifenbery), Terry Dawn 33, 219
State Theater 252
Steamboats in the Timber (Ruby El Hult) 109
Stedman, Dale 224, 227
Steele, Don 149
Steeple, R.C. 110
Stefani Brothers 281
Ste. Genevieve, Missouri 36
Stephens, Heidi 342
Stevens, Sarah (Eggers) 188, 191
Stevens, Tate Arthur 188
Stevens, Troy 188, 191
Stewart, Betty 153
Stimson, Art 245
Stockton, Mr. & Mrs. 328
Stoessiger, Gus 38
Stone, Harry 106
Stone, Maynard 258
Stone, Randall 258
Stoney Indian Tribe 137
Strebe, Dorothy (see Motie, Dorothy)
Strebe, Frank 37, 62
Sturtz, Amy 284 298, 300
Sturtz, Kathy 286, 291
Sturtz, Stefani 286, 287, 291
Sturtz, Steve 286, 291
Sullivan, Ed 219
Sutherlin, Frank G. (mayor) 132, 134, 194
Sweeny, Sharron 33, 219, 231

Tacoma, Wash. 216
Taft, William "Duke" (mayor) 183
Taft, William Howard (president) 86
Talbott, Claudia 342
Talbott, John (mayor) 323, 329, 333, 342
Tang (Adams), Jean 181
Tarbert, Berneice 258
Taylor, Sally Jo (see Dixon , Sally Jo)
Tenderloin district 10
Themopolis, Wyo. 323
There Never was a Girlie Like You, (song) 74, 106
Thompson, Dan 184
Thompson, David 161
Thompson, Emilou (Daubert) 179, 180, 184
Thompson, George 161
Thompson, Jack 161
Thompson, Madeleine 181, 185
Thompson, Mary 161
Thompson, Robert 161
Thompson, Sally 161
Thompson (Adams), Suzanne 33, 146, 178-82, 184, 185
Thompson, Ted A.L. 179, 180, 184
Thompson, William "Bill" 149, 154, 161, 162, 164
Thundercloud, Chief 134
Tiger, Wash. 101
Timons (Adams), Teresa 181
Tiplin, Deanna (see also Monte, Deanna) 231
Tiplin, Derek 231
Tiplin, Rob 231
Tiplin, Tiffany 231
Todd, Eileen 258
Todd, Lucille 258
Toplet, Alan 96
Tournament of Roses Parade 203, 206, 211, 216, 217
Town and Country Shopping Center 249
Trayner, Hampton 199
Treyz, Mrs. Oliver 140
Triple Trio 234
Truman Margaret 148, 159
Truman, Bess 148, 155, 159
Truman, Harry (president) 148, 155, 159
Tulane University 181
Tunstall, Cathy 301
Turner, Toni Lynn 238

Tyrone Power Motion Picture Corp. 100

Ulrich, Pat 325
Ulrich, Roy 258
Umatilla River 133
University of Idaho 180
University of Portland 181
University of Washington 59, 61, 114-5, 119, 124, 131, 211, 323
U.S.S. McDougal (ship) 119

Vancouver, B.C. 140
Vancouver, Wash. 211, 310
Van Heusen, Jimmy, 321
Van Inwegen, Patrick 315, 317, 321
Van Inwegen, Victoria (see Nicacio, Victoria)
Vanderline, Michelle 289
Vandersall, Myra 153
Vanessa Behan Crisis Nursery 331, 333
Ventura, Calif. 116
Vero Beach, Fla. 140
Vic Dessert's Oasis 245
Victoria, B.C. 205
Victory Corps 148
Vincent, W.D. 70
Vogue Clothing Shop 245

Waldorf Astoria 86
Wales, Ernie 252
Walla Walla Parent Teacher Assoc. 182
Wallace, Mary Kay 212
Walt Disney Productions 62
Walter P. Shiel & Co. 115
Ward, Bob 224
Ward, Charles 36
Ward, Ella (Motier) 36
Ward, J.C. 100
Ware, Al 96
Ware, Grant 96
Warner, Michael 228, 229
Warner, Michael 231
Warner, Scott 228,229, 231
Washington, DC 249
Washington Motion Picture Corp. 99, 100
Washington State College 88, 148, 149, 163, 179
Washington State Patrol 173
Washington State University (WSU) 180-2, 237, 269
Washington Trust Bank 309
Washington Water Power Company 20, 78, 88, 211, 214
Walla Walla, Wash. 133, 159, 180, 182, 188
Washtucna, Wash. 252
Wenatchee, Wash. 145, 157, 216, 289
Waterhouse, Constable 137
Waters, Donna 212
Welk, Lawrence 223
Well, Adolph 70
Wellpinit, Wash. 165, 169, 170
Wenatchee Valley College 288
West Coast Airlines 203, 205
West Valley High School 330
Western Car Advertisement Co. 72
Western Life Insurance Co. 88, 179
Western Pine Manufacturing Co. 249, 254
Western Union Life Insurance Co. 70
Westminster Congregational Church 145
Weston, Mildred 18
Wheat Growers, Association of 225
White, Aubrey 78
White, J.C. 109
Whitehouse, Martha 141
Whitmore, Hazel 103
Whitworth College 211, 213, 298, 300
Whitworth Presbyterian Church 260
Wickline, Leilani Ann 33, 234-237
Wickman, Barbara 175
Williams, Catherine "Cay" (see Betts, Catherine)
Williams, Jennifer 284, 290, 296, 299
Williams, Ray 133, 144
Williams, Thomas Sr. 133, 143, 144
Williams, Tom Jr. 133, 144, 145
Williams, Will 245
Willis, Tina 342
Wilson, Jay 257, 261
Witter, Earl 258
Witter, Marie 258
Wold, August 70
Woodward players 103
Woodward Theater 103
Wroe, Linda 235
Wurttemberg, Germany 228
WW I 87, 96, 115
WW II 133, 139, 141
Wynia, Joy Ann 258

YMCA 54, 115, 117
Young Life 264

Zuzelski, Sigismund 160